# THE INTELLIGENT ORⲤ

*The Intelligent Organisation* offers a radical model of organisation based on the integration of structure, individuals and information. In this game-changing book, leading consultant John Beckford proposes a different way of designing organisations in order to transform their performance and capitalise on the potential offered by contemporary information capability. This book demonstrates how an organisation designed *backwards from its customers* provides optimised autonomy for individuals and integrated, coherent information.

Drawing on ideas from management science, business information management, organisation theory and extensive professional practice, Beckford argues that organisations have not evolved to process and derive meaning from exponentially increasing availability of data, and that the use of data for optimum performance requires **fundamental organisational changes**, not incremental improvement. Beckford demonstrates how to effect these changes in real practice and the positive results these changes can yield, as well as the challenges in implementation and how to work around them. Beckford's style is lively and direct, but his arguments are academically rigorous, striking a persuasive balance between accessibility and authority. The text is supported by case studies throughout and a dedicated website, www.intelligentorganisation.com, with support materials for lecturers.

*The Intelligent Organisation* will be of significance to Masters and Undergraduate students reading Business Studies, Information Systems, Business Information Systems, Computer Science, Business Management and Management Science.

**John Beckford** is an independent consultant and Visiting Professor in the Department of Science, Technology, Engineering and Public Policy at University College, London, and in the Centre for Information Management at Loughborough University, UK.

This book goes beyond traditional thinking as often found in Operational Excellence and provides great insights to make organisations more viable. By adopting this fashion, organisations can engage the next level of business performance that we could call Viability Excellence.

—Joep Lauret, Senior Manager Performance Management at Wärtsilä

This book will become an inspirational and essential source for both teachers and students. The careful attention to theory, method and context is richly illustrated with useful real world case studies. Comprehensive in its scope and scale, and rigorously argued, it offers a provocative and masterful assessment of a wide range of issues confronting the modern organisation as the relentless drive for technological supremacy marches on.

—Dr Louise Cooke, Loughborough University, UK

With thirty years of practical systems thinking science put into one essential toolkit, *The Intelligent Organisation* must have over £50k worth of consulting in one handy manual.

—James Robbins, CIO Northumbrian Water, UK

# THE INTELLIGENT ORGANISATION

## Realising the value of information

*John Beckford, Ph.D.*

Routledge
Taylor & Francis Group

LONDON AND NEW YORK

First published 2016
by Routledge
2 Park Square, Milton Park, Abingdon, Oxon OX14 4RN

And by Routledge
711 Third Avenue, New York, NY 10017

*Routledge is an imprint of the Taylor & Francis Group, an informa business*

*British Library Cataloguing in Publication Data*
A catalogue record for this book is available from the British Library

*Library of Congress Cataloging-in-Publication Data*
Beckford, John, 1958–
    The intelligent organisation : realising the value of information /
John Beckford.
        pages cm
    Includes bibliographical references and index.
    1. Information technology—Management.    2. Knowledge management.
3. Organizational effectiveness.    I. Title.
    HD30.2.B443 2016
    658.4′038—dc23
    2015013827

ISBN: 978-1-138-84704-0 (hbk)
ISBN: 978-1-138-84707-1 (pbk)
ISBN: 978-1-315-72702-8 (ebk)

Typeset in Bembo
by Apex CoVantage, LLC
Printed and bound in Great Britain by Ashford Colour Press Ltd, Gosport, Hampshire

**Intelligent:**
**Able to initiate or modify action in the light of ongoing events**

Collins Paperback English Dictionary, 1992

# CONTENTS

# PREFACE

Living in the information age we continue to run machine-age organisations. For all our advances in technology, we still focus inward on making the machine work instead of outward on the value exchange with the customer. The result? We waste lots of money pursuing nugatory improvements. As Eliot (1934) asks in "The Rock":

> Where is the wisdom we have lost in knowledge,
> where is the knowledge we have lost in information?

We have been in thrall to technology since the early 1960s. Technology has delivered significant gains in performance, but those gains have been constrained by our adherence to a conventional form of organisation. We have at our disposal the technological means to transform our organisations but without radical change in the way we comprehend information we will remain trapped in machine-age thinking. Einstein (1946) suggests (in at least one version) that

> You cannot solve a problem from the same consciousness that created it.
> You must see the world anew.

Machine-age organisations are doomed to failure in a rapidly changing world. An Intelligent Organisation exploits the value of information and releases the capability of its people.

We need to invest ourselves in a new way of thinking, to understand the flaws in current practices and clearly see the unrealised value. There is a compelling business case for change; simply appreciating the latent value of information will allow us to realise potential for people and organisations. We continually tinker with our machine-age organisations to keep them running. How much better would it be if we designed them so that they modify themselves? If we built capability for adaptation in rather than bolting it on?

The machine-age organisation is functionally arranged and siloed. The Intelligent Organisation is systemic. Made up of four interacting, interdependent parts, those interactions generate emergent properties, properties which belong only to the whole, not to the parts. Those four parts are a value-generating system, a value-enabling system, an identity system (for maintaining a shared purpose) synthesised through the fourth part, an information system. That allows a trialogue (a conversation in three parts), ensuring that the organisation communicates with itself and its environment and enables it to do three things simultaneously:

- manage its present (efficiently carry out value-generating activity);
- create its future (enable new value by anticipating, influencing and responding to changing needs);
- nurture its identity (maintain alignment of its purpose, people and processes).

Every organisation exists for a reason. It is purposeful in pursuing its own sustainability and in fulfilling the needs of its customers. It fulfils that purpose through interactions with its customers, which deliver value to both them and itself – the relationship is dynamic and reciprocal, potentially symbiotic. Each organisation must understand what it does that provides value to its customers, what need it fulfils, what outcomes it seeks to achieve and focus on them and, as Wiener (1948) suggests:

> [T]he importance of information and communication as mechanisms of organisation proceeds beyond the individual into the community.

Designed backwards from the customer, the value-generating system is comprised of the end-to-end processes (together with their embedded tasks and procedures) that deliver goods and services. It is self-regulating, self-aware at the level of its processes, using information about its performance to control and improve itself in a known environment. This self-regulating structure is called a homeostat and is a core idea in the transformation. Its job is to ensure that we do things right.

The value-generating system is the customer of the value-enabling system which provides resources to support and enable it. It does this by understanding, anticipating and influencing both the organisation itself and what is happening in the world outside it. It enables its adaptation to ensure survival. The value-enabling system renders the whole organisation self-regulating and self-aware. It uses information about the performance of all the value-generating activities and about the unknown or problematic environment of the organisation to steer it towards the future. Custodian of strategy, its job is to ensure that we do right things.

These distinct functions combine to constitute a logical hierarchy based on information rather than positional or functional power. The whole is unified through the shared purpose, a common sense of identity amongst the human actors which needs to be nurtured and through which people's different perspectives and understanding can be reconciled. That whole is synthesised through an information system which has both hard and soft dimensions. The hard dimension is quantitative, addressing objective characteristics. The soft dimension is qualitative, addressing cultural and social characteristics.

In a logical hierarchy based on information, we also need to address the question of autonomy. Control is distributed throughout the organisation, decisions are made where the information is available and, to enable responsiveness, that needs to be close to the customer. The information available to the value-generating system is constrained (it can only see its own part), whereas that available to the value-enabling system provides a view of the whole. It is therefore essential to design appropriate autonomy into the organisation so that freedom to 'do things right' is preserved at the process level, whilst the prerogative to 'do right things' is exercised at the whole organisational level in a manner consistent with the shared purpose and values.

Now, if all that has been said so far is going to work, then we need to provide accurate, timely information in an appropriate format to the human actors in the organisation. As the Joseph Rowntree Reform Trust (2009) suggested:

> If you think IT is the solution to your problems, then you don't understand IT and you don't understand your problem either.

The information system must itself be designed backwards from the (highly distributed) decisions that need to be made throughout the organisation, so that it does not generate a costly and inefficient internal 'reporting' industry. At the operational level it must filter and segregate data to provide only that information which is required at each decision point, while at the strategic level it must aggregate, collate and interpret data to enable longer-term decisions. Only in this way can the information system and the people have requisite variety to make useful decisions. In essence, the Intelligent Organisation is defined by the way it uses information, and the organisation and information architecture need to be isomorphic images of each other.

In developing the organisational architecture, applying the notion of the homeostat, distributing decisions and creating an information system that supports all of that, we have to a large extent embedded in the organisation the essentials of performance management. It is self-regulating, is aware of its 'self' in relation to its environment and has capability for adaptation built in throughout. Nonetheless, there remains a need to explore how we should manage the performance of the whole. This is a paradox; we have built autonomy into the architecture, now we need to control it. That requires a deeper understanding of what we mean by performance, a richer understanding of how information can help us to understand and trace the roots of under- (or over-) performance and how we need to engage people in decision making. We also need to reconcile the short- and long-term aspects of performance from which may arise tension.

All that has been said up to this point can be addressed to any organisation from the ultra-large conglomerate to the individual (people are organisations too). The public sector, however, requires some additional consideration. Challenged as they are in most countries with the demand to 'do more for less', public sector organisations operate under different constraints and conditions than do the private sector and those constraints and conditions affect both how we can think about them and how the challenges can be addressed.

All that thinking is fine, but the point of thinking about organisations, the purpose of this book, is to enable us to address their challenges. So, having started by understanding the information challenge and explored how very differently we can think about organisations, we finish by exploring how we might take action to change them, to realise the Intelligent Organisation.

Mature economies struggle to deliver growth (increase in the total value of the economy); mature organisations fight to increase productivity (increase in the efficiency of use of all types of resources). Meanwhile, developing economies and developing organisations are mimicking the behaviour of both. Rather than proposing and developing a new way of doing things, they are replicating established practices with success often enabled by lower-cost labour rather than substantial innovation.

If, as is often attributed to Einstein,

> Insanity means doing the same thing over and over again and expecting different results,

then perhaps many of us are trapped in an insanity of tradition – following well-trodden paths, seeking and finding marginal, incremental improvements but closed to the possibility of real innovation. Finding it easier to remain within 'what is' and complain about it, we perhaps lack the insight or the courage to consider 'what could be' and embrace it.

The Intelligent Organisation is offered as a way out of this trap.

# ACKNOWLEDGEMENTS

This book was inspired by three groups of people. First are those who have gone before; their insights and wisdom created the opportunity for a new question to be asked. Notable amongst these is Stafford Beer, whose work inspired my initial research and on whose foundations this work is built. Second are those in the many organisations who have allowed me the privilege of working with them, testing theory in practice on them and their organisations, helping me to understand what appears to work and why. Third are the clients, consultants and academics on whose support and friendship I have drawn to test practice in theory, to understand how the practical pursuit of increasing effectiveness can be embedded in our theoretical understanding of organisations.

Particular thanks are due to the artist Annabelle Elford for the cover picture, a beautiful interpretation of the message of the book. A diverse group of friendly but demanding critics reviewed the drafts, offering support and challenge in equal measure. The book is much better for their contributions. My thanks to Alan, Andy, James, Joep, Jon, Keith, Louise, Matt, Peter and Peter. The mistakes, errors and omissions are all mine.

Finally, as always my thanks to Sara, Paul and Matthew, whose support through all my endeavours makes them possible.

# FIGURES

# VIGNETTES

# ABOUT THE AUTHOR

**John Beckford** is Visiting Professor in the Department of Science, Technology, Engineering and Public Policy at University College, London, and in the Centre for Information Management of the School of Business and Economics at Loughborough University. He holds a Ph.D. in Organisational Cybernetics from The University of Hull and is a Fellow of the Cybernetics Society, a Member of the Institute of Management Services, a Fellow of The Royal Society for the Arts and a Fellow of the Institute of Engineering and Technology. John's first book *Quality* (Routledge, 2010) is in its 3rd edition and John has published extensively, regularly delivering seminars, workshops and master classes.

He established Beckford Consulting in 1990 and works internationally with government and private sector organisations in a variety of industries including software, finance, publishing, social housing, steel, healthcare, paper, national infrastructure, energy, water and ICT utilities, food, manufacturing and transport.

More can be found at www.beckfordconsulting.com

# 1

# THE INFORMATION CHALLENGE

Gentlemen, we have run out of money. It's time to start thinking.

Ernest Rutherford (attributed)

## Introduction

The tsunami of 'big data' flooding through organisations is overwhelming us. Organisations, processes and decision making commonly adhere to norms developed when instant messaging meant sending a telegram and the telephone was a rare and exotic instrument. The whole notion of the paperless office seems ridiculous; emerging generations of technology continue to exacerbate the problem.

The revolution in our organisations since the 1940s has been technological, not informational. The development of data-processing machines, from 'Collosus', the first digital programmable computer in 1943, to contemporary wireless and highly portable devices, and contemporary communications capability via the internet has been astounding. Jackson (2015), citing Forrester Research, highlighted how the growth in our ability to process, retrieve, store and transmit data is stupendous, while our collective ability to make effective use of it lags far behind:

90% of data stored within a company is not available for analysis.

Data, as Silver (2012) suggests, is just that. We probably have too much data when what we need is information. Information is data which has been filtered, integrated, assimilated, aggregated and contextualised to enable decisions.

## Thinking inside the box

Technology and technologists are very good data providers; organisations and managers must become very good data converters and users. For many people and purposes the delivery technology is often quite irrelevant. What is relevant is the information. It is information that allows us to comprehend things, to understand them, to decide what to do. We need both thinking tools and organisations to do this with; information technology (IT) is simply an enabling system to convey it. What counts is what we, people, do with the data and information, that is, the processes, problem solving and analytical tools that we apply to and with information. There is far more potential information available to us and our organisations than ever. However, we appear ill-equipped to use it, either through the software tools of business intelligence (BI) or our own ability to interpret and understand it. Collectively we seem to neither appreciate the value of information nor design our organisations to exploit it.

Relative to the potential offered by information, many organisations are deeply dysfunctional. Their operating models are rooted in mechanistic, bureaucratic, functional, centralising structures, and managers frequently secure decisions through bureaucratic means using positional power:

'It's my decision, I may not be right, but I am in charge'.

For such organisations, much of the money they have spent on IT has been wasted. Structured and organised in line with "traditional models of organisation" (Beckford, 2010), they are not able to exploit their investment in technologies. Both the hardware and software work, the machines operate with extremely high levels of reliability (greater than six sigma uptime – 99.999%), parts and components are exchangeable and hot swappable; data is backed-up, mirrored and replicated; millions of messages are transmitted and received with almost no losses.

So, if that is all right, where is the failure?

IT has been attempting to deliver organisational value since the 1960s with the implementation of computerised accounting. Some substantial progress has been made but, typically, the IT has been retrofitted to the established organisations and structures, not used to create a new organisational paradigm. Technology has commonly been applied to automate tasks, previously carried out by people, which can be represented in machine logic (an algorithm or programme) as routine, logical, methodical, number crunching and, relatively, unchanging. Those tasks are not characterised as needing "ideation, creativity and innovation" (Brynjolfsson & McAfee, 2014), computers can only work inside the box. Automation has delivered some efficiency gain but has often deliberately, and even more often unconsciously, removed discretion from people in the organisation, particularly those who directly deal with customers.

Decision making travels further up the hierarchy as technology makes more data more available more rapidly to managers. This does not always lead to better decisions being taken but to more decisions being taken further away from the customer, problem source or need – and simply, perhaps inadvertently, through the capability to transmit data electronically. Many organisations are developing IT-enabled, dysfunctionally over-centralised structures, not through intent, desire or need but simply because the information systems enable it. No one notices it happening or thinks to stop it. Collectively we have not reexamined the notion of what it means to 'control' an organisation nor grasped that, particularly in service organisations, there is a significant element of subjectivity regarding performance. That cannot be controlled by an automaton, it requires people and judgement. Performance is a function of the customer as much as it is a function of the organisation.

Beynon-Davies (2013) determined that 67% of UK organisations have suffered at least one 'systems' project that has failed to deliver expected benefits or experienced time and cost overruns, while Gartner (webref 1) stated that 80% of SAP (Systeme, Anwendungen und Produkte in der Datenverarbeitung) clients are disappointed in benefits realised, the measurability of those benefits and the competency of system users. Gartner argue that 90% of IT projects do not return real benefit to the organisation and 40% fail completely. Meanwhile, McKinsey, the management consultants, is reputed to have stated that, historically, two-thirds of chief information officers have not had to defend their budgets because nobody else knew enough of the arcane language of IT to ask the right questions. Morgan Stanley (webref 2) estimated that between 2000 and 2002, companies threw away billions of dollars of their IT capital expenditure on 'shelfware' – software licences and systems never used – a situation that has probably deteriorated in the intervening years. Meanwhile, Carr in the Harvard Business Review (2003) suggested that "IT doesn't matter". HBR did not see IT as a source of strategic advantage; online retailers and other information-intensive organisations might not agree. Universities meanwhile continue to produce computer science graduates who rely on "geek speak" (Times Higher Educational Supplement, 14th August 2014), not having the communication or business skills to render themselves useful to organisations. However, if all this is true, then somebody somewhere must be doing something wrong – or maybe we are collectively valuing and focusing on the wrong things.

The contemporary convention in commissioning an information system or technology project is to identify a problem to be solved, measure the cost of solving it (that is the hardware, software, configuration, customisation, training, backfilling and business disruption), and capitalise it all. Because such projects have a value over time, the accountants can depreciate the investment. The payback is then measured through reduced headcount, increased system availability, better compliance with regulators, improved reporting, reduced 'clicks' to use the system, improved appearance and better toys. Typically, most organisations hold nobody properly accountable for any difference. Instead they consider that

'IT is a sunk cost, like drains and car parks, so let's just minimise the cost'.

Organisations (well, the people really) are often seduced into IT projects with the prospect of better equipment and faster data rather than better information.

The epiphenomena of an IT system are its gadgets – flat screens, mobile devices, smartphones, wireless transmitters and all the other physical, commoditised, ephemera. Software houses have modified their licensing models, lowering the initial cost while, often, increasing the cost of support, configuration and upgrades; the total life cost of the product increasing overall. Many 'upgrades' add little value; of themselves they often do not make the user more productive, efficient or effective in their role. They do not, in general, 'serve the customer better'; they do not make the individual better at their jobs. Often, all we get is a faster, more efficient way of making the same mistakes. Individually these mistakes cost less to make and we can make more of them more rapidly – is that an increase in productivity we want to celebrate? The total cost of all the mistakes is often greater than it was before.

The various integrated 'enterprise-wide' software packages in widespread use throughout the world still largely reflect the traditional, functional and siloed structures of the organisations that use them. This is partly a reflection of the preferences of the individual buyers . . .

'I need a better finance package'

. . . and partly a reflection of the challenges of developing applications that are truly comprehensive. It would be fatuous to deny the challenge of creating completely comprehensive programmes that 'do everything'. The proliferation of functional applications and the need (and it is a need) to use the same data in more than one functional silo often leads to replication of data across those silos. This generates a requirement to synchronise the data and maintain its integrity. However, because of the challenges of integration, and variously:

- inadequate understanding,
- poor control,
- limitations of budget,
- absence of agreed information architecture and
- haste,

data is often shared through unstable, insecure transfer and integration methods and taken from a context in which it has meaning to one in which that meaning is lost. These inadequacies compromise the integrity of the data and reflect our poor understanding of the value of information. Integrity becomes almost impossible, when even minor changes are applied to the arrangement or order of data in a spreadsheet or where it is merged with other data. Even where there is good intent, it is difficult to sustain a data maintenance routine and anyway:

'It won't have changed much, let's use last month's data'.

Organisations have accumulated more and more applications with more and more versions of the data so that it becomes nigh on impossible to determine which data set contains the 'truth'. Each (whether accurately maintained or not) is applied to a particular often functionally partial or siloed decision. Meanwhile everybody is relying on the usually unverified accuracy of the data; nobody is testing it. In one organisation there were more than 30 different versions of a particular 'truth' with consequently inadequate decision making and many arguments about which was 'right'. Of course, in this situation none were absolutely wrong or right; rightness (or not) depended upon the underlying assumptions and the question to be answered.

Multifold replication of data carries with it the likelihood of error. When we couple to that the absolute logical precision of algorithms, we discover potential for further amplification of those errors. When somebody, anybody, searches for stored data on the internet (or the corporate intranet) they find, simplifying greatly from MacCormick (2012), all the possible answers to the question they asked, ranked in order of the number of connected pages and the number of links to that page. The question they ask will probably not use the precise words or have the same precise meaning (to them) as the person, people or machines that populated the data sources being searched. The 'internet of data' is a global data-proliferation engine, massively increasing its data storage requirements every day and, very often, doing so by storing even more copies of things that are already there – and, as yet, it doesn't forget. Perhaps the internet is a Borgesian library (Borges, 1962) of wrong answers to poor questions? The simplicity and ease of use of web browsers attenuates our ability to ask good questions – if we let them.

Data has cost but is the raw material of information. We can use it many times. Information has value; we 'make' it from data, calculate it, present it, use it, exploit it.

However, our poor discipline in the management of data, coupled to multiple applications and devices, compounded by the use of the internet (especially for 'cloud' data storage), fuels this highly effective data-proliferation engine. We capture and store ever more copies of approximately the same data, but have less and less useful information to make decisions with. This leads us, or me anyway, to what I have chosen to call Beckford's Law, which is:

"The more data we have, the less information we have (relatively)."

Data and information exist in inverse proportion to each other. Data proliferates as a function of:

|               | the number of users |
| --- | --- |
| multiplied by | the number of devices |
| multiplied by | the number of applications |
| multiplied by | the number of backups |
| multiplied by | the ease of transmission (the propagation rate) |

Information proliferation is the inverse function.

Data proliferation is exponential in two dimensions, volume and frequency, and information declines in proportion. Because of the rate of data proliferation we probably have more information in absolute terms, but the rate of growth of information is much smaller than that of data. But we need information to make decisions – *not* data.

If data were treated, in accounting terms, as a 'material good', it would be acquired, stored, compiled, applied and used in a manner that respected its cost and value, just like a washer, nut, press or other physical element. It would be regarded as part of the assets of the business. Failure to do this (and I am not suggesting it is easy) undervalues those businesses whose stock in trade is data and which make their living from information provision. We don't do this because the data itself is often invisible and because the cost of data capture and storage is hidden, embedded in other things. If we consider the stock of data in the same way we consider the stock of raw materials or work in progress, then we should be horrified at the mess in the data warehouse and its inefficiency. I have tried this with more than one business – they were.

With each new generation of IT investment it appears increasingly difficult to generate substantial payback. We have reached a plateau in our ability to improve operational efficiency within the existing structures and norms. A new organisational form is needed, coupled to a fresh appreciation of the roles of managers, of systemic efficiency and of effectiveness. Doing more of the same is not and will not deliver benefits; we struggle to realise gains from previous investment and, once a cost has been saved, we cannot claim the saving again (although many try). Fortunately, as both managers and technologists consider the situation, there is an increasing recognition of and demand for new, innovative thinking about the situation. If the old solution is not delivering benefits, what might a new solution look like?

The key is this: information is more important than technology.

## Dissolving the information challenge

The information challenge is to escape the thrall of technology and to design whole organisations as adaptive systems embedding distributed control through information. The information system (in its broadest sense) is not simply an attribute of the organisation, it *is* the organisation.

Since their inception, information systems have been thought of as adjunct artefacts, bolted onto the core of the organisation but not integral to it. Early systems were often associated with telecommunications; extensions of the telephone system, sharing some of their technology, a faster means of moving data and calculating results. Others were associated with finance, the early accounting systems automating the work of bookkeepers and clerks. These systems have supplemented and sometimes replaced more traditional means of transmission or accounting, but the focus has been on the devices and the software, not the information content. Today, information flows define the true structure of the organisation.

Our organograms, job descriptions and reporting structures are, for the most part, refined evolutions of control mechanisms developed in societies long before the sort of formal organisations now seen. Many organisations continue to employ a somewhat militaristic command and control structure with decision power concentrated in the hands of a small number of people, perhaps increasingly so with flatter organisations and more task automation. While armies and religious orders have followed the same essential form for more than two millennia, large-scale civil enterprises have only really developed since the 1700s. The Industrial Revolution in the United Kingdom, powered by Newcomen's steam engine and its successors, enabled, perhaps demanded, a progressive urbanisation of the population as people moved to work in factories which depended upon command and control in order to function. With low levels of automation, the whole depended upon the conformance of the individual to the requirements of their task. The evolution of organisations, their success and the increasing "wealth of nations" (Smith, 1776) is coupled to that of social norms, values and expectations, including the emergence of a managerial class; people who are neither direct owners of the means of production nor directly productive workers but whose task is to be the control system of the organisation, quite literally the middle class.

The late Victorian era through to the Great War of 1914–1918 saw the emergence of formalised ways of thinking about managing. Henry Ford, inspired by mechanisation in abattoirs, developed the moving production line; Frederick Taylor (1911) developed the notion of "scientific management", thinking of the organisation as a "machine"; and Henri Fayol (1916) built on this with his proposals for the duties of managers, especially "unity of command" and "clearly defined duties". Max Weber's Bureaucracy Theory (1924) in considering the legitimacy of authority in organisations, reinforced this, suggesting that a bureaucratic approach was indispensable to the survival of organisations. Thinking developed through the work of researchers such as Mayo (1949) and Roethlisberger and Dickson (1939) with the Hawthorne experiments, emphasising the critical role of human behaviour in organisational success. Herzberg, Mauser and Synderman (1959) and Maslow (1970) developed theories of motivation, emphasising the role of people and challenging the notion that any organisation can be treated, simply, as a machine, their view being more oriented to the notion of an organism. In the second half of the 20th century, thinking about organisations as 'sociotechnical' systems developed, building on the early work of the cyberneticians Wiener (1948) and Beer (1959, 1979, 1981, 1985), while the human, soft systems perspective was heavily influenced by Ackoff (1981) and Checkland (1981). Each of these thinkers developed perspectives which addressed the systemic nature of organisations, but each emphasised a particular *weltanschaaungen* (a worldview or set of assumptions about the world) – political, human behavioural, structural.

Notwithstanding all of these ideas and experiments, most organisational management is conducted with some blend of the 'machine' and 'organism' models. The systemic perspective has not yet prevailed. However, if we are to tackle all of the challenges of contemporary, increasingly complex, organisations we need a

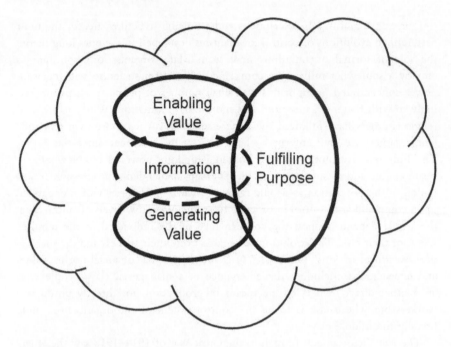

**FIGURE 1.1** The Intelligent Organisation

new approach. The Intelligent Organisation (Figure 1.1) recognises that information is the binding, synthesising feature that integrates fulfilment of purpose
through value-generating and value-enabling activity. It enables the alignment of
process, structure and decisions with people, that is, the values, skills and behaviours
that lead to organisational effectiveness and viability.

## The dialogue of the deaf

The ready availability and apparent cheapness of both hardware and software have
enabled a situation in which data is overwhelming us, but real information is
scarce. Rooted in a partial or functional understanding of a particular problem
rather than a holistic understanding of the information needs of the organisation
as a whole, information solutions often exacerbate the data-handling challenge.
The consequence is fruitless discussions and arguments in which the protagonists
are unable to resolve their problems because, working with different data, their
arguments are all right. A frustrated and frustrating dialogue of the deaf ensues,
in which the participants are unable to understand the perspective of the others
because 'that's what my data tells me'.

The challenge of inconsistent data needs to be resolved. While sound methods
exist for addressing this, such as master data management, the expansion of data
across multiple devices and 'cloud'-type solutions exacerbate it. The cost of growth

in data capture and the benefit to the organisation of useful information must be articulated; the value of solving it must be demonstrated. The many sceptics in the organisation must be challenged and encouraged towards a new way of thinking.

The complexity inherent in contemporary organisations must be recognised and embraced at a requisite level which matches that of the organisation's environment. We need to deal with the irreducible complexity so that the claimed benefits of information investment can be realised. Information must deliver value, that value must become obvious. This makes the business case for change. While both costs and benefits need to be explored in monetary terms, they also need to be considered in terms of the impact on the people in the organisation. An entire industry around 'change management' needs to be challenged. In an organisation run on information, which seeks dynamic ultra-stability through self-regulation, continuing adaptation and learning, managing change (the adaptation) is not an addition to the day job, it IS the day job. The Intelligent Organisation redefines the role of the manager as enabling allostasis; he or she keeps things the same (achievement of outcome) by making them different (internal adaptation).

Value does not solely relate to the monetary measure; behaviours (the ways individuals express their values and beliefs) and skills (the competences applied to the conduct of any particular task) inform and are informed by available information. Behavioural coherence and consistency in the organisation (how we do things) is driven by the alignment of the decisions made (what things we do), with achievement of purpose and the organisational goals (why we do things). Any mismatch between those dimensions will have psychological and monetary consequences. Those consequences will not be explicit or obvious but realised in hidden costs through inefficiency, low staff retention, high staff turnover rates, and very commonly, sickness and absence rates. Ultimately, all these things are expressible in monetary terms and are important to profit maximisation in commercial organisations, to cost minimisation in public services and to surplus generation in the third sector. Whilst the focus and purpose in each sector may be different and the benefits of effective information use realised in differing ways, the value proposition is the same for all.

Understanding the value of information creates the business case for adaptation, and realising that value becomes the imperative to ensure sustainability. This is particularly important in light of the challenge of mature markets and economic, social and technological change. Inspired by Beer (1981, 1985) and developed through theoretical and applied work since the early 90s, it is essential to think about the philosophy and design principles for the Intelligent Organisation; how it can be structured and developed, how information needs can be identified and how autonomy and empowerment can be embedded to address the continuously shifting balance of control, empowering individuals and increasing responsiveness and immediacy in dealing with clients.

## The interconnectedness of organisations

When we can articulate how much value is unrealised then that will provide the bedrock for exploring the philosophy and principles for the Intelligent Organisation. How does it work? Why does it work that way? What are the implications for job design, role articulation, responsibility, accountability and, ultimately, organisational performance?

We should perhaps begin by considering the interconnectedness and interdependence of the organisation itself. Traditional hierarchy leads, inevitably, towards silos of influence and control, a situation in which each manager is charged with improving the performance of the part for which they are responsible. The interests and performance of the whole organisation are only visible to those at the peak of the hierarchy. Any attempt to improve the performance of the whole by improving only the parts is doomed – real improvement is only possible through enhancing the interactions (Ackoff, 1981), for which no one appears responsible. Figure 1.2 indicates the level of internal interdependence for any organisation.

If you are not familiar with process diagrams this looks a bit daunting, so, try this:

> Find the heavily outlined box at the centre of the figure.
> For some reason (it matters not what) there is to be a change in process, skills requirements or standards. Now follow the arrows.

> Assuming first a process change, follow the vertical arrow upwards to 'Any Process'. You will find that has three exit arrows – follow each of them in turn to follow the impact around the organisation.
> Done that?
> Now assume a skills change and follow the horizontal arrow going towards the 'competencies' box and again follow the subsequent arrows.

> Nearly there . . .
> Assume a change in standards.

That's interesting. We can't get to the standards box from the 'change box' without considering first the consequences for process or skills. The ability to meet a standard will be a function of change in process or skill or both! Change in one implies change in the other two.

Now that you have pursued the interdependencies from one fixed start point, see what happens if you start in any other box . . . you will find that, eventually, regardless of starting point, you will work your way through every box. The point? It is simply not possible to change one aspect of an organisation without affecting many others. These interdependencies can best be conceived as information flows, a change in one relying on information being conveyed to another to activate the appropriate response, perhaps analogous to gene activation in cells.

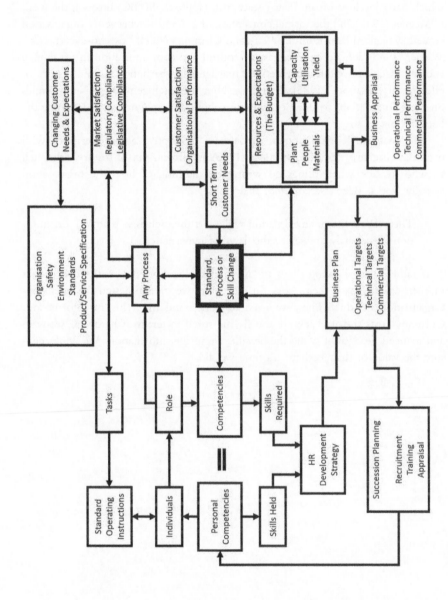

**FIGURE 1.2** The interdependence of organisations

## Summary

Radical though they may seem, the ideas explored in this book have a long history. The ideas are rooted in the concepts and ideas of managerial cybernetics which have developed from Plato's steersman (approx. 390 BC) through the work of Wiener (1948) and the formal conception of a "neuro-cybernetic" organisation created by Stafford Beer from the 1950s and Clemson's (1984) "psycho-cybernetics". Wiener (1948) defined cybernetics as "control and communication in the animal and the machine", while Beer defined managerial cybernetics as "the science of effective organisation" (1985). Thinking about the Intelligent Organisation builds on those foundations to draw on thinking about and applying the ideas over the last 20 years or so.

The established organisational models are descriptive and prescriptive with organisation charts described by Beer (1985) as "frozen out of history"; they tell us who to sack when things go wrong but nothing of how the organisation actually works. Beer asserts (1985) that:

> The cybernetics of any situation will assert themselves so that ALL organisations necessarily answer to the 'laws' of cybernetics.

If rather than allowing them to 'assert themselves' we design the cybernetics in, then we can make them work for us. Before we start to design the Intelligent Organisation on these lines, we need to understand the value of information. Currently costs and payback are usually measured in terms of hardware, software and reduced headcount while the benefits are in the information. We don't measure the value of that. Perhaps it's time we did.

# 2

# THE VALUE OF INFORMATION

Nowadays people know the price of everything and the value of nothing.

Oscar Wilde, *The Picture of Dorian Gray* (1890)

## Introduction

Information is valuable in its own right to organisations. It is a resource that we should capture, manage, retrieve and invest in for the benefit of the whole organisation. Its value is realised when it allows us to make decisions which enhance the effectiveness of the organisation in fulfilling its purpose. However, while we talk about the 'information system' and invest in infrastructure, software and hardware, we rarely think about the information itself and how we exploit it for value.

## Accounting for information

*An organisation operating a continuous production process has around 200 software applications, invests annually about £25m of capital and spends more than £20m of revenue on information systems (IS).*

*The value of the information provided to the organisation? Unknown. No one is held to account for it, the basis of investment is 'best endeavours' and, bizarrely, they don't have the information to make good decisions about investing in information.*

Many organisations conform to this example. They don't seem to know why they buy what they buy, they don't really know why they use what they use. Many have no real idea what the information systems cost to buy or run and cannot even estimate what value is generated. If the mantra that 'what gets measured, gets managed' holds true, then organisations need to get serious about benefits realisation from investment in information. They have much latent information in the form of data but do not use it in an intelligent manner, and many of the true costs of information systems are, in one way or another, lost in the budgets of other parts of the organisation.

## Feeding the monster

*A sweet manufacturer installed a state-of-the-art enterprise resource planning (ERP) system to improve production and financial control and reduce costs. Production staff, working within local budgets, all upgraded local PCs and spreadsheet software to generate the data to 'feed' the ERP. The costs of these upgrades were in the production budget, not the IS budget. Savings were claimed while costs went up.*

Often a system change in one part of a business does not remove a cost so much as displace it to another, so that while one manager is receiving a bonus for improved performance and reduced costs, another is negotiating for an increased budget whilst being criticised for overspending. The particular case mentioned above is from around 2004 and I was concerned about its continued relevance – until told in May 2014 of another organisation experiencing exactly the same thing.

All this happens for several reasons:

- Organisations (and budgets) are managed through functional silos, not as integrated whole systems;
- Interdependencies are not understood, observed or respected and the wider organisational implications of proposed changes are not recognised;
- Costs are often exported to other silos – displaced rather than reduced;
- It is easier to invest money in things we can see, the computers and their peripheral artefacts which we can count, measure and, if impressive enough, feature in the annual report than it is to invest in 'invisible' information and the thoughtful use of it.

## What's IT worth?

Organisations spend money on technology and systems when they should be investing in information to enable intelligent decisions. A change is needed; rather than measuring the cost of information systems provision, we need to measure the value of the information provided. That is a fundamental shift, a challenge to the conventional way of thinking, but relatively easy to express in terms that should make sense for the organisation and its customers. To support that challenge, let us think about the following questions: how much could the effective use of information

- improve response times to customers (external and internal)?
- enable recognition of and response to opportunities?
- enable better decisions, closer to the customer?

- reduce time on data collection and enable more effective analysis?
- reduce product development time and time to market for new products?
- enable effective recognition of and response to threats and adverse events?

Answers to all of these questions can be expressed in terms of the drivers of any particular organisation – its critical success factors. These might include profit, volume, customer satisfaction and social outcomes. Measuring the value of information not only allows for it to be both understood and realised, it also allows for more conventional technology questions to be tackled:

- How much easier is the system to use?
- How much duplication has been eradicated?
- How much more authoritative for decision making is the information?
- How much more efficient are we?
- How much more effective are we?

Value rests in our ability to deliver information to generate strategic or operational insights. That allows us to use it to deliver sustainable improvements in customer service, competitive position, costs and revenues.

That suggests that some further important questions need to be addressed:

- How much is a happy customer worth?
- What is the value of time in the market?
- What is the true cost of error or failure?
- How productive are we?

## The value of a happy customer

A happy customer offers two potential sources of value, one easy to measure, the other more difficult. In the first case it is reasonable to assume that a happy customer will be a repeat customer and that makes for a simple equation:

*Net Profit per Item * Number of Repeat Purchases = £V(☺C)*

This value is then amplified by the number of repeat customers.

However, in order to solve the sum (to provide the information as opposed to the data) we cannot work in silos, we need data from different parts of the organisation:

- Finance need to be able to state the net profit per individual item sold;
- Commercial need to provide the repeat cycle frequency;
- Marketing need to be able to state the number of repeat customers.

No functional silo can solve this apparently simple problem alone.

The second potential source of value is the number of other people the happy customer tells, who then go on to become customers. The data to calculate this is not easily available in the organisation's systems. It might be obtained through effective customer surveys, in particular through the idea of the "net promoter score" (Reichheld & Markey, 2011) which calculates the proportion of your customers who would recommend you to somebody else. It is equally important to recognise that the inverse question is also valid:

What is the cost of an unhappy customer?

Here the negative amplifying effect of telling others is often held to be greater than the positive cycle:

'If I am happy with the service I will shop there again. If I am not happy with the service I will tell everybody I know.'

And social media (another IT-enabled activity) means that a lot of people can be told very quickly.

Happy customers are not produced by sales, finance or marketing alone. They result from all of the interactions of the customer with the organisation, its collective ability to understand and inform the customer, to meet their expectations and needs. While the impact can be measured at the customers, it is the alignment of the organisation towards them that generates the value.

## The value of time in the market

The value of time in the market is vitally important when there are finite limits to the product or service life. These include shelf-life for perishables, patent life for pharmaceuticals and other protected goods and services, or 'first to market' advantages for technology-based products. Again, the equation is simple:

*Net Profit per Item * Volume per Day * Number of Days advantage*

For a pharmaceutical company, with strict time limits on a patent before generic competitors can enter the market, being faster is potentially worth billions in additional revenues. At the other end of the scale, fresh produce that does not hit the market immediately is valueless, generating cost but no revenue. That can mean not just profit or loss but survival of the business for a low margin producer. While the particular specification of information arrangements will necessarily differ widely between these situations, nobody likes a day-old doughnut.

Turning first to the pharmaceutical company. Information flows from opportunities for therapeutic treatments in a global market, through research and development, testing and regulatory compliance, marketing, production, 'detailing' to clinicians and, finally, prescription. The process may take around seven to eight years to be fully worked through to the first prescription, at which point the company has perhaps only six or seven protected years to exploit its product. The commercial benefit of being six months faster to the market for a product likely to generate billions in revenue is huge. The need for effective conversion of data into information across the whole process is evident, the challenge substantial, the benefits massive.

While the holder of a pharmaceutical patent has a legal advantage against competitors, the same does not apply, at least not as much, to innovators in technology markets. Whilst particular technical components might be protectable by patent, there is nothing to prevent a competitor marketing a product with similar or even identical functionality and, often, functionality can be replicated quickly. In this case, time to market needs to be complemented by rapid client acquisition; it is vital to be both first and fast. Information about the market and the customers is key to both and its value can be expressed in terms of products, market penetration and revenue. Each day that the product is in the market without competition, the revenue opportunity against competitors increases.

## The true cost of error or failure

Fresh goods production generates some particular challenges for information; there is a limited market for stale bread.

For the producer of perishable goods working with very short timescales, intelligent use of information is critical. Market demand and responses to changes in that demand, time to market, delivery times, prices (which are often dynamic) and current consumption rates are key. Producing too much generates unrecoverable costs, producing too little misses profit opportunities.

## Mushroom management

*Working with a mushroom grower, primarily a supplier to the major supermarket chains, we determined that there was a major process issue that might be solved by information. At best, mushrooms have a 48-hour shelf-life before they are unsaleable. The presenting issue was that the final order from the supermarkets was received at 7am for shipping by 12 noon. This shipping deadline was enforced to meet the 'just-in-time' delivery schedule for distribution centres and shop deliveries. An order not delivered to the distribution centre on time would most probably be returned and the product scrapped.*

*While the supermarkets provided 'indicative' purchase plans a year ahead, updated quarterly, monthly and weekly, they only committed to the product on the day. Actual order volumes varied to reflect unsold stock on the supermarket shelf from the previous day and changes in the weather; any sudden change in temperature or precipitation could trigger an immediate change in both the volume of mushrooms produced and the demand in the market, but these were not often consistent with each other.*

*The picking, packing and dispatch process had a maximum five-hour window and assumed availability of sufficient product in the growing sheds.*

*A mushroom, under the right conditions, doubles in size every 24 hours. In broad terms, the crop (combined volume and weight) is fixed by the combination and composition of components – compost, casing material, spores – and the growing conditions – temperature, moisture, draught. They can be flexed to give a +/- 24-hour change in crop readiness. Because of the overall growing time, the production volume decision is taken 42 days before the first cropping day and the decision about volume of compost is taken 5–7 days before that. The producer is therefore cropping on any given day a volume and weight of mushrooms determined 42–49 days beforehand against an order received that day. Every order not met is a lost revenue opportunity; every mushroom not sold is an unrecoverable cost.*

*Value of time in the market can be comprehended in this case by effective estimation 42–49 days ahead of the likely market demand and by accurate forecasting of the volume of mushrooms available from a given weight of materials under anticipated weather conditions. It is well known that weather forecasts are rarely accurate any more than three days ahead.*

*This is a substantial probabilistic challenge. Almost nothing can be known to a certainty. Realising value lies in eliminating as much uncertainty as possible while making defensible assumptions about the rest. The whole then needs to be brought together in a decision model, its accuracy enhanced by learning from experience such that, over time, the mean gap between volume produced and volume sold is reduced; a form of optimisation.*

*Critically, in this instance, the organisation needs to use data at two levels. The first level deals with the prediction of production and demand; an operational cycle. The second level uses data about the accuracy of the first level predictions to improve the utility of the model itself. This requires consistent, considered use of multiple data sets over time, not an attribute of most organisations or their information systems. The tradition of the organisation was 'judgement', a best guess based on experience. Whilst useful – experienced people are very good at making judgements – this tradition had its limitations.*

*An information model was developed that brought the disparate elements together in a systemic whole. The impact of this robust information model over time was to reduce the mean gap in value terms by around £1m per year, taking account of the cost of lost opportunity and the cost of scrappage. For a business with a turnover of around £20m and a net bottom line of £1m, that was a significant gain.*

Street traders in many tourist destinations provide a good example of market responsiveness. In the few minutes that it takes to observe an imminent change in the weather, they shift from selling parasols to selling umbrellas, or mini-copters, buckets and spades or caps and back again.

Success for either an individual or a large corporation rests in the ability to process and respond to changes in internal and external information at the same rate as the rate of change of the data. This is a truly dynamic requirement that will not be fulfilled through the traditional approaches of reporting, discussing and deciding. Adaptation must be done in something approaching real time, and when the organisation is really smart it can adapt in anticipation, it can be intelligent.

## How productive are we?

Assessment of productivity has been a key concern for organisations for hundreds of years and is of increasing importance in sustaining performance. Such assessment brings together a number of interacting factors:

- Capacity of plant and machinery;
- Reliability and 'downtime';
- Resilience of infrastructure;
- Process and job design;
- Application of skill;
- Attitudes and behaviours;
- Supervision and management;
- Use of information as an enabler of decisions.

These things are not always brought together to optimum effect.

## The benefit of understanding interdependency

*A manufacturer was fighting in a dynamic market to increase value to customers by increasing volume while holding its cost base static. Increased product availability had immediate sales benefit and every additional ton of sales generated revenue of around £350. Daily production volume was erratic and appeared unpredictable, the annual production and sales targets, around 300 kilotons (kt), were constantly missed.*

*A simulator (an information system) was built which analysed the production capacity of the whole plant and identified potential production volume both for each stage and the whole interacting process. This showed an opportunity to generate budgeted volume plus 30% if run effectively. Multiple simulations were explored with the management team to find optimum performance. One finding was that the yield losses between the first two stages of the process were stable at about 3%, i.e. to obtain 1 ton of product after stage two required 1.03 tons of product after stage one. However, the budgets (negotiated in silo fashion) required stage two to produce 10% more than stage one. This had a bizarre consequence – stage one could only succeed by making stage two fail and stage two could only succeed if stage one failed. In establishing the production plan, notice had been taken of the capacity of each phase but not their interactions.*

*A plan was devised to balance the throughput across the process and manage the plant to increase output to meet market demand. Within 12 months the plant was producing at the 400kt level and all output was sold. The value of information? 100kt * £350/t = £35m additional revenue in a full year.*

The simulation in this instance initially considered only the relationships between the physical artefacts of the system and their interactions. However, in addition to the 'simple' identification of the performance characteristics of the interacting machines (volumes, flow rates, downtime and reliability), the creation of the simulation tool depended on engagement with the people who actually did the work, the operational stakeholders. Sharing information about the relationships and interdependency of the whole system stimulated reflection on the design of operational jobs, limitations and constraints applied by 'management', the maintenance regime, construction of budgets and a host of other matters. All of these impacted on, and usually impaired, the achievement of the full potential of the

plant. Revealing 'new' information to the stakeholders about overall plant performance and their part in it led to significant shifts in their thinking about what
was possible. It was those shifts which delivered the change. This shows that we
can, must, use information as the link between processes and structures, skills and
behaviours. Neither will change without impacting on the other.

When we shift focus to service organisations the challenge becomes harder.
Services, like manufacturing, rely on good process, but the emphasis of service
delivery is on human interaction (Beckford, 2010). Unlike manufacturing, service
productivity cannot easily be measured to a highly precise level. A high level of
certainty can be obtained in a manufacturing process using quantitative metrics
and appropriately frequent measurement. Services rely for their completion on
the application of the necessary 'skills' to carry out the relevant task in conjunction with the appropriate 'behaviours' (of both service provider and customer).
Whilst there are tangible aspects to this which lend themselves to measurement,
there are significant intangibles which do not. Did the right things happen? How
did it feel?

The assessment of intangible aspects has a great degree of probabilism associated
with it. It cannot be modelled or represented in the same way as a manufacturing
activity. Key elements of service are ephemeral – they exist only in the moment of
the transaction itself and cannot be captured, monitored and measured quantitatively.
In these cases measurement may be obtained through a variety of qualitative tools
which, appropriately applied, can give statistically reliable indicators of performance.

Uncertainty can be reduced in relationship-based transactions by investment
in the development of both skills and behaviours. The first of these relies on
training operators in the skills relevant to the task, the 'what' of the transaction.
The second requires a behavioural focus, the 'how'. This is a sophisticated need.
It means that the individual must choose to adhere to the values and norms of
the organisation, the 'why'. They must also, insofar as it is possible (Wilson, 2002),
understand their own behaviour (and its impact on others) and the behaviour of
others (and its impact on them).

Modification of skills and behaviours relies upon effective communication of
information between the organisation and its employees: technical information
about how to carry out the process and behavioural information about how to
interact with customers and about values, why those things are done. Measurement
of a particular instance of a service transaction will always be problematic and to
some extent subjective. It relies on human interpretation of what happened, what
was said, what was meant and what was understood. Such transactions are highly
amenable to quantitative analysis in the aggregate and on an understanding of the
systemic rather than point impact of success or failure.

Service provision in a call centre (which is a very common means of providing
customer service) is often measured, expressed and incentivised in terms of:

- number of calls handled
- length of call.

The incentive mechanism, an expression of information about what is really important to the organisation, encourages a particular type of behaviour; that is, the call receiver is encouraged to terminate calls quickly in order to get to the next caller. If, as is often the case, the customer need is not satisfied during the first call, then a second call is received from that person. The call centre appears to be succeeding; lots of calls are being handled very quickly. The customer is increasingly irate.

Observation suggests that each subsequent call roughly doubles in length. The customer has to explain that they have called before, still have the problem and repeat the explanation of the problem. Because the call receiver is now failing (the call is taking longer), it is likely to either be escalated (*'your call is being held in a queue for . . .'*) or to receive a promise for action in order to clear the line. The call operator can then get back to the original queue. The information about performance (and the incentive) given to the call receiver is driving precisely the wrong behaviour. The costs of service are increasing because the number of calls is driven up. The organisation risks losing the customer to a competitor, another cost.

Now, if your call really was important to them? The call centre performance would be measured on 'first-time resolution'. The operator would be incentivised to stay on the call longer, fix or immediately escalate the problem and satisfy the customer. The measurement of productivity would not be about how many calls were handled (efficiency – an internal measure) but about how many customers were satisfied (effectiveness – an external measure). The Intelligent Organisation would capture useful data about the content of the calls to understand what drives the volume, and use that information to modify behaviours and processes in other parts of the organisation. This 'feedback' of information would drive overall performance improvement.

## The perpetually failing problem-solving engine

Typically, because most information systems reflect the functional, siloed structure of the organisation, data is difficult to bring together in a coherent way to inform valuable decisions. Data definitions vary widely; the same word may in any organisation have different meanings for different people and the same data may be differently defined in different functional silos.

Because data are distributed in this way we end up with a "perpetually failing problem-solving engine" Figure 2.1 (adapted from Beckford, 1993). The ability of the organisation to respond to changes in data does not match the rate of change in data (volume, frequency and content). Decisions are made which are designed for the problem we had (an assumption that nothing has changed), not the one we have now. The "mean time between perturbations of the system" (Beer, 1974) is shorter than the time it takes the organisation to respond. The goalposts are necessarily moving but the players cannot keep up. Simply, in Figure 2.1, at T1 a problem is identified and modelled, M1, leading to a proposed

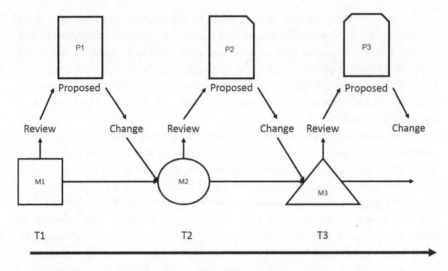

**FIGURE 2.1** The perpetually failing problem-solving engine

solution, P1, and a change process ensues. However, by the time this has happened the situation has evolved to M2 and the P1 solution is no longer suitable, the proposal fails. At T2 a fresh look is taken, M2, and a further solution, P2, is developed. Meanwhile, the situation, in this dynamic organisation in a dynamic environment, continues to evolve so that at T3 the situation is different again and the P2 proposal no longer holds. The cycle continues because the organisation is developing and applying solutions to problems more slowly than their rate of change.

To resolve this cycle and ensure that the organisation can respond effectively to necessary change it must, through use of information, respond to the 'Conant-Ashby Theorem' (1970):

> Every competent regulator of a system must be a model of the system.

This suggests (Conant and Ashby did the mathematics so I needn't bother here) that for an organisation to be effective in self-regulation, it requires an internal 'model of self' (MoS). That is a representation of its ideal state against which effectiveness can be measured and which provides the basis for change. In order to act intelligently, the organisation must create an informational representation of itself which is much richer than the traditional financial 'budget'. In effect, it needs to be able look at its own reflection in a mirror. It must be able to change its processes, behaviours and systems to become better at being itself and to do that at least as fast as the situation is changing, preferably faster. It must anticipate rather than simply respond to change in its situation. To become truly adaptive it must maintain an internal model of its environment, all those market, technical, social, political and environmental issues that affect its viability and use that to adapt itself to the environment and adapt the environment to itself.

## Summary

This chapter has shown how we commonly fail to realise the value of the information already held by organisations and how we might come to comprehend what that value is. We have seen how the functional orientation of our structures, systems, processes and behaviours acts to inhibit effective use of that information.

The Intelligent Organisation is a dynamic, self-reflective, adaptive system, understanding both the cost of information and the value generated from it. In the next chapter, we shall see how it can overcome the limitations of our current models.

# 3

# GENERATING VALUE

The world in our heads is not a precise replica of reality.
Daniel Kahnemann, *Thinking, Fast and Slow* (2011)

## Introduction

We have established that the Intelligent Organisation relies on an understanding of integrated information as the key to organisational survival and that there is substantial value to be realised from that integration. That requires us to conceive of an organisational architecture for the information age. The initial stage is to think about the first major element of the Intelligent Organisation, the Value-Generation System.

## Thinking about organisation

Survival-worthy organisations are conceived as purposeful, adaptive, self-aware and dynamical systems. The conventional organogram is unhelpful. It tells us who to fire when things go wrong but says nothing of how the organisation actually functions, the processes, tasks and procedures, skills we bring to bear or values that underpin our behaviour. The organogram tells us who reports to whom and who is (at least notionally) responsible for what, but tells us nothing of how the organisation becomes bound into a purposeful entity. However, an organisation is of necessity 'organised'; without structure and some form of hierarchy arising in its internal relationships it will be chaotic, perhaps anarchic, each part struggling to interact meaningfully with others, maybe attempting to create rules and impose them on the other parts. Neither the organogram nor anarchy appear particularly useful.

A little philosophy is essential here, some thinking about the whole organisation as self-regulating, adaptive, self-aware and dynamical. Self-regulating means that it is able to manage itself towards its goal. Adaptive means that change capability must be designed in, not added as an afterthought, an initiative or a strategy. Self-aware means that it must be able to see 'itself' as a whole in its environment, that is, its customers, its market and the economic, social and political circumstances in which it exists. Dynamical means that it must be able to interpret the evolution of its environment and have internal capability to change itself in relation to it – built in, not bolted on. The organisation, its customers and its environment must co-evolve.

It may need to offer different products or services or the same products and services in different ways. This implies it must be able to adapt itself locally in its immediate interactions with its customers. That will require a significant level of autonomy for customer-facing individuals, since the organisation cannot adapt at a very local level without it. A 'one-size-fits-all' procedure cannot offer a solution to this. It doesn't matter how long we make the procedure chart, it will never quite reach the customer whose needs will nearly always fall between two possible outcomes. That causes tension; while adapting itself to the needs of individual customers the organisation needs consistency and coherence around its processes in order to *be* an organisation. The Intelligent Organisation must achieve a dynamic level of autonomy in its operation that is best described as tight–loose control. It must tightly constrain those things which define it as itself and nothing else, while at the same time exercising only loose control on other factors, creating conditions under which individuals can empower themselves. This is not an invitation to anarchy. A logical hierarchy will emerge from the design, a hierarchy based on information, the need for both constraint and autonomy and a more adequate definition of what management means.

## The Intelligent Organisation – overview

In the Intelligent Organisation, effectiveness (Figure 3.1) is a function of the interactions of processes, structures, people (the values, skills and behaviours they apply to the processes and structures) and information. These are integrated to provide three perspectives:

* What: the 'hard', quantitative processes, structure and numbers;
* How: the 'soft', qualitative, skills and behaviours; and
* Why: 'purpose', the expression of personal and organisational values.

Effectiveness is given meaning in the interaction of these perspectives.

Effectiveness is not a measure of financial performance or profitability, but a measure of how well the organisation meets the expectations of its customers and its capability to survive. Financial performance is subsumed into this richer understanding. We shall return to performance measurement later on, for now let it

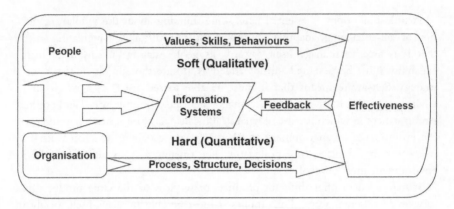

**FIGURE 3.1** Organisational effectiveness

suffice that, within the legal and financial conventions adopted in most economies, *all* organisations are constrained, over time, to generate at least as much revenue as cost. Financial performance is best thought of as one of a basket of measures and is just as important to public and third-sector organisations as it is to commercial enterprises.

While we must deal with the organisation as a whole, we do need to break up the story into manageable parts; it is not a linear discussion. In the rest of this chapter we deal with the value-generating parts of the organisation. They interact directly with customers; they fulfil the fundamental purpose of the organisation.

## Generating value: the fundamental activity

Designed backwards from the customer, the Intelligent Organisation is process based. The customer is the ultimate beneficiary of the process however many steps there may be. Processes, and there is usually more than one, are sets of activities (tasks and procedures) that integrate to produce goods and/or services that meet the desired customer and organisational outcomes (Figure 3.2). Represented generically here for the purpose of explanation, the work of a process is to convert inputs into outputs that meet desired outcomes. The process design must be rooted in understanding the needs and desires of customer(s) (who may be internal or external) and the extent to which the organisation is willing to fulfil them and then determining what activities and inputs are required to meet them.

Outputs include not only the products and services required by the customer but also the by-products – residual materials, cash, waste, data and experience which should be utilised in the next iteration of the process. The input–process–output is shown for convenience at this stage as a single line; don't worry, it will get more complicated soon.

Looking at the process, we find that it is broken down into a series of tasks or subprocesses, and those tasks are further broken down into detailed procedures.

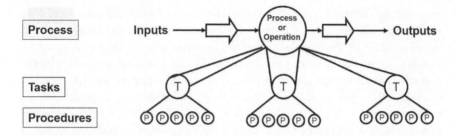

**FIGURE 3.2** The process, tasks and procedures

A core process is end to end, usually company-wide (Feigenbaum, 1986), and its output is something of value to a customer. A helpful starting point for identifying core processes is to understand what constitutes 'value' for the customer.

For a water and sewerage company, the customer expects potable water from the tap and the removal of dirty water via the drains. This suggests a minimum of two core processes for the company; one which collects, cleans and delivers water and one which removes used water, treats it and disposes of it. The process for potable water then can be considered as a series of tasks, working from the beginning of the process as:

Collect Water – Treat Water – Distribute Water

The sewerage process tasks can be considered as:

Collect 'Used' Water – Treat Water – Dispose of Water

The water company probably needs to add to that a customer service process for repair and invoicing. It will have a lot of assets connected to create its network (a highly distributed water factory), and it can be argued that maintenance of that 'water factory' is also a core process. Alternatively it can be argued either that 'maintenance' is a task within the production processes or that it is an 'enabling' process (see Chapters 5 and 6). The 'right' answer, to some extent, depends upon how we choose to interpret the organisation and how responsibility and accountability for performance are to be managed. In essence, a choice needs to be made about whether the activity is understood and managed as value generating or value enabling.

For a motor car manufacturer, the thing that the customer values is perhaps the car, so the overall core process tasks can be considered as:

Design Car – Manufacture Car – Distribute Car

Another good argument ensues here, does the customer value the car or the journey (or personal convenience) that the car enables? The manufacturer sets a price for the car; that is what they value. The customer may well value something else. In the UK, the greater part of the new car market is for leased company vehicles, while in the private market a significant proportion are acquired on personal contract plans or hire–purchase. The focus for all these sales is on periodic cost rather than outright purchase price. The manufacturer receives the capital at once via the dealer or the finance company, whilst the user is paying for the vehicle over time. It may be that each party is valuing different aspects of the transaction. It is important to understand the perspectives of both the customer and the organisation in establishing the purpose of any process. The solution probably rests in understanding the purpose of the organisation from the perspective of the customer; the need or opportunity it exists to fulfil.

In the service context the outcome does not sustain as it does in manufacturing, it is largely created and consumed in the interaction of the organisation and customer. The same essential logic applies, however. The 'output' of a dental practice might be considered as 'completed dental treatments'. While the process which produces that has both curative and preventative characteristics, the 'outcome' is patients with healthy teeth. The greater part of the output rests in the application of professional knowledge, skill and judgement; it relies more on skills and behaviours than on pure process, but nonetheless relies on a simple statement of the process steps:

Receive Patient – Assess Patient – Treat Patient

These are, of necessity, massive simplifications. Processes must focus on delivering the purpose of the organisation, the reason it exists and, ultimately, their performance define its effectiveness. However, as the following case shows, whilst the process is critical, it is not the whole but one part of the essential 'triple' of what, how and why.

## Visiting the dentist

*While considering the effectiveness of a dental practice, the dentist was asked to define the detailed tasks and procedures that underpin the high-level process description. The detail of 'Receive Patient' was quite short and simple, essentially the verification of identity and appointment. The detail of 'Assess Patient' took a dozen pages of written description just to get the patient into the chair. It required the dentist to assess everything from the mood and demeanour of the patient (determining in what manner they should be dealt with) to the clinical requirements (the overall apparent health of the patient to the specific condition of every individual tooth). Thereafter, 'Treat Patient' consisted of over 180 different things that might be done for every individual tooth. It was neither useful nor practical to attempt to document in procedural terms every possibility. That was best left to the judgement and skill of the dentist. That is rooted (pardon the pun) in extensive initial training, continuing professional development and experience.*

Life can become more complex again. Public services (whether directly provided or through an agency or nongovernmental organisation), often have multiple parties who might be considered as the customer. Is the customer the funder? The beneficiary of the service? Both? Does one process satisfy all needs? In healthcare, especially with commissioning of services, is the process focused on patient benefit? Referrer benefit? Funder benefit? Understanding organisational purpose is fundamental to adequately addressing these challenges. If the role of the police in the UK is to 'preserve the Queen's peace' who is their customer? Society? The Home Office? The 'citizen'? The police and crime commissioner (as representative of the citizen)?

It might be argued that the police have two core processes. First might be the prevention of harm and crime, second the detection and arrest of criminals – the final output of which is a 'prosecution-ready' case file, because the prosecution itself is undertaken by a separate service. The answer chosen has implications for both design and management of 'the process' and for understanding performance. If 'harm and crime prevention' and 'crime detection and arrest' are treated as the 'core processes', then complete success on the first (zero crime) renders the second redundant, whereas complete failure on the first will (probably) mean that the second is overloaded.

There is an emerging theme here of the need to achieve the most appropriate (under the varying circumstances) definition of purpose and clarity of process. In a knowledge economy, we must understand how to balance the constraints necessary for process standardisation and compliance with the freedom necessary to allow professional judgement to be exercised.

It is critically important that work starts with the customer-oriented process(es); the fundamental activity flow. Once the core processes have been defined, they can then be disaggregated into the discrete tasks and contained procedures required for their completion. This ensures that all of the activities of the organisation at this level are focused on the customer and that improvement at either the task or procedure level is measured in terms of contribution to process performance. This avoids the risk, so commonly experienced, of an improvement that answers to Hutber's Law (1970s) – "improvement means deterioration"; we don't simply do the wrong thing better.

## The homeostat: the logical emergence of hierarchy

The process so far described will produce only the outputs it has been designed for. However, as with any system, left to itself the process will change and, most likely, decay. Materials, people, skills and data all change over time. The customer perception of the value of the service or product and the social, economic, political and environmental circumstances all evolve. Left to itself the process will tend towards either chaos or crystallisation. For the physicists amongst you, this answers to the Second Law of Thermodynamics which states, roughly, that the amount of free energy in a closed system will decrease over time. In our case, the free energy (usually money) will be wasted sustaining a chaotic system (anarchy) or consumed in an inflexible way of working (bureaucratic crystallisation). The latter

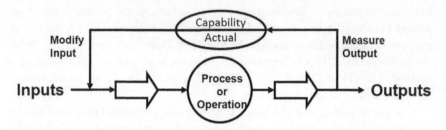

**FIGURE 3.3** The emergence of hierarchy

arises when the organisation does not adapt to the environment, the former when the attempts at adaptation are individually arbitrary. Either way it dies. There is therefore a logical need to regulate the process. This enables local self-regulation (how did I do?), adaptation and moderation to ensure that the process remains aligned with its environment and continues to be efficient and is called a homeo-stat. The process output that enables this is information and that is used to make decisions (Figure 3.3). The regulator, the logically necessary activity of 'management', is essential to keep process aligned with the customer and organisational expectations.

In Figure 3.3, the manager as regulator (the divided oval) is shown as receiving feedback (measurement of output) from the end of the process. The manager compares what was achieved (actual) with what was desired (capability) and acts to close the gap between them by changing one or more of the inputs (i.e. materials, energy, cash, skills, behaviours, data). If done right, on the next iteration of the process cycle the gap gets smaller. The manager is using feedback about the process embedding self-correction and constituting Ashby's homeostat (1952). This same approach applies to the contained tasks and procedures.

Management is the name we give the activities of those responsible for 'regulating' our organisations. It consists in closing the gap between things as they are (actual) and things as we desire them to be (capability) and is logically necessary. How that management is exercised is not yet considered. We are not yet exploring the 'how' of management, simply the 'what'. Readers will be very familiar with comparators, they exist in heating and cooling systems (thermostats for regulating temperature), lighting systems (rheostats for regulating light levels) and in motor vehicles (cruise control systems and anti-lock braking systems). These are very simple regulators, typically operating with a single externally generated goal and an on/off response. In the organisation the regulator needs to be more sophisti-cated, it needs to deal with a range of possible goals and a range of possible responses. This needs judgement and that needs people.

Figure 3.4 shows the regulators in place at the task level and how the process constrains both tasks and procedures. These and their regulation may all be con-ducted by a single individual (self-management is entirely legitimate and highly

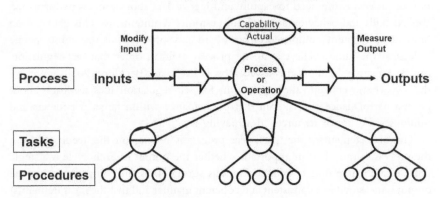

**FIGURE 3.4** Process and task regulation

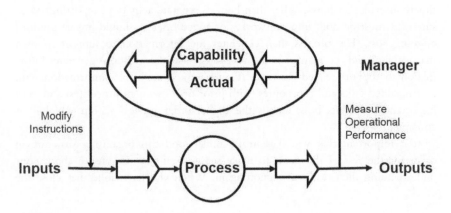

**FIGURE 3.5** The process of management

desirable) or may involve hundreds of people in a large organisation. For now, it is the principle of this integration of process and regulation that is important.

Figure 3.5 opens up the regulator so that the management task can be seen. It shows that the input to the management process, at this level of consideration, is the output performance metrics of the operational process.

The explicit task of management (a process running backwards from the output to the input) is to compare actual with desired output and modify the inputs to close the gap. It is important to appreciate that management is limited in the things it can modify:

- the process itself (the what) – tasks, procedures, materials;
- the skills and behaviours to be applied (the how and why);
- the desired output (standard) – (perhaps in response to a change in customer requirements or market conditions or even the internal capability of the process itself).

Management does this through the use of information. Implicit in this regulation of process is the need to capture and report data about process performance, applied skills and behaviours and about customer requirements. This demands an 'information system' comprised of both hard and soft elements that must operate at least at the same cyclic rate as the process itself, in order that 'self-regulation' can be effective. Shingo's quality idea of 'Poka-Yoke' (Beckford, 2010) embraces this cybernetic concept; the mechanism for self-regulation uses feedback about process performance to maintain that performance within target parameters and minimises the use of resources in achieving it.

The management of any particular process is relying on the 'feedback' from the process output. It is unimportant whether the output of each cycle is a single unit, a batch of products or a continuous stream. It is only important that the output is measured in a consistent and coherent manner and that the measurement(s) is useful to the manager (regulator) in modifying the input to the next cycle. A well-designed process will embed data generation, as one of its outputs, to support timely information flows, rather than being a separate activity of reporting. Measurement must be built into the work, not added on, and should impart minimal ongoing cost. The process then generates the information to support its own management and the management process (the act of regulation) generates information to support related processes (Figure 3.6). It exchanges information with its embedded tasks and procedures, with prior or subsequent process(es) and, very importantly, with its boss, that is the higher-order process within which it is contained.

It is important that you have really understood this organising structure in order for the rest of the book to make sense, so, if you are unsure about your understanding then read this section again. When you have done that, close the

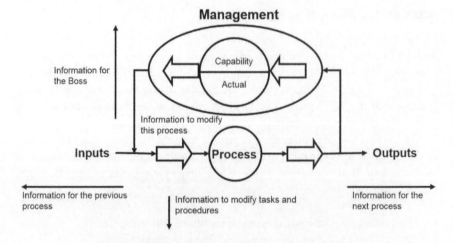

**FIGURE 3.6** Information dissemination

book, lean back, stare at the ceiling for a while and think how different it is to convention. When I was first working with these concepts, I called my Ph.D. supervisor, saying "This is really hard", to which he replied, "Yes it is" and put the phone down.

Now I suggest you take some time out from reading and attempt to map your organisation into the model . . .

What are the outcomes sought?
What are its outputs?
What are the core processes?
How is information used to manage them?

## Requisite complexity

The 'homeostat' will be regarded from here as the fundamental unit of organisation. It replaces the functional hierarchy to which we have become inured with a hierarchy based on managing process performance through information. It is a 'permeable loop'. Closed enough to allow it to be self-regulating, as long as it is provided with appropriate forms of energy it will keep on doing whatever you designed it to do in the first place. Open enough to exchange information with its environment of customers and predecessor and successor processes. It contains subprocesses (tasks and procedures) with which it also exchanges information and it is, itself, a subprocess of a higher order regulator (it exchanges information with its Boss). So it is informationally permeable and its information exchanges need to be structured. It needs information, not data, with which to inform managerial decisions.

The understanding developed so far is good but not yet rich enough. The homeostat so far presented has but a single arrow, implying perhaps a single channel for information flow. This has been a convenience to help with the writing. In any real situation the homeostat must have requisite complexity to deal with variety, the range of possible conditions or states it can be in, thrown up by the whole process. The process is productive through the interaction between all the elements of production. I have 'arbitrarily' chosen six factors of production to represent the general case of a process in an extended homeostat (Figure 3.7). I know that 'we are different' – everybody is a 'special case' – but every actual process will be a particular case of this generic one.

The manager, as regulator, is receiving information (aggregated and contextualised data) about all the outputs of the process, expressed as measures of operational performance, and understanding the performance gap. Typically we call this a measure of efficiency or productivity. We ask how well did we utilise the various inputs compared with the desired or target level of utilisation? When there is an actionable gap (utilisation will rarely be 100%), the appropriate managerial response is to consider which of the inputs to modify for the next cycle of the process in order to close the gap. This is *not* about punishment or retribution for past

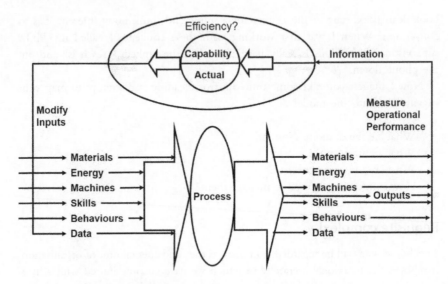

**FIGURE 3.7** Expanded homeostat

performance, it is about error prevention in the next cycle. The manager needs both to receive information and respond to it sufficiently quickly to achieve this.

It is critical to remember interdependency at this point. Changing any one input may have consequences for the others. It is inadequate management to change one parameter ('use less materials') without understanding the impact that may have on others ('apply a higher level of skill' or 'use more energy').

Working through this systemic understanding, we can now make effective use of all of the conventional tools and techniques of operations management (Slack et al., 1995). It may be appropriate to apply the tools of Business Process Improvement (Tucker, 1996), Business Process Re-Engineering (Hammer & Champy, 1993), Lean Manufacturing (Ohno, 1988) or Lean Administration (Seddon, 2005, 2008). If considering skills and behaviours, it may be desirable to apply ideas around organisational learning (Senge, 1993) and knowledge management (Hislop, 2013) and organisational psychology (Schein, 1988) and to draw on the established work concerning motivation and performance such as that of Herzberg et al. (1959), Mayo (1949) and Maslow (1970). The works of the quality gurus (Beckford, 2010) collectively offer a range of tools and techniques, many of which would be useful with this challenge.

## The management of management

Adding further complexity, now that we have one homeostat we can envisage that there will often be more than one of them. We need to start to think about how they combine. Each is, in and of itself, relatively simple; however, when we

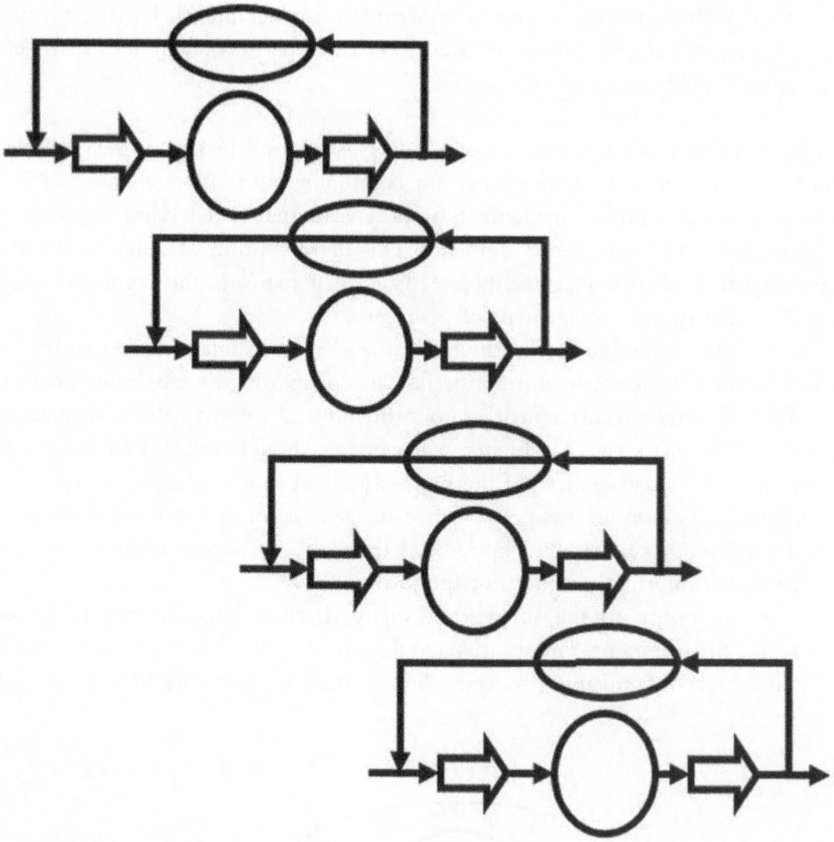

**FIGURE 3.8** Multiple processes

connect homeostats through information flows, they interact and become interdependent. Like flocking birds or swarming bees they become capable of exhibiting
apparently complex behaviour. What we have is lots of (relatively) simple things,
each doing (relatively) simple things but all joined together and activated by
information. In physical terms, each might be thought of as a simple cell which
joins together with other simple cells, collectively acting in ways which display
apparently complex, even emergent, behaviours.

It is unlikely that an organisation of any significance (even an individual) will
have only one process. There are likely to be two or more divided on some basis.

Looking at Figure 3.8, the homeostats might represent:

- four identical processes operating in different geographical markets, e.g. USA,
  Europe, Middle East, Asia-Pacific)
- four different processes in the same market (e.g. a utility company providing
  power, gas, telecommunications and water)

• four different market segments in a common geographical domain, e.g. the division of banking customers into mass-market personal, high net worth personal, small business and corporate.

In each case it is essential to recognise that because of the size of the organisation or the nature of its environment (or commonly both), it is necessary to find useful ways of discriminating segments of the environment and developing processes which are focused into those segments. This division stimulates the need for a next higher level of management, a regulator that regulates the regulators (Figure 3.9), that is, the management of managers.

If the role of the manager at the process level is to maintain performance and ensure local adaptation, within constraints, to changes in the environment, then the role of 'Senior Management' is to maintain and improve the management process. That is to say that higher management should not, indeed must not, intervene in the management of the process itself. It should observe the effect of managerial action on process performance and take action to modify the management process. Note how in Figure 3.10 the flows to higher management are linked to the information flow, not the process flow.

Thus, no doubt to the surprise of many, there *is* a useful, two-fold role for senior management. First to manage the process(es) of management, second to manage across multiple processes. Senior management should balance and

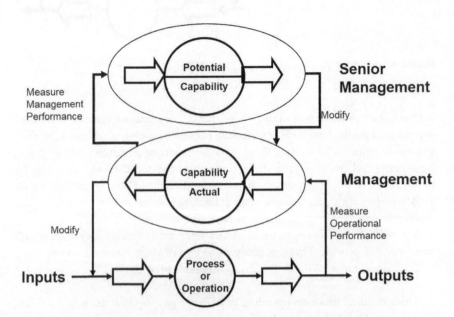

**FIGURE 3.9** The management of management

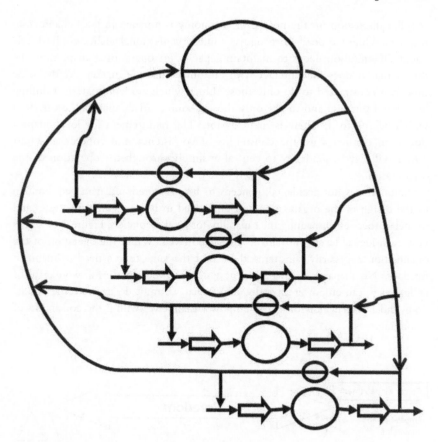

**FIGURE 3.10** Higher management observing management

optimise performance for the benefit of the whole organisation. This higher order management manages the present of the organisation, managing the delivery of current products and services to current markets in a known environment.

The hierarchical 'superiority' of management can now be seen for what it is. It is logically necessary to sustain the coherence of the whole system. It is able to make decisions *not* because it is more 'politically' powerful, but because it has more appropriate information. This information is available because it has an overview of the entirety of the processes and is the guardian of established standards and goals. In the Intelligent Organisation, information truly is power.

That does not make senior management omniscient nor all-powerful. For the organisation to be survival-worthy, power must be devolved to those who deal with the customers, otherwise the capability for local adaptation is lost.

A fuller discussion on the notion of autonomy is pursued in later chapters, in the meanwhile we need to recognise some organisational realities. The Intelligent Organisation needs to maintain capacity for operational adaptation, the things that it does that interact with customers and the market. At the same time, it is constrained to do only those things which are legitimate in fulfilling its defined purpose and to use only those resources (data, materials, skills etc.) which belong to it. There is then tension. The requirement for local adaptation is in conflict with the constraints of consistency and coherence, whilst power will have a tendency to centralise simply through the operation of the organisation.

Autonomy is not accidental; it needs to be structured and managed, built in to the design of the organisation and embedded in its operational processes and its meta-processes, enshrining the capability for local adaptation. Figure 3.11 shows how each logical level constrains its contained levels. Whilst the operation of the organisation necessarily constrains, there is at the same time a need to maintain freedom. No manager or management system, however powerful, wonderful or enlightened, can empower an individual. What we must do is create the conditions under which individuals can empower themselves within the constraints of belonging.

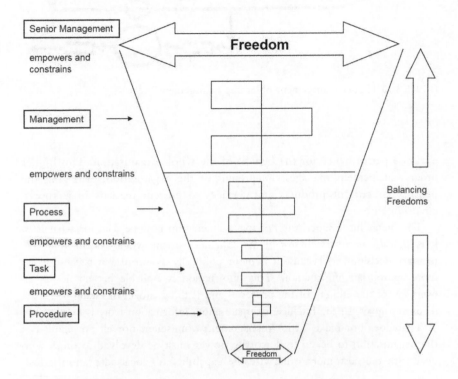

FIGURE 3.11 Managing autonomy

## Summary

This chapter has started to build the whole of the Intelligent Organisation around the central idea of the homeostat, the device using feedback about performance to enable self-regulation. It has introduced the idea of both an organisational form and the logical necessity of a hierarchical decision structure based on information.

You should perhaps spend a little more time now thinking about the implications of what you have just read before you look at the examples in the next chapter.

# 4

# GENERATING VALUE

## Cases

The purpose of the system is what it does.

Stafford Beer, *Diagnosing the System for Organisations* (1985)

## Introduction

Introducing a way of thinking holistically about organisations that challenges the traditional approach so radically, it seemed important to lay out the whole value-generating system in a single flow, rather than in a fragmented way. Hopefully you have taken a few minutes to think about your own organisation before we put theory into practice by considering three case studies:

- Fusion21: A third-sector procurement and training business;
- Southern Mill: A paper manufacturer;
- ChemCo: A research and development organisation.

At the end of the chapter, we will consider the individual as an Intelligent Organisation using me as the example. As you read, I encourage you to think how these ideas would translate to your organisation or others you know well.

Each of these case studies is revisited in later chapters to build up the whole picture.

## Profits into people not into pockets: Fusion21

Fusion21 is a social enterprise that promotes efficient public procurement as a means to generate social value and reduce costs. Originally established on Merseyside, its aim is to create demand-led training and employment. It achieves this by offering an intelligent procurement service to its clients, reducing their costs by operating cost-effective procurement frameworks and by training unemployed people in relevant skills, placing them in work with the contractors and suppliers fulfilling the contracts. A pleasing, circular outcome; the more the members spend through the frameworks, the more people in their own communities are able to find work. Fusion21 sets itself the goal of being the market leader in procurement efficiency and social value with the business objectives being:

- Maintain and support existing clients;
- Attract and retain new clients;
- Undertake research and development in improving products and services;
- Fitness for purpose.

Achieving the first two of these objectives is the focus of this study, and it works towards them through:

- Procurement Services
- Training and Employment Services
- Consultancy Services

Fusion21 looked at through a conventional organogram is represented in Figure 4.1.

As we have already established, that tells us remarkably little of how the organisation works and how it generates value for its stakeholders. How much more helpful might it be to consider the organisation through the processes (Figure 4.2) it engages in to generate value?

This shows us how each of the individual homeostats is focused on the environment in which Fusion21 seeks to do business. While each has a unique process, they draw on a shared pool of organisational resources for their completion. They share data (about customers, contractors, suppliers, tenants and job seekers), they have shared beliefs and behaviours (the culture of the organisation) but they require different skills for each process. At least some of the skills required for delivering an efficient procurement process are different from those required for training or

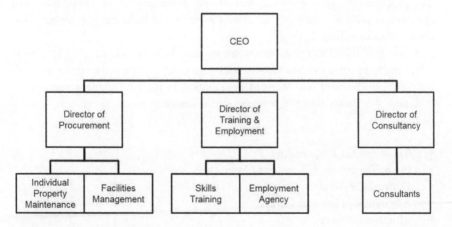

**FIGURE 4.1** Fusion21 hierarchy

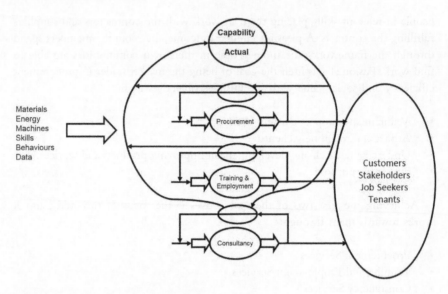

**FIGURE 4.2** Fusion21 process perspective

consultancy. Each process can be locally managed whilst there is a view of the whole (senior management) attempting to balance performance, the demand for resources and so on.

It is critical to recognise the legitimacy and necessity of shared data in this context. Remembering the 'circular outcome', the environment of the organisation (the social and economic context in which it undertakes its business) is common to all processes. Sharing of data enables a situation in which the procurement process generates a surplus. That surplus is invested in the training of job seekers who can be offered work in the delivery of the project. Indeed, in some cases Fusion21 has employed the individual rather than placing them with a contractor. The 'Training and Employment' process needs to be aware *both* of the opportunity, the 'procurement' of a contract, and of the availability of an individual with appropriate skills so that they can close the circle and place the job seeker. That demands information sharing.

It was established in the previous chapter that these overall processes are themselves made up of embedded homeostats (the tasks and procedures), so we shall now explore the next two levels of organisation in the procurement process.

Figure 4.3 shows that the process of 'Procurement' breaks down into a series of tasks:

- Recognise the Opportunity
- Invite Tenders from Suppliers/Contractors
- Evaluate the Tenders
- Appoint Supplier and Contractor
- Monitor Delivery

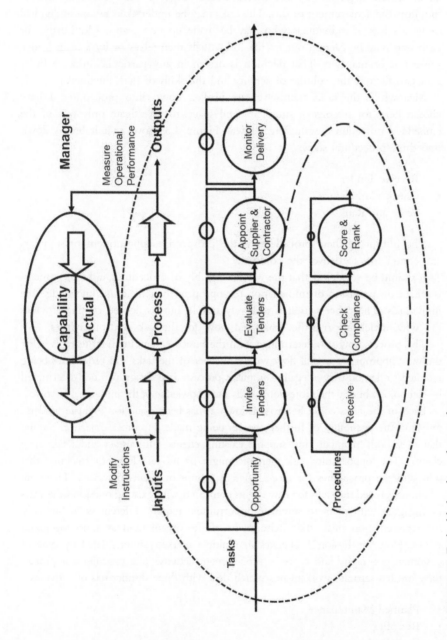

**FIGURE 4.3** Embedded tasks and procedures

Each of these tasks is itself embedded in a homeostat which receives 'inputs' from the previous step, is self-regulating and generates 'outputs' for the next step, all of which aggregates to the overall output desired. The process homeostat monitors the achievement of this. The tasks may be undertaken by one individual or by a series of individuals who may be made up into teams. Monitoring for each step may be carried out by the individuals themselves or by a team leader, supervisor or manager. That decision is driven in any particular instance by at least two factors: the volume of activity and the skills of the individuals.

Meanwhile, the tasks themselves are broken down into procedures. I have chosen here, for reasons of simplicity and space, to investigate only one of the embedded procedures, evaluating tenders. Figure 4.3 shows that it breaks down into three procedural steps:

- Receive Tender
- Check Compliance
- Score and Rank

The output of these procedures is the prospective appointment of suppliers and contractors to deliver the contract.

It should be very clear that the whole assembly of procedures, tasks and process is reliant on provision of information to appropriately skilled and knowledgeable individuals. The process itself is relatively simple, but its desired output provides the 'why' which informs the 'what' and 'how' for the tasks and procedures.

This process flow was determined with the Fusion21 procurement team as being the most appropriate overall flow, with a number of the tasks and procedures being required to demonstrate a legally compliant process. The design was not determined by technology but by the professional skills and knowledge of the individuals involved.

Each of the tasks could be broken down as has been done for 'evaluate tenders', revealing the possibility of further choices being made. Fusion21 objectives require that they both 'maintain and support existing clients' and 'attract and retain new clients'. The 'opportunity' task therefore might be broken down to recognise that split, and the procedures for those different groups of clients may vary. There are additional procedural steps for new clients compared with existing ones, and the ways of engaging with them to stimulate opportunities require different skills. Similarly, the representation treats the environment of the organisation as a homogeneous whole. However, Fusion21 operates in multiple markets, differentiated by type of customer, geography and types of procurement activity. The procurement process therefore has separate workstreams which deal with three distinct sets of activities:

- Planned Maintenance
- Retrofit
- Facilities Management

The overall process for each of these is as represented in Figure 4.3, while at the task and procedural level there are significant differences. This workstream breakdown is shown in Figure 4.4.

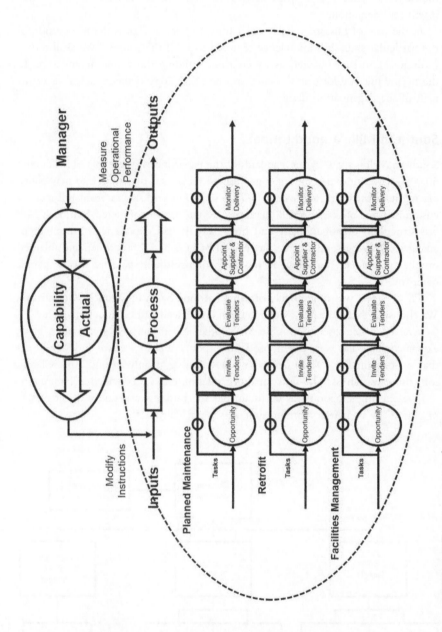

**FIGURE 4.4** Procurement workstreams

In designing the Intelligent Organisation, it is essential to grasp the needs of the particular situation and to understand how to build requisite complexity into the design to address it appropriately, whilst at the same time developing a consistent representation.

In the case of Fusion21, a key determinant of the design is the recognition of the particular skills and knowledge required to fulfil the process. We shall return to Fusion21 in later chapters as we continue building the whole organisation. In the meanwhile, we look at a case where the technology is the principal determinant of the organisation design.

## Southern Mill: 'a good tonne'

Southern Mill is small by the standards of the paper industry, capable of producing 50,000 gross tonnes per annum. The business recycles waste paper into new paper, placing it in the market in over 3,000 sizes, colours and shapes, from full reels to customised and packaged small quantities. When first encountered, Southern Mill was struggling organisationally and financially. It had experienced a number of changes of key personnel in a short period of time and a fall in demand (blamed on the global recession), and it was not an investment priority for its parent company.

The business was functionally organised around Sales, Production, Conversion, Warehousing and Dispatch with representative 'Head Office' functions. The site General Manager, also responsible for another larger business some miles away, explained that sales were down, production poor, stocks excessive and, despite all that, on-time in-full (OTIF) deliveries were running at only around 70%. Clearly something was amiss. The functional organisation chart is provided as Figure 4.5.

The existing situation was unsustainable; the business was under threat of sale or closure by its parent if improvement was not delivered.

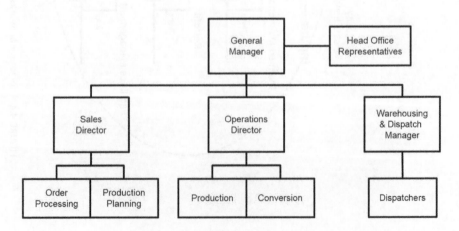

**FIGURE 4.5** Southern Mill organisation chart

A detailed review of performance highlighted that the functional management of the business coupled to inadequate information systems had generated a situation in which processes were suboptimal, and none of the key functions had the right information to support their decisions. Each was making decisions to optimise its own performance while potentially being damaging to the overall output.

The production function was charged with producing '100 good tonnes per day', and for themselves, had defined 'good' as being paper of merchantable quality. If a particular paper was running well on the paper machine, they would keep making it in order to reach target even though they had exceeded the amount of that paper required by the plan and despite the delay to fulfilment of other orders. Stock was rising because unsold paper was accumulating in the warehouse while orders were left unmet.

Meanwhile, the sales team were pushing volume, offering increasing ranges of colours, weights and sizes and offering discount for bulk orders whilst having no clear picture of the production cost or profitability of any given line. A 'quick and dirty' early analysis showed that, for at least some products, they would have been better off sending the order back with a £50 note attached to it than actually providing the product.

Customers were taking advantage of discounts by placing orders for large quantities to be called off, and then not calling them off. The increasing range of colours, weights and sizes being offered by sales was exacerbating the production challenge. A complete cycle through all of the colours and weights stretched to 16 weeks, while the supposed delivery cycle was 4 weeks. This ensured that OTIF would continue to deteriorate.

Every significant change of product on the paper machine required a 'change off' period which would cause at least one hour of lost production (about four 'good tonnes' lost) and the conversion activity (splitting reels into sheets) was very labour intensive, further increasing costs. Customers, relying on just-in-time deliveries to keep their own plants running, would contact Southern Mill and demand order fulfilment. The production team would interrupt the flow, insert an urgent order, disrupt the cycle, lose more 'good tonnes' and further delay output. If a significant colour change was required, then the mill might experience two 'change-offs', losing two hours production (8 tonnes), for order quantities commonly less than 5 tonnes. The cost of the change-offs (or lost production) was not factored into the price of the inserted product and more paper was being made for 'waste' than for the customer.

The conversion activity was some distance from the mill, as was the Dispatch and Warehousing operation, making both difficult to manage. Meanwhile, missing and inaccurate information about stock levels meant that Sales were reordering items already in stock. Lack of accurate information meant that Dispatch and Warehousing staff, unable to identify the existence or whereabouts of stock, would either dispatch incomplete orders or newly produced paper. Meanwhile, existing stock aged and deteriorated.

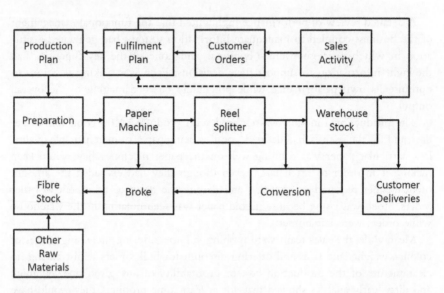

**FIGURE 4.6** Southern Mill, process view

It was clear that the challenges of Southern Mill could not be addressed in a linear fashion, but needed to be tackled through a process which recognised its dynamics and adopt both process control and appropriate information to dissolve the problems. Figure 4.6 shows how integrated the organisational processes were and how inappropriate was their attempt, in this particular case, to manage it from a functional perspective.

For those unfamiliar with process flow:

- Sales Activity stimulates Customer Orders
- Customer Orders goes to the Fulfilment Plan
- Fulfilment Plan checks Warehouse Stock and *either*

  - If stock is available generates a Dispatch Order directly to the Warehouse
  - If stock is not available generates a requirement for the Production Plan

- Production Plan informs Preparation which allocates Fibre Stock and other Raw Materials to the Paper Machine
- The Paper Machine produces Reels of Paper which are Split with three channels for output:

  - Reel Direct to Warehouse (increasing stock)
  - Reel to Conversion (cutting the paper into sheets and packing it)
  - Broke (paper damaged during production and reel trim offcuts)

- Warehouse Stock goes to fulfil Customer Deliveries

It should be clear that this overall process of 'Meeting Customer Orders' needs to be managed as an integrated whole.

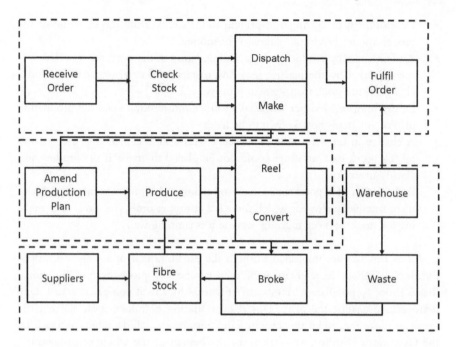

**FIGURE 4.7** Southern Mill, key processes

With the manufacturing processes essentially fixed by the nature of the technology (the paper machine only makes paper one way; what can be varied is the machine speed, paper weight, width and colour), we had to consider effective process control (the natural activity of the homeostat) and accurate, useful information as the basis of improvement. While there were three distinct key processes (Figure 4.7), their interdependence and interrelationship meant that any attempt to manage them within the functional silos was doomed to failure. At the same time, attempting to fully integrate them and manage them as a single process was not appropriate; they were too large, too diverse and too physically separate.

The interrelationship needed to be fully articulated, accepted by the business and a mechanism established for information sharing to enable better decisions. The cycles could then be synchronised, using information effectively to optimise the whole. The best performance of the weakest link will always act as the bottleneck.

A number of critical steps were taken. A model of the whole process was developed, shared, tested and agreed with the management staff to both confirm understanding of the overall situation and to allow discussion of the challenges. It was agreed that the 'purpose' of the business was to fulfil customer demand for speciality papers. That could only be done if the business itself was financially, organisationally and informationally sustainable. This generated a flurry of activity:

- Development of a formal, mathematical statement of the capacity of the whole process from end to end (a demand-driven process perspective);

- Development of costing and pricing models replicating the structure of the process model, but in the 'language' of money;
- A stock audit, by product and age, and updating of the stock records. This was accompanied by the placing into raw materials of deteriorated stock and a change to the stock management process;
- Dispatching ordered but 'uncalled' product and removal from the production plan of any items now known to be held;
- A change in the 'Check Stock' process, with a lock step, so that, using now-reliable stock data, an order could not be placed to 'make' if the product was already in stock;
- Redefinition of a 'good tonne' for production to become 'a tonne of paper of merchantable quality for which there is a customer order', i.e. no longer 'making for stock' or 'keep it going because it is running well'.

All of this was accomplished through the establishment of a daily 'operations meeting' at which representatives of each of the key processes (not functional 'heads') met to populate a 'dashboard' (Figure 4.8) which compared actual daily performance against the plan. This regular sharing of information allowed the teams to make the cycles synchronous and ensured that all decisions, overseen by the Operations Director, were taken for the benefit of the whole organisation.

Over a period of about eight months, stocks were reduced, bringing substantial cash into the business (destocking generates cash). OTIF increased to 96% compared with only 70% at the outset and product complexity was reduced through negotiation with customers. Accurate costing allowed the sales team to have fact-based discussions with customers about the price of certain products. The production cycle time was brought down to six weeks and was progressing towards four.

All of this was brought about by the effective use of information.

## ChemCo: the dog that didn't bark

In beginning this section, I am reminded that information is our friend, a point best made by Kipling:

> I had six loyal serving men,
> they taught me all I knew
> Their names were What and Why and When
> and How and Where and Who.

There are an increasing number of organisations, and parts of organisations, where the meaningful 'product' is information itself. These include policing, research, insurance, financial services and advertising. Similarly, sales businesses, particularly 'online' retailers, gather and collate information about potential customers to provide information to sales staff, and the defence and security forces gather and use information to identify, substantiate and eliminate threats to peace.

# Daily Dashboard: Southern Mill

## Production

| Plan | Actual | Diff to Plan |
|---|---|---|
| 132 | 138 | 6 |
| Net Tonnes | | |
| Planned | Actual | Diff to Plan |
| 80 | 100 | 20 |
| Hold | Over-make | Broke |
| 20 | 50 | 5 |
| Shut | | |
| Plan | Unplan | Diff to Plan |
| 48 | 56 | 8 |

## Conversion

| Product | Plan | Actual | Diff to Plan |
|---|---|---|---|
| Sheeted | 4 | 3 | -1 |
| Laminate | 3 | 4 | 1 |
| Coated | 2 | 2 | 0 |
| Colour | 1 | 1 | 0 |
| Coiled | 1 | 1 | 0 |
| Coiled SS | 2 | 3 | 1 |
| Collated | 3 | 2 | -1 |
| Guillotine | 5 | 5 | 0 |
| BPOP | 6 | 6 | 0 |
| Packed FP | 4 | 4 | 0 |
| Packed BP | 5 | 5 | 0 |

## Sales

| | Plan | Actual | Diff to Plan |
|---|---|---|---|
| Stock | 600 | 630 | 30 |
| >180 | 0 | 45 | 45 |
| >365 | 0 | 0 | 0 |
| Dispatch | 104 | 100 | -4 |
| OTIF | 98% | 96% | -2% |
| Orders | 100 | 105 | 5 |
| Rev | £90000 | £94500 | £4500 |
| Credits | £0 | £3000 | £3000 |
| Unplan £ | 0 | £500 | £500 |
| Complaints | 0 | 1 | 1 |
| Accidents (LT) | 0 | 1 | 1 |

FIGURE 4.8 Southern Mill dashboard

Despite this, the data or information is not itself 'purposeful'. It enables decisions in the pursuit of the 'job', whether that be preserving peace, selling products or prosecuting criminals. The achievement of the outcome is the reason why the process exists, but its operation and management requires knowledge and skill to be applied to the information. In such cases, each iteration of the process cycle must be explicitly informed by the learning arising from the previous cycle.

ChemCo (a chemical research company) provides a good case here, one in which knowledge management happens in at least two ways:

- The learning arising from each iteration informs the enquiry of the next, modifying both the process and the result being sought;
- The knowledge of the scientists undertaking the enquiry is increased. Whether or not the process of enquiry leads to the desired output, the state of knowledge of the scientist is changed. That is, the simple practice of doing their job relies upon and increases their knowledge and skill, the application of which is the core process.

Both the organisation and the individual can be said to be learning. They are adapting their behaviour in the light of new knowledge. Figure 4.9 displays the process followed by ChemCo.

The Product Development process consists of four stages, each of which contains tasks:

- Trawling:

  - Commercial Evaluation and Technical Evaluation;

- Evaluation:

  - Commercial Evaluation, Technical Evaluation, Regulatory Evaluation;

- Product Development:

  - Market Evaluation, Rigorous Chemistry, Process Development;

- Testing:

  - Marketing, Absolute Chemistry, Production Testing.

The research scientists, usually obsessed with smells and bangs, follow the scientific method in their work. They develop a hypothesis at Stage One for a molecule or compound to address a particular problem or need (the output that is pursued) and trawl for possibilities, evaluating them from both technical (will it work?) and commercial (will it make financial sense?) perspectives. A wide range of compounds may be evaluated at this stage and each has a value. Knowing that compound X doesn't work is as valuable as the knowledge that compound Y does.

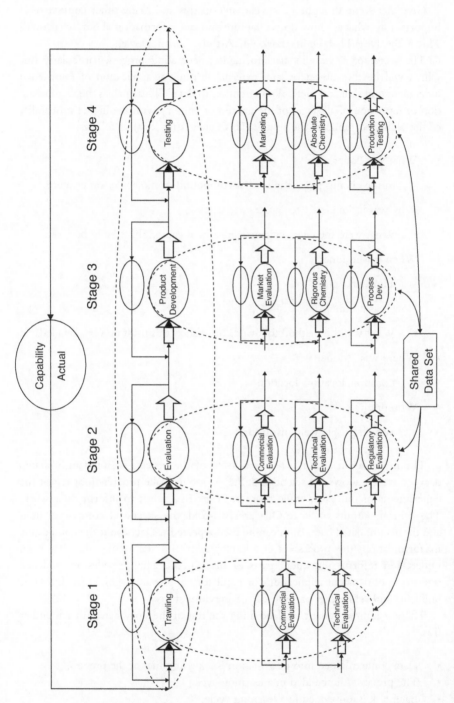

**FIGURE 4.9** Product development process and tasks

Give that some thought . . . 'what isn't' in this and many other contexts is as important as 'what is'; how do we capture and use information about 'what isn't'? This is the Dog That Didn't Bark (Sir Arthur Conan Doyle).

The secret of success in an information-generating process, particularly one which will be the subject of later external scrutiny, is application of knowledge, judgement and skill and meticulous attention to detail. This enables the reconstruction or repetition of all stages of the process of enquiry with the higher probability of the ability to replicate the results. This detail is (at least) as follows:

- What was done?

    - In the chemistry example what compound or molecule was created?

- Why was it done?

    - What were the clues, evidence, ideas that caused this step to be taken?

- When was it done?

    - Time, date etc.

- How was it done?

    - What was the method followed? In science, this must be very detailed.

- Where was it done?

    - Location, location, location

- Who did it?

    - Which people were involved?

The information accumulated as a result of the process is stored in a 'shared data set' which allows the scientists at Stage One to make progress (not repeat the experiments of the past), while those at Stage Two use it to inform their work. The critical outputs of Stage One are two-fold, the successful compound itself and the accumulated data. Both can be used repeatedly. Data about the compound, its formulation, the process of its development and the testing that has been undertaken inform subsequent parts of the process. This provides an evidence trail to support patent applications or regulatory approval. Stages Three and Four build on and refine the learning of the previous stages.

There is limited benefit in elaborating the rest of the story here, just remember this:

- Data contextualised into information is a key product of the process;
- The process is embedded in a learning cycle;
- Each task is embedded in a learning cycle;
- Each procedure is embedded in a learning cycle.

Success in the overall process both at each iteration and over time depends upon the effective capture and application of information within the process; the state of knowledge about the chemistry continually changes. At the same time the process, tasks and procedures improve themselves, optimising resource use, aiming to improve efficiency.

## "It's Tuesday, I must be Kate"

It is common for us to grant equivalence to processes and roles (one role = one job) especially in a functional hierarchy. However, what has been described is about processes with a logical informational hierarchy; it said nothing of people or body count.

Thinking about Intelligent Organisations applies as much to individuals as to larger organisations. Indeed, with continuing growth in the number of small enterprises and uncertainty in the continuity of employment, we should all consider ourselves from the perspective of Intelligent Organisations. To enable individual sustainability, we must generate value, organise ourselves, deliver outputs, achieve outcomes, manage our information, balance our resources and, importantly, do that in the context of 'not-work' relationships. We must also create our own future, something we will turn to in Chapters 5 and 6.

One day, as my wife was leaving the house to go to work, I asked her what she was up to that day. She stopped, thought for a while and said:

"It's Tuesday, I must be Kate."

She understood that people fulfil roles and those roles often differ from day to day. That day she would be fulfilling another's teaching duties. While we are each indivisible, we each carry out multiple roles typically as employees, partners, parents, children. We need to think about how we organise our 'selves' in order to fulfil those roles, minimising tension, maximising effectiveness. We need to be able to see ourselves as organisations.

I imagine many readers will have placed themselves in the model of the Intelligent Organisation like this:

I am a worker, what is my process, what are the tasks and procedures, who is my manager?

Or

I am a manager, what process do I manage, what output am I trying to achieve, what are my inputs?

An individual carries out the process, task, procedures *and* the management of themselves. We are both worker and manager. The requirements, activities and skills may be different for each part but all must be done. We shall be brave (well, *I* will) and use me and my microbusiness to help think about this.

There is only one physiological 'self' (that eats, sleeps, drinks and ages), but I fulfil a number of roles. I am contemporaneously (and sometimes simultaneously):

- Husband and Father
- Researcher and Scientist
- Consultant and Educator
- Volunteer

Each of these instances of my 'self' represents a way in which 'I do what I do', actions through which my 'purpose' (of being myself) is fulfilled. It is through these that I express my identity to the world and that world engages with me (it is my environment). This is all represented in Figure 4.10.

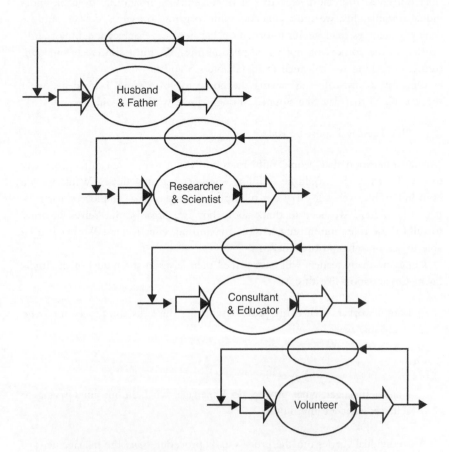

**FIGURE 4.10** Processes and roles

Some of these processes are more obviously 'work' than others, but they cannot be separated from the aggregate, indivisible me and I must balance my energy across them. Each has a desired output. Each has inputs, process, structure and decisions, requires skills and behaviours and generates and uses information. All of that must be managed. While the process of being 'husband and father' leans on behaviours and skills, 'consultant and educator' relies more heavily on process and structure. 'Researcher and scientist' has a strong process element, but again draws on a slightly different set of skills and behaviours to the others. 'Volunteer' employs a similar range of skills and behaviours to my other 'selves' but modified to suit the particular circumstances of working with young people. Fortunately, many of the skills required by each 'self' are common to the other 'selves'.

For each role I must:

- Understand what the desired output is;
- Provide the various inputs necessary;
- Observe the output of the activity and modify the inputs to improve my performance – to be a 'better' self.

Being self-managing, I must hold myself to account:

- Did I achieve the output expected by my wife, client, research community and stakeholder?
- Do I need to change my skills, processes, standards and behaviours to improve myself?

It is critically important that the corrective action is applied to the right characteristic and that I do not apply the wrong skill to the particular process. When my wife is telling me about something happening in her workplace, it is perhaps unhelpful for me to explain to her how she could go about resolving it (consultant role) when what she wants is to be listened to (husband role). Think about this in relation to your boss? Your partner? Your children?

Equally, I need to balance my resources across these four 'selves'. I must manage each individual process *and* manage the management of them, so that effort and outputs are balanced to meet the needs of all of my stakeholders – wife, children, clients, students, collaborators. That necessitates a higher order control loop (Figure 4.11), (meta)self-management.

I am then quite a complex self, living what Handy (1985) called a 'portfolio' life. In order to remain in a state of relative calm, I must balance the priorities of each role against the others. I must consider the ways in which process, skill and data need to be blended to allow each to happen and how to manage my knowledge. How do the things I experience and learn about in one of my roles inform both that role and others? This deals only with the things I do already, it says

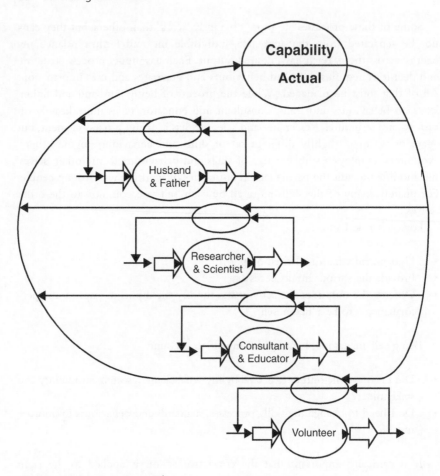

**FIGURE 4.11** Managing my selves

nothing of other things I might do tomorrow. How do I adapt? The human being is a supreme learning machine if we allow it to be.

Before you move to the next chapter, you could usefully spend some time thinking about your own life in this way:

What processes are you responsible for?
What roles do you fulfil (in work and out of it)?
How do you balance your time and effort?
How do you hold yourself to account?
How do you adapt and learn?

It may be that in considering those questions, you may find sources of tension in your life which could be resolved through this understanding.

## Summary

We shall be returning to each of these case studies later in the book. The intention of this chapter has been to encourage you to think about how you might apply the ideas outlined in the previous chapter to your own organisation. I hope you had some success.

Everything covered in the last two chapters has essentially been concerned with the operation and management of the Intelligent Organisation – it has been focused on managing the present. In the next chapter, we shall focus on how the Intelligent Organisation can create its future. And that is something that most are very poor at doing.

# 5

# ENABLING VALUE

I'm from Head Office and I'm here to help.

Anon

## Introduction

The second major part of the Intelligent Organisation is Value Enabling. Value-enabling processes are designed backwards from their customer (the value-generating part of the organisation), consistently improving performance with each iterative cycle by synthesising information about the present with desires and intent for the future.

The highest level of the logical value-generating hierarchy is in a position of internal informational omniscience. At that level, the performance of the whole operational organisation can be seen and inputs modified to improve it. That is good. However, if we stop there, what we have is an organisation in which learning and adaptation are limited to generating a slightly better version of 'now' in the existing environment. It will be autonomic, doing what it has been designed to do, but nothing else. Without capability to understand and evolve to interact with the problematic future, any organisation is not adequate for a rapidly changing world.

So we had better do something about it.

## The head office challenge

It is time for a little more organisational philosophy. Every organisation, whether a sole trader or a global corporation, needs what are usually thought of as 'head office' activities if it is to survive and thrive.

However, these functions (and this may come as a bit of a surprise to the actors who populate them) are not purposeful in their own right. Their purposefulness and utility is measured by the extent that they enable value in the rest of the organisation.

Unfortunately, it has been awhile since anybody told them this, and often 'Head Offices' have become self-serving. That is, many decisions are made which 'work' for the folks in the centre but not for some, or all, of the rest of the organisation.

## Distributing information

*A large company operates across multiple sites in the UK and Europe. Many of those sites are distant from centres of population due to the nature of the product and the production process. The CIO proposed that, as part of the IT strategy, the business would adopt cloud-based solutions for core systems such as email, finance and so on. The proposal was duly adopted and rolled out across the company.*

*Everything works well . . . except at the multiple remote sites where internet connectivity is based on bandwidth-limited copper wire or mobile telephony. In these cases the local staff, frustrated by slow data transmission rates, must leave the site, drive to the nearest area with a strong mobile phone signal, make and receive their transmissions, then drive back to the site. The 'benefits' claimed at Head Office are no doubt real, the IT system works really well, for them. The information costs and value are hidden in the inefficiency imparted to the operating business.*

This behaviour sounds absurd, but it is common, and it is not just in the IT space that it happens. My younger son was rejected at the age of 16 by the online recruitment system of a major DIY store chain because his answers indicated he was not team player enough to stack shelves on Saturday afternoons, a task mainly requiring the ability to work independently. The 'system', owned by the HR department, no doubt increased efficiency in HR processes; a cheaper way to get the wrong result? I doubt it was doing much for either efficiency or effectiveness in the store itself.

Whether it is the imposition of a solution that only works for one part of the organisation, undertaking activity that is only good for the particular Head Office function while imparting cost to other parts of the organisation or, in effect, penalising the customers by reducing the level of service offered, this whole suite of behaviours is analogous to 'pathological autopoiesis' (Beer, 1985).

Autopoiesis (Maturana & Varela, 1987) is the natural process by which an organism sustains its own existence. Pathological autopoiesis – sickness – occurs when those essential activities become self-serving. They thereby impart damage or harm to the host organisation either by failing to fulfil their own purpose or by consuming resources which should be used elsewhere. When the value-enabling functions are investing in their own preservation to the detriment of the value-generating functions and the customers, they are, in effect, cancerous.

These necessary functions need to be focused on enabling the whole organisation to add value to all stakeholders. By understanding how they contribute value to the whole they can avoid imposing nonvalue-adding, unnecessary or bureaucratic burdens on the organisation and its customers. If the value added by an enabling function is properly understood, then the costs that necessarily go with it can be properly appreciated.

A little more sympathetically, the tasks of the value-enabling processes are valuable, necessary and often not that simple. They must do several things in parallel in order to maintain the organisation in a state of dynamic balance (allostasis):

- Deliver value to current customers in current markets through existing services and products;
- Modify the future market to more closely align it with the current service and product offer;
- Develop or enhance services and products to appeal to future customers in future markets;
- Modify the internal arrangements of the organisation to enhance its viability in the changing environment.

It therefore must:

- Understand the performance, current and relatively short-term needs of the value-generating parts of the organisation in the context of the present market environment;
- Understand the opportunities and threats emerging in the problematic future environment;
- Reconcile the two;
- Develop strategies and plans for simultaneously adapting the organisation (internal) and modifying the environment (external) to ensure its future;
- Synthesise the changes across multiple value-enabling functions, e.g. HR, Finance, IT, Property, Marketing;
- Negotiate with the value-generating parts of the organisation to deliver the necessary changes.

Doing all that successfully is quite a trick.

The first challenge is that the value-generating parts of the organisation typically have the biggest share of the resources. They will assert their autonomy and, with their focus on the 'here and now', will not want to 'fix today what ain't yet broke'. Humankind has a general tendency to respond more willingly to threat than opportunity (Kahnemann, 2011), but the threat in this case is perhaps only visible to the value enablers, not the generators.

The second challenge resides in modifying the environment, the activity often called marketing. Its first pursuit is to influence the market to demand 'our' products and services, it seeks to modify the buying behaviour of customers. Its second pursuit is to interrogate buyer behaviour so that we can understand:

- what is being demanded now and into the future;
- what environmental conditions are changing;
- in what ways the market is seeking to modify the organisation:
  - social, demographic, technological, financial, political.

The sustainability of the organisation rests in it enjoying a mutually beneficial relationship with its environment; and that means adaptation for both.

The third challenge is the development of new services and products. The value-generating processes of the organisation are adapting and modifying things; they are using information about customers, products, services and performance to 'do things right'. The value-enabling processes have the responsibility to 'do right things'. That provides a useful, if rather porous, delineation between the sets of activities, but also provides the basis of potential tension or conflict. Value generation can improve product or service quality, it cannot define and develop a whole new product or service; it has neither the resources nor the skills to do this and it would not be considered organisationally legitimate.

Hence a mechanism is needed, the fourth challenge, through which the internal arrangements of the organisation can be modified to enable its adaptation. Such mechanisms are often cast in change or transformation programmes, managed by 'change management specialists', consultants and various other hired hands and are, frequently, enabled or driven by information system changes.

Intelligent Organisations are thoughtful about this external expertise. They recognise that if adaptation is an ongoing requirement (and it is), then they need to develop in their own workforce and managers the capability to deal with it. Continuing to hire in short-term expertise to "unfreeze, change, refreeze" (Lewin, 1947) is expensive and doomed to failure. It may be that the temporary engagement of particular technical, managerial, training or consulting skills is a necessary part of accelerating a transformation, but ultimately the capability must belong to the host.

Very large organisations may have within their boundaries all of the skills and knowledge that they need. It is certainly the case that they should employ enough people with the right skills and knowledge to address the vast majority of areas. However, unless they wish to close the organisation off to innovative, new or different thinking and ideas or simply to challenge, then there is a legitimate role for external or specialist internal expertise, so long as it is genuinely value adding. Without such expertise, the organisation risks remaining informationally closed, only able to deal with that which already exists within its boundaries. In a rapidly changing environment that is probably more weakness than strength.

Ultimately it is critical that the process of change is owned, sponsored and driven by the people inside the organisation, however difficult that may be. Often the help that is most needed is to support them to become intelligent managers, to help them recognise that stability arises through change and, perhaps for the first time, to deal with the new and unknown and all of the risks and challenges that go with it.

The role of management in the Intelligent Organisation, regardless of position, seniority or size of empire, is to enable its continuous adaptation to changing circumstances at the same rate (at least) as is demanded by the changes in the external environment. They must keep things the same by making them different, i.e. to maintain dynamic stability through managing change. Each can be thought of, perhaps, as a gyroscope, a device for maintaining orientation. While mechanical gyroscopes generally consist of a spinning wheel or disc (the energy in the system) in which the axle assumes any orientation that achieves dynamic balance, in the organisational gyroscope the axle is the managerial posture (the orientation), the spinning wheel is the flow of information (energy). In both cases the desired outcome is dynamic stability.

## Enabling value: dealing with the problematic future

It will, I am sure, come as no great surprise to find that at this point we revert to the homeostat and recognise that the desired output of the value-enabling processes is to create the future of the organisation.

Value-enabling activity needs the creation of a higher order homeostat containing a 'model of the model of self' (MoMoS) which consists of more highly aggregated information. The MoMoS reflects the structure and performance of the organisation at the operational level, but filters out the operational detail. This aggregation acts to sustain autonomy at lower levels. It avoids being overwhelmed with data and unnecessarily, unintentionally or incompetently constraining freedom to adapt.

A second need is to generate a 'model of world' (MoW), a representation of the environment in which the organisation exists. That must contain a requisite abstraction from everything that surrounds the organisation – whether political, social, economic, environmental or competitive – i.e. all those aspects which impact upon it and those on which it seeks to have impact. This is necessarily an abstraction, "the only perfect model of a cat, IS a cat" (Wiener, 1948), the only 'complete model' of something is that thing itself. So, we must accept imperfection and the need for judgement. We should be conscientious in our model building while recognising that, to some extent, the model built will reflect the preferences, prejudices and biases of the model builders.

These two artefacts, the MoMoS and the MoW, constitute a representation of the organisation in its world and generate the potential to understand possible outcomes from changes in either. The generic question is 'what happens if . . .?'

The combined models act as the centre point of two processes. The first captures data about the performance of the organisation, compares it with the desired performance and understands the gap.

The second captures data about the changing external environment of the organisation, compares it with the current MoMoS and understands that gap. The decisions that emerge from those processes are relatively simple (in principle anyway):

* Change the organisation in *this* respect
* Change the market in *that* respect
* Use a combination of actions that do both.

In Figure 5.1, starting at the extreme right, the MoS becomes aggregated into the MoMoS, the informational abstraction of the essentials of structure and

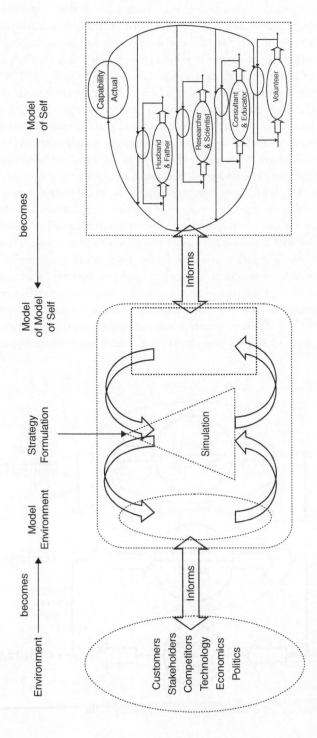

**FIGURE 5.1** The value-enabling process

performance. At the extreme left, the exploration of the environment generates the MoW, an abstraction of its essential characteristics as they impact on, or are impacted on by, the organisation. The 'simulation' at the centre allows the development and testing of hypotheses about the possible futures of the organisation and the formulation of strategy for realising them. It is a thinking space.

For those of a conventional turn of mind, these can be recognised as the core activities at the corporate level of formulating and implementing strategy. The environment-facing actions arising from this are often limited to marketing; the organisation-facing ones can cover a range of things from research and development to product development to structural change (often undertaken in the absence of any more thoughtful approach) and change in skills and/or behaviours.

Figure 5.2 presents the managerial homeostat, an alternative way of considering the argument. The lower loop represents generating value with the management continually striving to improve operational performance. Meanwhile, the value-enabling activity is considering the gap between current capability and potential, the performance that could be achieved if constraints were removed. Their output is fed back to value generation to enable further change, and that stimulates debate about the allocation of resources between current and possible future activities.

For ease of description, this is treated here as a single process. The reality for most organisations is that the value-enabling process happens across multiple functional areas, e.g. finance, property, information services (ICT), research and development, product development, marketing, human resource management and so on.

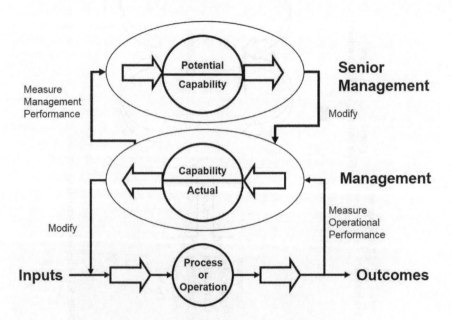

**FIGURE 5.2** Enabling value interacting with generating value

These parallel processes need to be synthesised, integrated, synchronised and coordinated. All too often an organisational change process, stimulated by one functional team is pulling (or pushing) the organisation in one direction while another is going the opposite way! Figure 1.2 (p. 11) showed how a change reverberates throughout the organisation. Now think about the complexity when multiple processes are stimulating multiple asynchronous changes. Is it any wonder it feels chaotic at times, that 'Head Office doesn't know what it's doing' and that the value-generating parts of the organisation respond with 'keep your heads down', 'ignore the latest fad', 'there will be another one along next week'? The 'resistance to change' in the organisation may simply be a function of too many inconsistent change requirements from too many sources overwhelming the capacity to cope.

In Figure 5.3, the information abstraction necessary is segregated into 'disciplinary' channels, each discipline is exploring the organisation and environment and drawing data into a model. In creating a simulation (thinking about alternative futures and actions that happens in the centre of the figure), these discipline-based data sets must be synthesised in a shared model. The data becomes shared information and the implications of possible changes can be explored in a mutual dialogue that focuses on the whole, not the parts. Any one discipline 'doing its own thing' and disregarding the implications for the others will engender tension rather than value. It may bring about damage to or the demise of the whole organisation.

In a recent experience with a pharmaceuticals organisation, the commercial function was determined to do things its own way. While there was much merit in the ideas being proposed, they were not tested or agreed with other functions (especially regulatory and finance) and, as a result, far from being successful in the long term, they generated an 'immune system response' in the regulatory and finance functions which acted to inhibit the commercial strategy.

## Corporate strategy

Enabling value in an integrated manner relies upon good process, appropriate information (structure and content) and appropriate skills in data gathering, synthesis, analysis, reflection and debate. It requires a willingness to take time, to explore, test and reflect. Strategic decision making should not be measured by short-term responsiveness ('how quickly we can make a decision?') but by long-term contribution to 'survival worthiness'. In biological terms, it is about how well the organisation adapts its environment to itself and how well it adapts itself to its environment.

There are a wide range of tools for strategic thinking which, whilst good in isolation, can have far greater value when used in the context of this argument. Underpinning all is the common language of accountancy, used for the conveying of information about certain aspects of performance. It should be noted, however, that the 'financial position' is a product of the activity of the organisation and financial reports are a proxy for describing only a single perspective on performance.

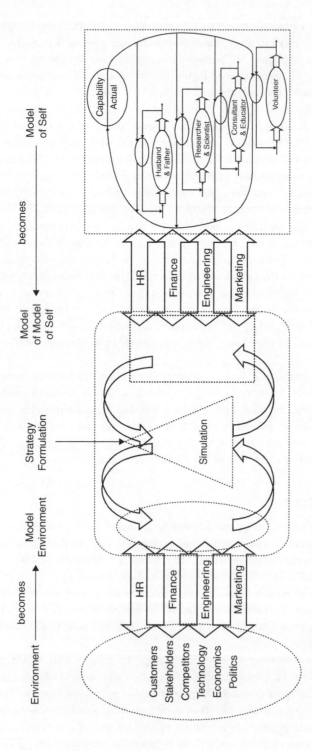

**FIGURE 5.3** The multi-channel value–enabling process

Financial reports are a product of the organisation's activity, not a driver of it. Anyway, not everybody understands what the accounting numbers mean.

Porter's "Five Forces" model (Porter, 1980) is powerful in helping to interpret the position of the organisation in its environment relative to existing and potential competitors as well as in the value chain of the industry. Ansoff (1987) offers models for considering choices about growth, looking at present and future markets and products, possibilities for further penetration of existing areas and development and diversification into new areas. Adding further to this area is the Boston Consulting Group Matrix (Johnson & Scholes, 1989) and others like it, which seek to help understand future possibilities in terms of the market position of existing products and services and how they might be adapted to ensure future success. This includes the action, often regarded as heretical by the 'value genera-tors', of stopping unprofitable products or services. It seems inherent in many organisations that we continue flogging a horse until well beyond the point where there is any hope of it springing back to life. Adjacent to the strategy literature is that of marketing. Here the work of Kotler and Armstrong (2015) is probably of greatest value and significance. They focus on formulating a marketing strategy, looking at the information required to understand the market and consumer behaviour. Since we have designed our organisation backwards from the customer, the approach has much resonance.

The tools and rules of accounting and financial management are spread across a wide literature and, in some cases, statute law. The most obvious and frequently used tools with which most readers will be familiar are budgeting, forecasting and reporting. There is limited benefit in rehearsing that material here; I could never work out what to include or exclude. Interested readers might look at Bender and Ward (2008) for inspiration.

The people also need to be thought about – how many, what skills and knowl-edge are required now and tomorrow? How will they be recruited, developed, retained and rewarded? Torrington, Hall and Taylor (2008) offer a range of tools and ideas for developing what is now known as a 'human resource strategy'.

The methods, approaches and ideas for formulating strategy need to be brought together in a supradisciplinary conversation – one which integrates and synthesises the discussion into coherent and cohesive organisational adaptation. Here, the organ-isation can again draw on the whole body of systems thinking (see Beckford, 2010) and a wide literature from risk analysis (Vose, 1996), operational research modelling (Moore, 1986) and simulation and modelling (Goodwin & Wright, 2004). These tools allow for the development of decision models and demonstrably valid, integrated and harmonised solutions that use the information in a consistent and coherent way.

## Managing tension

In the meanwhile we have created a source of tension. While the value-generating homeostat is managing the present, the value-enabling homeostat is creating the future. The first acts to 'do things right' and it usually has control of the bulk of

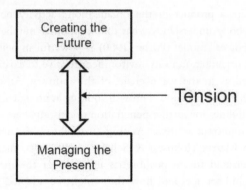

**FIGURE 5.4** Managing tension

the organisation's resources. The second acts to 'do right things', redefining what 'right' means in terms of organisational purpose, opportunities, products, services and all the myriad things that define the organisation. The two processes may be in conflict with each other (Figure 5.4), perhaps pulling the organisation in different directions.

In many organisations the value-enabling activity is addressed sporadically, usually after something has gone wrong. Typically falling sales of existing products, an economic downturn or a shift in customer behaviour are unanticipated because the organisation as a whole does not scan its problematic environment effectively. If we think about information systems and managerial activity in the organisations with which we are familiar, we should recognise that much management decision making about the *next* period is done by considering what happened in the *last* one and assuming a continuation of that into the future. This is, quite a lot, like driving a car down the road whilst only looking in the rear-view mirror – you can see in great detail what has already happened, can align your vehicle with the forecast flow of the road based on what just happened (this right-hand bend will go on forever) and can see all the obstacles you didn't hit. What you can't see is what is happening ahead of you. Organisations which do not have an effective process for creating the future (and there are many of them) necessarily become dominated by short-term, reactive decision making – and fail.

The tension cannot be effectively resolved in the 'traditional' manner. That, for many organisations, comes down to an adversarial boardroom battle in which there are winners and losers, with the losers 'moving on to explore alternative career opportunities'. That approach to resolving the tension is often more about benefit to individuals (promotion and bonuses) than it is the organisation. Decisions arising from it will often contain a 'political' element. There must be a better way.

Two things are missing. The first can be solved within the information structure we have already created. In the Intelligent Organisation information is available to deliver a level of objectivity into the discussion. Stating things objectively distances the discussion from often irrational or ill-informed 'I think' conversations and allows all parties to view the facts and assumptions, rather than attacking individuals and defending personal views. The information of course can never be perfect. The future is inherently uncertain and any discussions or decisions about what to do must acknowledge that uncertainty. The information entering the debate from within the organisation should have a higher degree of precision in reporting what has happened. There will be less certainty about what might happen in the future since there is limited insight into that. The second element that is missing and that will allow resolution of the debate is an understanding of the purpose of the organisation. Its mission, the reason it exists and the societal values it brings to bear.

It is easy to say that, for commercial organisations at least, the purpose is to 'make money'. However, as was established earlier, making money is but one part of the 'value exchange' between the organisation and its environment. So, yes, generating a surplus of income over expenditure is important to shareholders but, from the perspective of the survival of the organisation itself, making money is a consequence of being good (efficient) at what it does and what it does is done by the core processes that deliver services and goods to the customers.

So, if we are in doubt about the 'purpose' of the organisation we can, at least as a beginning, look to its activities to guide us.

The third and, somehow, more difficult element of this is to consider the values that underpin decisions. Bear in mind that the overarching objective is organisational survival in a world where both customers and actors within the organisation can exercise choices about what they buy and where they work. It would be reasonable then to adopt a set of values that support sustainable coexistence, a set of shared values that we can call our 'identity'. We should perhaps look to the literature on ecology here for inspiration as words like collaboration, cooperation, co-evolution, symbiosis and partnership might most usefully define the style of behaviour most likely to succeed.

This conversation in three parts, inspired by Beer's (1985) "meta-system", was defined by Dudley (2000) as the "Trialogue" (Figure 5.5). It allows the logical

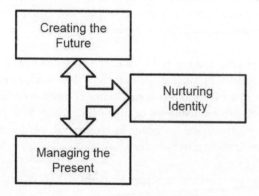

FIGURE 5.5 The trialogue

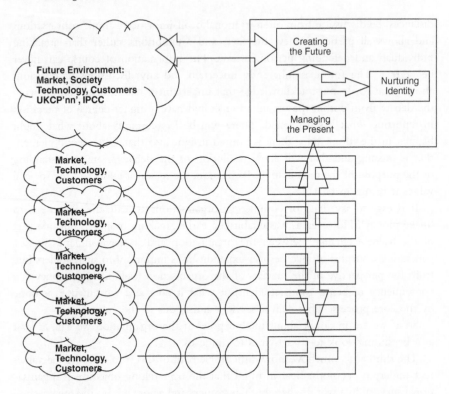

**FIGURE 5.6** The Intelligent Organisation (adapted from Beer (1985) and Dudley (2000))

*Note*: UKCP'nn' is the United Kingdom Climate Projection and its year (e.g. UKCP09). IPCC is the Intergovernmental Panel on Climate Change.

closure of the internal conversation whilst sustaining the dynamic, open relationship with the environment. The whole organisation is brought together in Figure 5.6.

## Thinking about growth

Economic theory has it that the enabler of growth is savings, that is, the excess of income over consumption reinvested. We are not going to argue with that convention here, but we are going to explore and, perhaps, extend the definition of growth.

The Intelligent Organisation seeks viability (Beer, 1985). It is designed to act in ways which enable its adaptation and survival in a changing environment. Thinking about that purely in economic terms is inadequate because it fails to consider all of the other dimensions of organisations and their place in complex societies. If our organisations are going to be survival worthy, then we need to think about growth in at least two dimensions:

physiological: getting fitter or bigger (or both);
psychological: getting smarter.

Conventional thinking only really addresses the first of these. Physiological growth is the stuff of market penetration, product penetration and product development and of mergers and acquisitions. Market and product penetration means that the organisation sells its products and services to a bigger audience in its existing markets, whilst market development takes those products and services to new audiences. Product development is concerned with the creation and sale of new products and services primarily to existing customers. These can of course be combined in a variety of strategies, all of them intended to increase the revenues flowing to the organisation, and they are equally applicable to commercial organisations, charities and not-for-profits. The sources of the revenue may vary, but the intent with all is to increase both market and revenue share. The economic benefits may be several – improved cash flow, improved profit, lowered unit cost through volume increases; the net effect is to increase the surplus of income over consumption. For the avoidance of doubt none of that is necessarily a bad thing. Mergers and acquisitions are, in effect, shortcut attempts to acquire additional surplus through access to larger volumes of sales, a new market for products, complementary products and services, complementary cash flows or, sometimes, to take a competitor out of the market. A business that sells heating products in the winter might well want to sell cooling products in the summer; the customers are the same, the market needs are different.

A word of caution, there is some evidence that mergers and acquisitions do not 'add value' to shareholders because of the difficulties and challenges associated with such transactions. It sometimes appears that they work better for the executives than they do for the companies and their shareholders. We would do well to understand whose interests are truly being served by such activities.

Untrammelled physical growth is not always good. Once the organisation exceeds a particular position in the market or is in a position with few or no apparent predators, then through its sheer size and weight it may become lethargic, slow to recognise and react to threats, perhaps even culturally complacent, convinced of its own 'rightness'. It will certainly become more self-interested. It may act to preserve the status quo and be less able (and willing) to respond to opportunities (oooh! too risky) or threats (oooh! 'too big to fail', 'hmmm, not big enough to harm us'). Alternatively it may become so convinced of its own greatness that it ends up:

> Taking over the world! Tech giants are blowing billions.
>
> *(Daily Telegraph,* 20th February 2015)

These constraints may apply to organisations whose dominance, in effect, enables them to slow product progress (particularly in applied technologies). This can occur where the cost (capital requirement or customer acquisition) of market entry is very high, e.g. aerospace and motor vehicle design and manufacturing, where natural predators are inhibited by structural lack of meaningful competition, e.g. rail franchising or regulated utilities. In some of these cases, the only true predator is the regulator and it is not in their interest to catch the prey.

That takes us to thinking about psychological growth.

Here again we can start with the conventional thinking. If one of the keys to survival is economic fitness, then being smarter is a good start. That might mean pursuing strategies such as 'operational excellence', 'quality' or 'lean thinking' (Beckford, 2010). That has been built into our process and structure. All such strategies are intended to improve the efficiency and productivity of the organisation, doing current things in current markets, increasing output and lowering (relative) costs to increase the surplus of income over cost. That, at the organisational level, can be seen as a good thing.

These conventional thoughts though rely on the assumption that 'growth' is in itself a universal good, that being bigger will ensure the survival of the organisation. It is interesting to note that the economic growth (accompanied by inflation) that has been seen over the last century is an aberration in the very long term. The norm over many centuries has been much greater stability of value, with increased savings arising from genuine productivity improvement rather than price rises. So, a challenge to convention arises from the lethargy, inertia, bureaucracy, risk aversion and, perhaps, power that results from dominance. The human actors in the organisation may come to believe in their own 'rightness', use that power to manage (manipulate) the market, the products and the customers, potentially ending up, in effect, abusing their position. Some banks and bankers may be considered to have achieved such power during the early part of this century as the inquiries into 'rate fixing', 'payment protection insurance' and other financial 'scandals' have suggested. The good news is that, however powerful they may be in the short term, these organisations ultimately always seem to fade, to struggle, to collapse. This is brought about by the emergence of new competitors coming to the market with innovations that are disruptive, whether through technology, process, service, product design or some other factor. The invulnerable, dominant player or players are ultimately unseated, though that may take some time and is delayed, if not stopped, by the barriers to entry, particularly those of capital and regulation (and sometimes by government intervention).

So, those organisations are not survival worthy. Large they may be, but they fail to truly build a sustainable position. Why? Because they are often not smart. We need to think about psychological growth – organisations getting smarter, learning, learning about learning. It also means that we who give the organisation life need to be (encouraged to be) smarter. We constitute a "brain", an organisational "collective consciousness" (Wilson, 2002). Instead of 'throwing bodies at problems', we should throw intelligence. We are the agents of the organisational memory, its connectivity, knowledge and self-awareness. Brains are neuroplastic, they change and evolve through new knowledge. Perhaps, psychological growth can arise by us raising the organisation to consciousness of its actions and impacts, and that will occur through individual psychological changes in affect, behaviour and cognition. We should be smart about being smart.

Psychological growth means that the organisation can apply its collective intelligence to improving itself informationally. Perhaps this is what is really meant by knowledge management? We have already demanded this in the shape of the MoS, a representation of 'how well I am'. This must be honest, perhaps brutally so, otherwise it is, at best, unhelpful. The human actors interpreting the MoS must be aware of the risk of "black swans" (Taleb, 2010), 'optimism bias' ('that was a one off, it couldn't happen again') and "availability bias" (Kahnemann, 2011). We typically react to the most recent events as if they are either 'blips' or a long-term shift in things, and there often appears to be little between these reactions other than the interpretation of a rapporteur. We must consider the trends and shifts in the environment to which a response is required and, unlike individuals, information in the organisation can give access to the unconscious organisational self (Wilson, 2002). All this is enabled by the constructive use of information, data filtered through tools, techniques and models that aid understanding. They should have their biases exposed by the honest challenging of their underlying assumptions and assertions about the organisation and its world which, inevitably, influence them.

I accept the argument of one discussion about this, that 'any CEO explicitly not aiming for physiological growth is likely to be sacked'. However, psychological growth may mean recognising that the organisation has reached an optimum physical size relative to its competitors and its environment. It may be that it has reached a size which actually suits the human actors, its philosophy or the opportunities available to it. It may mean accepting that a technology, product or service is reaching the end of its life and understanding how the pattern of changes around it will demand a new approach. This contrasts sharply with the apparent application of market power to hold back innovation, delay technology or inhibit competition through lobbying and the application of perverse standards which preserve the status quo. The reality is that the innovation, the disruptive technology, will ultimately find a way through and, in the medium term, leave the organisation exposed.

The Intelligent Organisation recognises that, with the aid of contemporary technology, it is in a position, through its people, to use data to develop a robust, honest model of itself and its environment and can use the resulting information to support decisions about the future which are able to maximise opportunity whilst minimising risk. That requires that the autonomy of individuals within the organisation is maintained.

## Summary

Some readers will no doubt object that I have reified the organisation, that is, I have apparently given it a life independent of its human actors. The story has been represented that way consciously and deliberately. People give life to organisations. Within the limits of current technologies and for most purposes it is largely people that make decisions. Nonetheless, it is a useful artifice, just for the time being, to suggest that we can both observe the process and be part of it. The complexity entailed in observing a process in which we are ourselves actors will be pursued later. It is also sad but true that in the absence of any particular individual, most organisations and processes will continue to function regardless. The established organisation, particularly a bureaucratic one, will have a momentum, an operating rhythm that will suborn the efforts of the individual. Large organisations do seem to develop a 'life' which is beyond the capabilities of individuals to influence (Robb, 1989).

That has been quite a walk through the essential principles and logic of the value-enabling activities. In the next chapter we shall bring it to life by looking at some case studies.

# 6

# ENABLING VALUE

## Cases

> Consult not your fears, but your hopes and dreams. Think not about your frustrations, but about your unfulfilled potential.
>
> Pope John XXIII (in Paddock, 2003)

## Introduction

Maintaining the rhythm of the book, we can now revisit the case studies considered in Chapter 4 to see how they enable value.

## Fusion21: creating the future

Two corporate objectives were left unfulfilled in our first look at Fusion21:

- To undertake Research and Development in improving products and services;
- To maintain 'Fitness for Purpose'.

The fulfilment of these objectives is led across the business by the Heads of Corporate Services and Business Improvement. They work together to constitute a nexus for the interaction of the present with the future. Corporate Services leads the challenge of maintaining fitness for purpose and deals with a range of matters:

- Operational and Strategic Finance;
- Operational and Strategic HR Management;
- Applied Information Systems.

Business Improvement meanwhile leads the Research and Development agenda, including:

- Marketing;
- Product and Service Development;
- Information Strategy.

The whole enabling activity relies on the aggregation of information from value generation and its integration with that discerned by value-enabling activity. This whole is represented in Figure 6.1.

We needed to develop an understanding of the current operating status of the company, its MoS, and interpret that not just through the operating activity but also by understanding how well Corporate Services were enabling that through the provision of:

- Skilled and knowledgeable people;
- Budgets and operating finance;
- Information systems.

The directors of the three business units, Procurement, Training and Employment Services (TES) and Consultancy, were in parallel able to provide performance information about each of the units. Taken together these information flows enabled the creation of the MoMoS, a rich understanding of the current situation from all perspectives.

The Heads of Corporate Services and Business Improvement developed, through processes of research and enquiry, information about the problematic future. To enable Fusion21 to expand the fulfilment of its mission, they looked outside the company to explore:

- the opportunities in the markets served by the company (by segment and geography);
- information about competitors and customers (in particular their apparent strategies);
- sources of government and other funding opportunities.

In parallel they looked inside the company to find opportunities:

- for different approaches to strategic finance (especially in the light of the business ambition);
- for extending the use of information throughout the business (with associated technologies);
- to enable improvements in operating performance (especially through reduced transaction costs);
- for delivery of strategic growth.

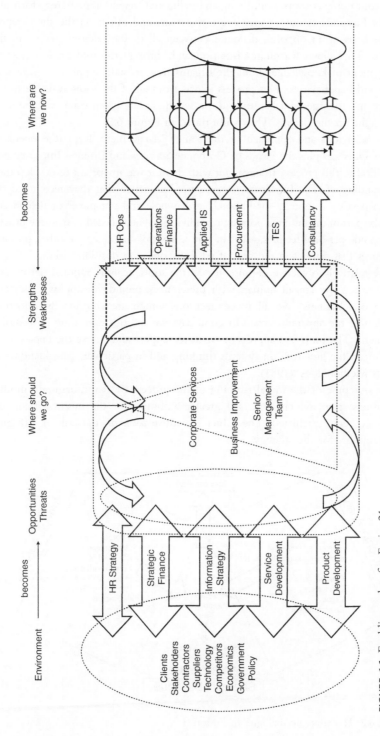

**FIGURE 6.1** Enabling value for Fusion21

All that information was brought together in a rich, complex and, very importantly, continuing conversation. Being an Intelligent Organisation, strategy formulation for Fusion21 is not a 'once every five years and put it on the shelf' report but the basis of an ongoing dialogue between all of the relevant people in the business. This allows learning, adaptation and, through the information systems, management of knowledge about the organisation, its staff, suppliers, contractors, clients and beneficiaries. This process selects from all of the tools available in the strategy and management literature those which, at any given time, cast the most useful light on the debate. This is illustrated in Figure 6.2.

The behaviour and approach of the Senior Management Team (the operating business Directors plus the Heads of Corporate Services and Business Improvement) was critical to this process. In engaging with them it was important to develop their understanding of 'The Intelligent Organisation' model so that they recognised the need to develop a strategy for Fusion21 as a whole and not prefer or defend any particular part of the business, position or individual. They needed to trust the process and set aside personal feelings, issues of power, control and all of the other, personal preferences that can get in the way of relatively objective decision making.

I say relatively objective because, for all the tools, analysis, rational debate and quantification, we are all human with preferences, prejudices, hobby horses and bees in our bonnets. We all make decisions which are emotionally informed regardless of the apparent facts. On good days we call this exercising professional judgement. The tools and approaches used to support and enable the debate were drawn from the literature on systems thinking and in particular, Checkland's Soft Systems Methodology (1981).

The outcome of the initial running of the process was to inform and modify the business plan, which expressed greater ambition for the business than had previously been articulated. The Chief Executive took on the task of engaging Board support for the strategy.

**FIGURE 6.2** The strategic dialogue in Fusion21

Implementation of the plan had its challenges, not least because the continuing process maintains openness to debate. This has been accompanied, as it always will be for every organisation, by changes in personnel and skills, by competition in the market place(s) in which Fusion21 does business and in changes in the overall economic position of the country. The process persists, as does Fusion21.

## Southern Mill

We left Southern Mill in a state of recovery – vital performance characteristics were improving but the whole business remained under risk of sale or closure.

Considering this organisation, we have to realise that whilst effective enabling activity is critical to its performance and survival, it did not enjoy the strategic freedom seen in the Fusion21 case study. Southern Mill was constrained in a number of ways:

- A single (and old) paper machine with a limited capacity and product range;
- A 'speciality' market requiring high frequency, small batch deliveries;
- Capital investment controlled by the owning group;
- Group control of raw materials' supply and cost;
- A rural location (with limited workforce options).

Acting within those constraints, the strategic choices were effectively limited to market growth and market penetration. Either selling more product to existing customers or finding new markets to which the existing products can be sold. Physiological growth would, ultimately, be limited by the capacity of the paper machine, but might the existential threat be overcome through psychological growth? Could a 'smarter' Southern Mill achieve sales volumes that would utilise all the capacity? Could it use information to manage itself better, to make better use of skilled and knowledgeable staff? Could it improve processes and systems and increase overall revenue, reduce unit costs and increase margin?

Frankly, being smarter looked like the only way forward.

The costing and pricing model in conjunction with the daily dashboard and the operations meeting were taken as the key starting point for the 'smarter' strategy. The first provided actionable, unarguable information which informed decisions about:

- What products should be made;
- What products could be eliminated from the range:

  - very small demand, difficult to make, unprofitable;

- What priorities should be set for:

  - customers, products, conversion, delivery;

- Production order (the sequence of colours and weights).

With a range of around 3,000 shippable products, two sites and the knowledge that the Finance Director had been unable to produce an accurate costing model in two years, this might sound like the wrong place to start. However, in the absence of accurate costing and pricing, Southern Mill was doing business blind to the implications of each purchase or sale decision. It was unable to respond to increases in supply costs (energy, materials) and incapable of a meaningful pricing conversation with its clients.

Building on the process understanding, the first step was to review the costing work already undertaken to see if it could be made useable. A number of significant flaws were discovered in the structure, organisation and utilisation of data which inhibited the accuracy and speed of the established costing model. It was jointly agreed to start again. A new approach was developed that replicated the process structure but was expressed in the languages of both finance and production. The two functions have a direct informational equivalence but use different languages. The approach was developed and tested tracking a single product through from inbound materials to dispatch. All functional and enabling areas were included in the development, each making a contribution and pushing the limits of the model. The initial manual costing approach produced what looked like reasonable answers but took 30 minutes per product at the first attempt. Several days were subsequently invested manually costing each product. The validity of the model was established by applying production volumes to the total production costs for the year to date generating a difference of under 1%. The model as constructed very faithfully reflected the actual situation. Once that test was completed and signed off by the relevant Directors, the costing process was automated so that it was possible to reanalyse *all* 3,000 products in under five minutes, given any change in input costs or conditions.

The pricing model was built using the manufacturing cost results with the addition of dispatch costs, exchange risk and flexibility on pricing (enabling management of margins). This meant that the sales team were not only able to understand product costs but also to negotiate from a position of knowledge with customers, understanding for the first time the implications of discounts and the sensitivity of the business to price. All of that work was designed to enable the senior managers of Southern Mill to be more effective in decision making. All of it drew on existing information sources and the final version was deployed across the corporate network.

It may sound a little complicated, and there were numerous challenges in bringing the whole model together. What you may find more remarkable is that the costing and pricing models were not built by a qualified accountant (who had failed miserably), but by a 19-year-old engineering undergraduate (with a little guidance), who understood process and information. It took only a few weeks from problem definition to implemented solution. Thanks, Allen!

The second focus was to look at how the skills of the 'enabling' individuals in the organisation might be enhanced. Drawing on the generation of more useful information on a more regular basis, the daily operations meeting became a learning, knowledge-sharing event. Using the information presented each day, the attendees were able to objectively explore what was working well or less well, what perhaps had gone wrong and, crucially, the cross-company effect of errors or failures in one area. Initial interventions were facilitative, but moved rapidly to a coaching approach as the participants began to learn from each other, to develop and test ideas, to behave differently together (for example, being collaborative rather than competitive) and, for the sales team, to take different ideas and propositions to customers.

Great progress was being made, the work together was bearing fruit and the results were showing through on the bottom line. Production, sales volumes and revenue were increasing, stocks were falling (in particular eradication of old stock and previously uncalled orders), low-volume and/or high-cost products were being eliminated through substitution, reducing product and production complexity and increasing throughput. All was going in the right direction.

Unfortunately, at this point Southern Mill was sold to a new owning group and the intervention ceased, but we know the mill is still there and has received some of the strategic investment it so sorely needed.

## ChemCo: the dog barks

We previously considered how information was generated and used in a chemical research and development process to stimulate learning both about the chemicals themselves and about the process of developing chemicals, embedding process control, adaptation and self-regulation.

Southern Mill has shown how value was enabled by representing information about process in a form that allowed managers to make different decisions based on a new level of insight and the informational equivalence of the production, costing and pricing models. The challenge for our chemists revolved around how to express the value of the R&D process to their Board. Delivering current value through current products to current customers is relatively straightforward, the worth of the work is evident in the short term through sales volumes, market share and other traditional measures. Research and Development is an activity of enabling future value – in the short term everything it does looks like a cost. When times are tough, it is an easy cost to reduce along with staff training and biscuits at the Board meetings.

What we needed was a means to express the future potential value of the outputs of the R&D process (new products or services) in terms of the current value of the investment to date. That is:

- we have invested £xxx in the development of future products;
- they address an, estimated, future market of £yyy;
- We have $n^n$ new products in development;
- The net present value (npv) of those is £zzz.

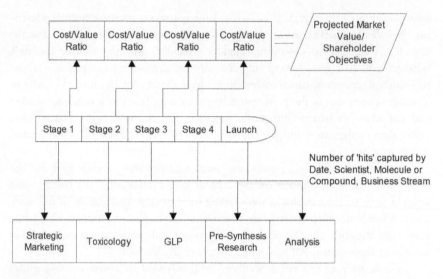

**FIGURE 6.3** Estimating future value

With appropriate and well-managed R&D, the npv (a number the accountants love) will exceed the cost, thereby making the business case for continued investment.

As with most enabling activity, this required sharing of information between different teams. A shared MoS capable of expressing its outputs in the varying languages of the interested parties was developed. At its heart was the research process, which you can see (Figure 6.3) has four stages, and every potential product will go through each of those stages.

At Stage 1, the researcher undertook work against a research plan to develop products that met the opportunities identified by the strategic marketers. They had identified opportunities but also stated approximate future market sizes (volume, price, scope) against them. As the researchers captured appropriate data about both the items (volume, type, success and failure rates) under development and the work involved in developing them, then, at Stage 1, the cost/value ratio of the work done against the market potential could be stated. This transformed 'work done' into an estimate of future value against an estimated future market which was matched against shareholder objectives. At each 'stage gate', a decision was made to proceed or not with each potential product. That decision could be made in the knowledge both of how well the product was likely to work and what it might be worth.

The future value of those potential products that made it through the stage gate also had to exceed the cost of all those that didn't; the whole R&D proposition, not just individual items, had to make financial sense. To put that into perspective, a pharmaceutical company may well carry out Stage 1 testing of over 500,000 molecules, with only 20,000 making it out to Stage 2 and only five or six making it as far as Stage 3 and ultimately only one getting into the marketplace as a product. Those are tough numbers. Being both efficient in the research process and effective in evaluation are critical. Because of the way the MoS was built (and there was an underlying process model that enabled the whole), data was captured once and used many times and for many different purposes. It made it possible to evaluate the work of individuals and teams, track the progress of molecules and evaluate the future worth of the products under development, *all* without creating any additional work or cost. All the chemists had to do was record their experiments and results as part of their process. The reporting and stage evaluation was built in. It is important to appreciate:

- The probabilistic nature of any R&D process in terms of value and risk;
- The degree to which information from multiple sources was integrated;
- The informational equivalence built into the model so that Chemists, Accountants, Marketers and Directors could have a meaningful conversation;
- The ability to use one carefully designed MoS to generate decision-supporting outputs for a range of information users without overhead.

## The individual as organisation: self-actualisation?

In the last visit to this idea we developed an understanding of the individual as fulfilling a number of different roles, articulated as 'selves' and drawing on a complementary set of skills and knowledge.

The enabling challenge is to think about the future, to consider the challenges and opportunities in our individual environments and consider what changes may be necessary, or desirable, to continue to fulfil our individual purposes. That requires

The creation of a MoMoS; an understanding of 'who I am';
The creation of a model of 'my world' to comprehend how that influences who I could be;
Comparison of the two to determine what changes are necessary or desirable.

There is a big distinction between necessary and desirable. 'Necessary' is a response to any threats to the continuation of my current selves. 'Desirable' is a response to opportunities and unfulfilled aspirations. It could demand the realignment of 'what I do' with 'what I wish to do'. The outcome is to develop a strategy which leads to a better 'self', one which is more closely aligned to 'the person I want to be'. In simple terms, it would, perhaps, make 'me' more content. There is a debate in the psychology literature about the extent to which we can really understand our 'selves', given that we all have what Wilson (2002) calls an 'adaptive unconscious', an inner self that we cannot access. However, our concern here is with the things that we do, the ways we express ourselves to the world. These are, or can be, a matter of conscious choice, whatever the underlying 'story of me' that we tell ourselves to justify them. Our operational selves, how I express myself to the world, are largely (for me) a function of the choices I make, not fate or the dictat of any other person. Value, for an individual, needs to consider both intrinsic and extrinsic factors. Intrinsic factors are those, such as the sense of self-worth, that arise from being true to one's self. Extrinsic reward means being valued for who we are, not simply what we do, and having a sense of belonging, esteem, prestige and, of course, earnings.

Given finite resources, I must operationally balance my energy across my four selves as long as they exist. Strategically, I can make choices about them. I could change or rebalance the investment of resources around 'Researcher and Scientist', 'Consultant and Educator' or 'Volunteer'. The role of 'Husband' and 'Father' are subject to change in the way they are articulated over time (Handy, 1989). Like any relationship, they must be invested in if they are to be sustained.

The operational environments of my four selves are relatively discrete, but they are likely to have some overlaps either of clients, relationships, services, skills or geography. However, when it comes to considering the whole self and the problematic future, they come together in a single place. This is partly because of the overlap but mainly because opportunities or threats in one implies potential for change which necessarily has implications for the others; remember, resources are finite.

It is rather too grand to suggest that every individual has anything as formal as a 'strategy'. There is though a need to pursue personal growth, psychological rather than physiological. For me, I want to be a 'smarter' business not a bigger business (or indeed a bigger person). No individual can remain static. 'Business as usual' means, at the very least, continuing adaptation to the changing circumstances of the environment. That requires us, however informally, to reflect on ourselves following the same essential pattern as any other organisation:

- Where am I?
- Where do I want to be?
- What risks do I face?
- What opportunities are there?
- What constraints are there?
- What could I change?

We can all perhaps dream about possible alternative futures. Indeed, Maltz (2001) argues that we must visualise the future we want and then we will change our actions in order to achieve it. He may have a point.

The challenge for each of us is to understand how we should adapt our 'posture' in relation to our world. Where there is tension between these things, that tension is resolved by reference to our identity – the sense of 'self' – and choices about those things which we value most, which include time, energy, money, but perhaps most fundamentally are about relationships and contentment.

The first information we require is about the future environment(s) in which our operations will be carried out. These consist of networks of professional relationships, the changing needs and desire of family and so on. Each of those networks of relationships needs to be authentically invested in, managed and farmed for long-term sustainability, otherwise they will decay. Meanwhile we must distinguish between those relationships which reward investment (increase contentment in one way or another) and those which simply drain energy and then make sensible choices about them. Wrapped around all of them are the political, technological, social and economic factors that influence each of them.

The second information we require is about our 'selves'. What desires and ambitions can be fulfilled through the network of relationships? What skills and knowledge can be used (or need to be acquired) in order to maintain mutual value exchange? What is the capability to provide value to each? What is the capacity that might be available to each one – and how does that balance against the possible demand? This covers our 'HR' function – skills, knowledge and behaviour.

In a perfect world there are perhaps more opportunities than there is capacity. The decisions then become about allocation of scarce resources to most rewarding opportunities whilst effectively countering any threats and balancing opportunity against desire and intent. The overall process is outlined in Figure 6.4.

Development and maintenance of authentic relationships requires investment of time over time with significant fluctuations in both workload and cash flow. As many self-employed individuals and small businesses will confirm, there is a tendency towards famine and feast. There is either too much to do and a struggle to deliver it or not enough to do with consequently poor cash flow. We must manage our finances to ensure that there is sufficient funding to support current costs and investment in the development of existing and new relationships. Funding is a key enabler of both current and future activity. Any attempt to shorten the 'new business' development cycle risks moving from an authentic relationship based on mutual trust and respect to one which is purely transactional with possible short-term benefits but a high risk of long-term loss.

The thinking equally applies to every individual seeking personal sustainability, whether self-employed or employed. We each must keep adapting to survive, the question is whether with each year passing we gain new and different experience, which perhaps implies making new mistakes, or whether we simply repeat the experience of the past?

It is not enough, of course, to have authentic relationships and enough working capital to survive. We must determine what work we will do and, if appropriate, with which organisations. Choices here depend upon both a rich understanding of the self in terms of skills, knowledge and competencies and the set of preferences that support their effective application.

I made a number of choices in order to be where I am – I like to work *with* larger organisations but appreciate that I did not like working *for* them – there is a difference. It follows therefore that the opportunities I am seeking in my problematic environment and the relationships in which I am investing time, energy and money must contain challenges and problems amenable to my skills and

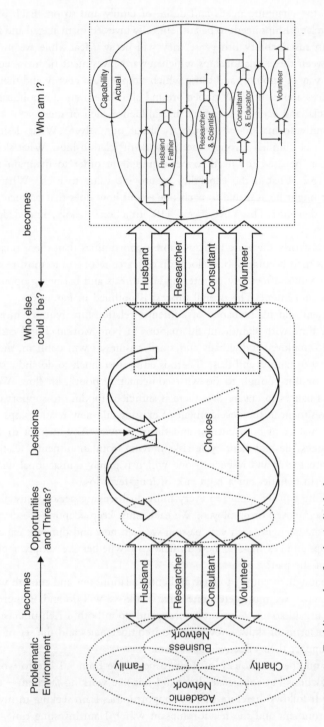

**FIGURE 6.4** Enabling value for the individual

knowledge. I must find individuals and organisations which share my essential values and are willing to 'rent' those skills to apply to suitable problems.

So much is common sense?

## Summary

We have shown in practice many of the ideas about the value-enabling parts of the organisation and how they can be applied to the individual, to full strategy formulation, to using information as the key to value and to understanding how we can use information about the present to understand potential value in the future. In the next chapter, we shall look at the autonomy of the individual in the organisation and how to exercise tight–loose control.

# 7

# MANAGING AUTONOMY

People are at the heart of the enterprise.

Stafford Beer, *The Heart of Enterprise* (1979)

## Introduction

Having established the value-generating and value-enabling structure of the Intelligent Organisation it will be evident that within that structure we run the risk of either overconstraining the organisation or having it run riot. We can have insufficient autonomy or too much. The dilemma of the Intelligent Organisation as Wiener (1948) expressed it is that, rooted in changing technologies, it

> embraces technical developments with great possibilities for good and for evil.

The information-processing capability of contemporary technology has the potential to massively centralise control, or it can guarantee our freedom. For now we have a choice, just because we can do something doesn't mean we should!

For me, we must ensure that we are free to exercise our skills, knowledge and judgement. Doing this effectively will allow the people in the organisation to be "all that one can be" (Maslow, 1970). It will also enable us to reduce costs, flatten structures and devolve decision making. In our Intelligent Organisation we need to manage what people do, not where they are and, as far as is possible, we need to equip them with the skills and knowledge to manage themselves.

## Power, communication and organisation

Power and control have a tendency to centralise in organisations of all types (Beer, 1993) and ultimately that will have a deleterious effect on performance. Quite apart from anything else, if the small group of people at the centre of the organisation are going to make all the decisions, then:

- Why do we need all the other people?
- Who wants to work where they are not trusted or valued?
- How big will managerial heads need to be to contain all the information needed to competently make all decisions?

Woodward (1965) suggests that organisational form (the structure and hierarchy) is determined by the technology employed by the organisation. It is true that technology constrains some aspects of organisational form; however, that research was undertaken before the revolution in technology of the last 50 years. Perhaps it is time to reconsider?

Contemporary technology enables the radically different form of the Intelligent Organisation which, if it is to be truly sustainable, must

- distribute decisions widely;
- have a shallow logical hierarchy;
- have wide spans of control.

Enabled by the effective use of information, such organisations are leaner, faster and more responsive to both customers' desires and their own needs. Distributed information enables local empowerment and effective self-regulation.

So, what gets in the way? We do.

The Industrial Revolution, from about 1760 in the UK, saw the formation for the first time of 'manufactories', large-scale organisations bringing together significant numbers of often unskilled or semi-skilled people to carry out a range of tasks. Dark, dank and dangerous places (no labour laws in those days), the owners understandably drew on the only organisational models available to run them. These models were essentially either religious or military. Both drew on strict hierarchy, centralised command and control, adherence to orders and severe (but different) disciplinary controls.

This approach was possibly necessary at the time. Only a lucky few people were educated or skilled and communication was primarily oral, not written. Communicating with large numbers of people simultaneously meant giving a speech or, in a noisy environment, shouting. The limited new skills of the majority of the workforce, together with unsophisticated, dangerous, unfamiliar, unguarded machinery, made close supervision essential. Of course there will always be some people (at every level of organisation) who would rather talk about work than do any.

Historically, then, large organisations relied upon a command-and-control hierarchy simply to continue existing. Knowledge and power were held by a very small, educated and often business-owning elite at the peak of the hierarchy. Orders were expressed orally and in writing through intermediaries (middle management). It was perhaps, given the limits of communication and the skills and knowledge of the workforce, the only way to run things successfully. Compare and contrast, as they say in the exams!

What is different about our circumstances?

Globally, and of course to different levels in different countries, many individuals are much more highly educated and skilled than was the case in the 1700s. Organisations are often several orders of magnitude larger than they were. Walmart (webref 3) employs around 2.1 million people globally (more employees than the population of some countries) and operates about 11,000 retail units under 71 brands in 27 countries. Microsoft (webref 4) has 'only' 128,000 employees and operates in about 123 countries. The number of individuals and PCs using its products changes so rapidly it is probably subject to Heisenbergian uncertainty. Even Jaguar-Land Rover (webref 5), one of the world's smaller motor manufacturers (and owned by Tata in India) has five sites in the UK, 25,000 employees and distributes its products to 170 countries.

Nobody can shout loud enough to be heard across such vast distances; no centralised process can manage such numbers. It is essential to distribute control. Contemporary information technologies enable that distribution but also enable the opposite. Whether through 'smart' phones, tablet, laptop and personal computers, corporate applications, intranet, internet or rapidly multiplying social media platforms, transmitting a message (and verifying that it has been received) has never been easier. Verifying that it has been understood and acted on as hoped is a different problem. Where is the equivalent mechanism for upward transmission?

Absolute centralisation of control will calcify the organisation. Absolute control by the individual militates against the idea of the organisation as a purposeful, unified entity, in which is implied a number of people working in concert to achieve a shared end. To have complete freedom within the organisation would be anarchic. However, once individuals become spatially or temporally distributed, even for relatively small organisations, control necessarily distributes itself (e.g. a policeman on the beat). Individuals with different levels of skill, knowledge and experience will, simply because they are operating at a distance from the command centre, interpret things in different ways and need to exercise discretion and judgement. If we want to both achieve coherence *and* accept that individuals will necessarily exercise some level of discretion, then we must reflect on freedom and belongingness and build them into the logic of the organisation. We cannot regulate, legislate or manage them out and survive.

Much has been written over many years about freedom and belongingness in organisations of all types. This ranges from the aristocracy of the philosopher kings in Plato's Republic (Plato, 390 BC, in Lindsay, 1906) to Mill's (1974) discussion of liberty, Sampson's (1993) concern with what he called Britain's "democracy in crisis" and Beer's (1974, 1981, 1993) insights into "designing freedom". There are explorations of this in the 'human relations' school of thought in the management literature, e.g. Mayo (1949), Maslow (1970), Herzberg et al. (1959), the soft systems work of Checkland (1981) and others and the critical systems work of Ulrich (1983).

The individual, in many situations and in circumstances where the choice truly exists, expresses their ultimate freedom by choosing whether or not to work with (or for) a particular organisation. Making the choice to join a particular organisation means we relinquish some portion of our freedom. When we choose to belong we commit, at some level, to follow organisational norms. Those norms include values (beliefs about how to operate in the world) and certainly include rules. This will extend to using the technologies provided for us and for some organisations, clothing. It used to be said of individuals joining the armed forces in the UK that

> if you take the Queen's shilling, you agree to wear the Queen's uniform and follow the Queen's orders.

Whilst being able to recognise a member of the military forces by way of his or her uniform seems reasonable, the widely reported requirement by Disneyland Paris in the 1990s that attempted to specify the employees' underwear seems somewhat less so!

The challenge for contemporary leaders is to create the behavioural and cultural conditions under which individuals within the organisation are able to empower themselves. The legalistic meaning of empower is to 'invest with authority, to authorise'. Might we consider that as the basis of developing appropriate autonomy throughout the organisation? What is the scope of empowerment? What are the conditions and opportunities that need to be created? What skills and knowledge do individuals need in order to empower themselves?

We cannot empower people; that is a nonsense. We can however create the conditions under which people can choose to empower themselves *and* act upon that choice. That is, we cannot simply state that 'you are hereby empowered' but must create the whole situation under which that 'authorisation' can be exercised. What might that mean for leaders?

In the Intelligent Organisation the logical hierarchy is based on the flow of information. It follows therefore that the individual best placed to make any particular decision is the person who can resolve three dimensions of any decision simultaneously:

- Dimension 1: What is the optimum solution for this specific instance?
- Dimension 2: What are the implications of and on that decision for the wider organisation?
- Dimension 3: What is the impact of the outcome of that decision upon the environment and what is the impact of the environment upon that decision?

That of course is a very bald, simplified statement. There will be simple decisions, ones with obvious, simple or transparent information and implications; they need not detain us here. However, many decisions will be complex, rooted in uncertainty, perhaps fraught with risk. In these cases being the Boss doesn't make you right, it just makes you the Boss. It seems that in order to make effective, risk- and judgement-based decisions and to engage the support of others, it will be helpful to the decision maker to amplify his or her own capability by leveraging the knowledge and capability of others. This will also reduce the need for a manager to have a brain the size of a planet and either or both an eidetic or photographic memory.

That means it is OK, in fact it is essential, to acknowledge that other people may know far more about something than you do. It means it is essential to recognise the talents and capabilities of all the people in the organisation. Perhaps it requires a certain Socratic humility on the part of leaders and managers to accept that a hierarchically 'superior' position does not demand of them that, sophist like, they have all the good ideas, solutions and answers. What it demands of them is that using the best information available they make the best decision they can that steers the organisation towards its desired outcome. That requires human judgement; if it didn't require judgement we would probably buy a machine to do it.

That judgement means that we, as managers, have to allow ourselves to be wrong. We have to allow ourselves to simply not know an answer. We must support, educate, encourage, teach, coach and rectify in such a manner that we continually develop the capabilities of others and invest in their freedom to apply them. Whilst management is also work, creating the conditions under which each individual will empower themselves will mean, over time, that the 'work of management' is much more interesting, productive and fruitful.

If our Intelligent Organisation is going to survive and thrive, then populating it with people blindly following orders will not suffice. Those so able will exercise their choice and leave; those in charge will not have requisite capacity to control everything. Equally, an organisation populated by anarchists, or perhaps prima donnas, each doing their own thing, will not suffice either.

## How much autonomy is enough?

Some? That is probably not an adequate answer. At this point it would be great to say 'here is a simple rule' – I wish it was so. In the absence of such a thing, I shall have to try and explain how I see it!

Beer (1985), not terribly helpfully, states the rule that each individual part of the organisation should have

as much autonomy as is consistent with cohesion of the whole.

We can take that to mean that constraints upon any individual within the organisation should be minimal. They should be free to fulfil their tasks so long as they act in a manner consistent with its espoused purpose, its values and the legal, regulatory and performance requirements which constrain it.

An Intelligent Organisation develops autonomy based on sound, repeatable, reliable, sustainable principles. We must create conditions under which people can 'know' the right thing to do in any particular circumstance without having to be told on each occasion. Those principles, developed and jointly owned with each individual, will themselves increase the perceived level of autonomy.

The organisation and the individual can, in effect, jointly determine the degree of autonomy, and both can actively seek to modify it as desirable. That is a good starting point for the discussion; enough freedom to do the right things, not so much that it damages the cohesion of the organisation. When we work within agreed constraints because we recognise and accept them, because we see them as self-evidently appropriate, we will be low cost to manage. We will most likely manage ourselves within the boundaries and will be able to develop authentic, consistent relationships with customers and colleagues. Very importantly, having chosen to accept the constraints, we will be likely to wish to remain with the organisation in the long term. Contented people appear to have higher levels of satisfaction, resulting in lower staff turnover, reduced absenteeism and sickness. These things are good for the financial health of the organisation.

One of the very interesting aspects of military management (and similar 'disciplined' organisations) is the extent to which it is outcome focused and operationally decentralised. Such organisations seek to recruit people whose values are aligned with those of the service – they set out to find 'people like us'. All recruits, whether commissioned or not, go through basic training designed both to turn them into soldiers, sailors, airmen or marines *and* to help them identify for themselves whether or not they fit (sometimes I am sure with a little guidance). Only once the civilian has been turned into a serviceman does the focus shift to training in the technical content of the particular service, whatever aspect that might be. Once the individual both 'belongs' and is fully technically trained to a very high level, then he or she is deployed into active duty. Such active duty will be specified in the form of an outcome, 'achieve this'. It matters not what the particular activity is. The officers, with inevitably the occasional exception, know that the servicemen, with inevitably the occasional exception, are willing and able to achieve the outcome (the what) and of developing the means for themselves (the how). The 'why' is a given, it is ingrained in their belongingness to the organisation. In simple terms, having trained and tested them thoroughly in advance, great autonomy can be allowed in the delivery of the outcome. An interesting paradox, the more tightly certain aspects are controlled in the early stage (selection, alignment, behaviours, skills), the more freedom the individual can have later.

I am sure you will remember Figure 7.1 (you saw it before in Chapter 3). It shows how in the logical hierarchy of the Intelligent Organisation each level is constrained by belonging to the level above and in turn constrains the level below.

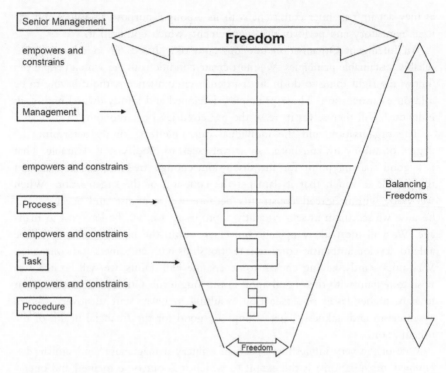

**FIGURE 7.1** Managing autonomy

Autonomy, in terms of the purpose for which the particular level exists, is constrained by belonging to the next higher level and constrains the one below it:

- Procedures are constrained by the required outputs of tasks;
- Tasks constrain procedures and are constrained by the outputs and outcomes of processes;
- Processes constrain tasks and are constrained by the required outputs of management;
- Management constrains process and is constrained by its required contribution to senior management.

Recalling the homeostat, the information about outputs and outcomes flows from each level to the next higher level as the enabler of management activity. The regulatory activity of the homeostat works to maintain it within the defined limits. Any tendency to move outside given parameters is rectified by control action already embedded in the system and keeps the system under control. All of which sounds potentially terribly oppressive. However, having already embraced Beer's principle, an oppressive regime cannot be the answer.

Maximising autonomy acts to:

- decentralise the organisation;
- enable local responsiveness to local customers;
- minimise the cost of supervision;
- maximise the sense of control for the individual.

Efficient manufacturing is very reliant on a high level of automation. This creates conditions in which, in general, people are employed only to carry out those tasks that cannot be completed by automatons or it has been determined will not be automated. In such circumstances the work of the individual is controlled by the work rate of the production process to which they contribute. Autonomy in relation to the task or procedure is low, it is governed by the machine. Individuals may be making some specific, limited choices and should have the power to stop the process if they observe it to be failing (Shingo, 1987). Here the technology (automation of the process) largely governs autonomy, although even the most automated process relies on the skills of individuals, for example, those required to set up the technology and keep it operating within its constraints.

Fast food outlets rely on production technology, repeatability and process optimisation. Reliable low-cost, high-volume output is the basis of the business model. There may be only one machine process to cook a burger, but the staff member must apply his or her skills to assembling it according to the instructions and the required presentation. That is something only a human can currently do; it requires judgement. Equally, the counter clerk is constrained in their process by the operating method of the till, but they also deal with the customer.

The blend of skills required by the burger assembler and the counter clerks are different. The autonomy required by the counter clerk is greater. They are not simply dealing with the need to follow the process in a consistent manner but also with the vagaries of the requirements of individual customers (largely but not completely constrained by a menu). Given that customers will not arrive at regular intervals, they must deal with varying arrival rates and the variances in behaviour of those customers who will, inevitably, range from delightful to downright rude. One junior banker I met very early in my first career had all these skills, back to front. He was a delight with the customers and could always handle any mood or situation however strange, but he couldn't cope with process, his till never balanced. More often than not he did the wrong thing for the customer but they loved him anyway!

The less the organisation relies on process technology, the more it relies on individual skills and behaviours and the greater the autonomy or discretion required by the individual in order to fulfil the task. Even in a notionally 'pure' service environment, such as banking, there is still a significant constraint imposed on the individual through process technology, the banking system. Customer service cannot be built in to the process, it has to be part of the authentic skill set of the staff member. Stupidities arise in any human system, even with the best of intent.

## Thank you for shopping at . . .

*A chain of neighbourhood shops was keen to improve relationships with its customers and decided to run a Customer Service Improvement Programme. It decided that whenever a customer used a credit card or cheque, the employee must address the customer by name and thank them for shopping with the chain.*

*The employees were predominantly low paid. They mainly worked at the chain for convenience to their personal lives, proximity to their homes, availability for their children, or in some cases because they were insufficiently qualified to apply for jobs elsewhere. The job was not necessarily what they wanted, it was what they could get.*

*The Customer Service Improvement Programme was run and all employees were trained in the new approach. After some time had passed they surveyed customers to evaluate success. They were disappointed in the results.*

*To enhance success, they made failure to follow the new standard a disciplinary offence. The chain experienced a rise in staff turnover and customer service deteriorated.*

Ultimately, employees were given no choice; the training focused on 'what' and 'how'. Perhaps it would have been more successful if it had concentrated upon 'why' and invested in obtaining genuine commitment from its employees rather than procedural compliance through what would look to many like oppression. Binding employees in to process compliance through overbearing scrutiny has, ultimately, the same effect as bottling gas under pressure. It is very expensive to achieve and will inevitably find the weakest point and leak or be triggered by a spark into an explosion. Sustainability for any organisation demands that it build harmonious relationships with the people that make it real. The Intelligent Organisation rests on an underlying assumption that most individuals, most of the time, want to do a good job, reflecting Theory Y (McGregor, 1960). They want to help the organisation succeed; that is good for both parties.

Greater reliance on skills implies greater autonomy. That, in turn, drives an opportunity for further skills. These skills are not technical – the ability to carry out the task – but self-managerial, requiring judgement and discretion, the ability to decide which task should be carried out, when and to what standard with what level of risk.

## A decision model for autonomy

We, in our organisations, desire that people do at least four things with their autonomy:

- Deliver: apply requisite skills to the process and achieve the required output and outcome;
- Learn: reflect on how well they applied the skills and ran the process and teach themselves how to do it better next time;

- Communicate: provide relevant information to prior, subsequent, contained and containing activities about performance;
- Alert: highlight to management those constraints on the whole system (skills, process, information) which limit performance and where they do not have the power (the limits to autonomy) to change the system.

How much autonomy is enough is perhaps largely determinable by certain characteristics of the whole organisation:

- business model;
- processes and their degree of automation;
- competences and skills of the individual;
- probability and consequences of error or failure;
- alignment of individual, organisational and professional interests.

We shall consider each in turn. The business model is probably best represented in the form of a grid (Figure 7.2 below).

In this grid, different business types are categorised according to two dimensions: volume and value. Our fast food franchise is considered as making money from high-volume, low-value transactions. It needs a process which is repeatable and reliable, likely to drive down unit costs and enable survival on a low price and margin. This suggests low cost per transaction, which typically implies a low level of skill or a very high volume relative to cost. Sales of power stations are

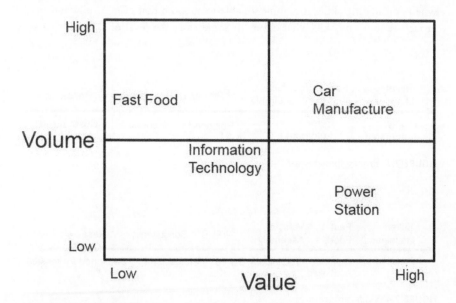

**FIGURE 7.2** The business model

considered high value and, at least relative to fast food, low volume. The high value of each power station suggests that whilst it is important to have a process for design and construction, the unique circumstances of each one will demand a more customised approach. This implies a significantly higher level of skill. Information technology products are seen as lower volume than fast food (most people buy more burgers than they do laptops or tablets). As relative commodities, value is higher but reliability must also be high. Technology products are either 'right' or 'wrong', they either work or don't. This suggests sound technical design and again a repeatable reliable production process with a medium level of skill. Car manufacture is considered high on both dimensions. A car, in the hands of the purchaser, is a high-value item (the second-most significant purchase for most consumers after their home). Whilst individual cars are low in value to the manufacturer, their total volumes are high (around 10 million cars per annum for the largest manufacturers). The technical complexity of the individual product needs to be matched by the technical skills of those assembling the product.

Taking this into consideration, we can now look at the processes and their degree of automation (Figure 7.3).

At the left-hand end of this continuum are processes in which the level of automation suggests that a low level of individual autonomy will be appropriate. Those towards the right-hand end (requiring higher levels of skill or judgement) will enable a higher level of autonomy. We can apply this to the skills of the individual as shown in Figure 7.4, in which we represent a progression from unskilled worker to seasoned professional.

It is important to note that these continua will never reach 0% or 100% on a scale. However customised a process may be, there will always need to be some level of process consistency, otherwise there will be no effective output. Equally, when considering skills, it is unreasonable to suppose that even a fully automated process requires no skill whatsoever. In some cases the level of skill may be very

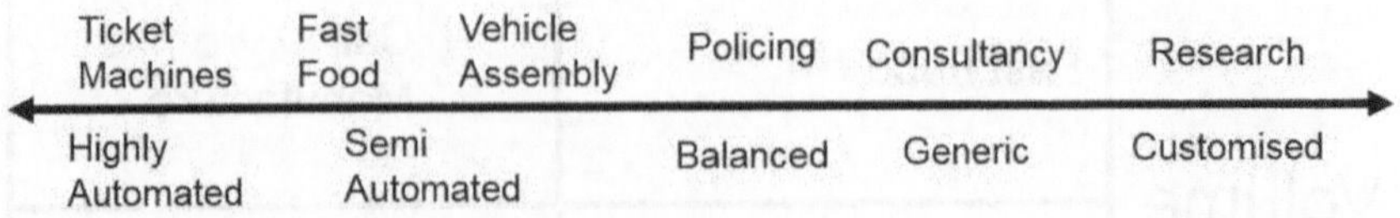

**FIGURE 7.3** Process progression

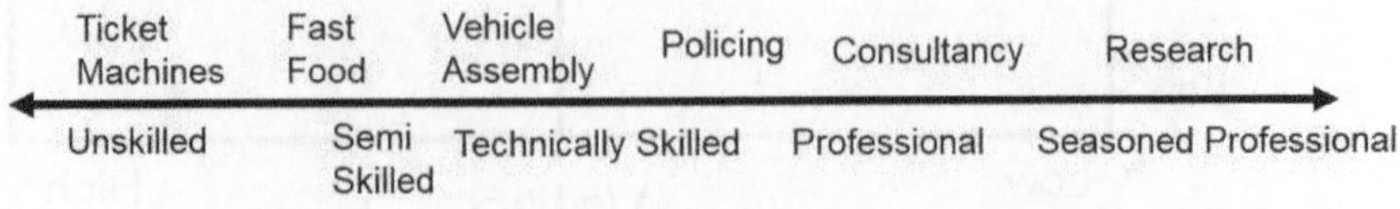

**FIGURE 7.4** Skills progression

small, in others (and automated ticket machines are a good example of this) the skill requirement is outsourced to the operator (the customer). Think about this next time you are queuing to use an automated checkout in a supermarket or DIY store. It is not the case that no labour is required for the process, the store has simply outsourced the skill, and the cost, to its customers.

The fourth element in the decision model is to consider the probability and consequences of process error or failure by individuals, i.e. risk. Represented in Figure 7.5, this works best as a grid. I suggest that fast food production is a low-probability but high-consequence activity (food poisoning). Demonstrable adherence to an approved process will mitigate risk, reducing scope for autonomy. Information technology, on the other hand, is low probability, low consequence. While the risk to life from information technology is low, the risk to reputation will be higher. However, the latter is likely to have less immediate consequences and the manufacturer will have the opportunity to rectify matters.

A power station carries a much higher probability of incident in all its phases. The consequences of unmitigated risks are significantly higher, not least the potential for loss of life. These present a particular problem, needing reliable, repeatable processes in all of the design, build, operate, maintain and decommission cycles over 50 years or more. At the same time they need technically skilled and professional people to operate them. The power generation technology of the station will delimit the extent to which autonomy can be possible.

Finally, we can consider alignment of individual, organisational and professional interests. Represented in Figure 7.6, this gets a little tricky; I have identified three sets of interests that somehow must be reconciled.

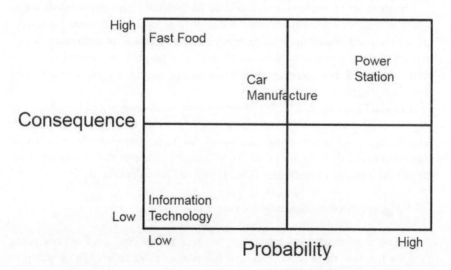

**FIGURE 7.5** Risk, probability and consequence

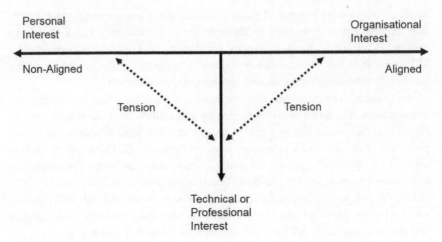

**FIGURE 7.6** Alignment of values

First is personal interest. An individual for whatever reason may be disengaged from the organisation's values. Those not so aligned are likely to act primarily in their own interest. Autonomy is likely to be minimal, but such a situation imparts a duty to those managing the organisation to consider how to rectify it.

Second is organisational interest. Individuals in this position are wholly aligned with the values of the organisation and likely to act primarily in its interests but may neglect their own interests in so doing. Here we may wish to constrain autonomy to mitigate the risk of damage to the 'self' through overcommitment to the organisation. Members of religious orders and 'Type A' personalities tend to be here.

The third set of interests is technical or professional. Here our interests are in a state of tension. The primary interest alignment is professional, second and third are personal and organisational. Doctors are a good example of individuals whose primary loyalty is often to their profession. The hospital or medical centre in which they work is a convenience rather than one to which they necessarily feel they owe allegiance.

And yes, I have made all those choices a little stark, exaggerated for effect. For most of us, in most situations, we are trying to manage the tension between our self, organisational and professional interests. We must appreciate the existence of that tension and then design in the 'right' amount of autonomy to dissolve it for all parties. That, to quote Henri Fayol (1916) on centralisation, is

a question of continuously varying proportion.

Pulling all of that together what do we need to do? And no, I am not going to make this easy, there is no arithmetic solution or silver bullet. We are going to have to think and then exercise our judgement:

- Locate your organisation in the business model, is it:

  - Low Volume: Low Value
  - Low Volume: High Value
  - High Volume: Low Value
  - High Volume: High Value

- What does that suggest to you would be a good way to use process?
- Locate the process(es) on the process progression continuum:

  - Where do you think it fits?
  - Is that consistent with the business model?

- What does that suggest to you would be a useful level of autonomy for individuals?
- Locate the skill levels on the skills progression continuum:

  - Where do the skills fit?
  - Is that consistent with the business model?
  - Is it consistent with the process progression?

- How does that modify your perception of the level of autonomy?
- Locate the organisation on the probability and consequence grid, is it:

  - Low Probability: Low Consequence
  - Low Probability: High Consequence
  - High Probability: Low Consequence
  - High Probability: High Consequence

- How does that modify your perception of the level of autonomy?
- Locate the people on the interests alignment chart.

  - Where do you believe they fit?
  - What evidence do you have to support that belief?
  - What, if anything, is being done to manage the alignment?

It would be surprising if in many organisations there were not favourable overlaps. That is, overlaps where the skill level of individuals is higher than is required to safely operate the process. In these circumstances it may be appropriate to increase levels of autonomy, to allow for further delegation of decisions, to increase the sense of freedom within the organisation.

It may also of course be that there is unfavourable lack of overlap. That the extent to which the process is automated is insufficient to compensate for the lack of skills being applied to it. Usually there will be evidence of this in poor product, failing customer service, complaints and so on. The interesting thing is, what do you do to fix it? Do you reduce autonomy (quick fix, looks cheap and feels powerful) or do you invest in resolving the skills deficiency and preserve the autonomy in the system?

It is usually the case that once autonomy has been removed (usually on cost or risk grounds) it becomes impossible to restore to its previous level.

## Summary

What this decision model alerts us to is the need to link back to the 'value-enabling' activities of the organisation. Where we have discovered a bias towards automation and process, then value-enabling activity needs to focus on ensuring that these aspects are appropriate and robust and that the people have the appropriate skills to deliver the required outcomes. Conversely, where the organisation has low reliance on process and high reliance on skills, the value enablers need to ensure that they are investing appropriately in employing the right people with the right skills and that both the organisation and the individual are investing in them suitably.

Both of these actions can be conceived as addressing the matter of 'risk'. Appropriate investment in processes and skills will be one of the tools for mitigation. One measure of success in this regard might be *not* that individuals have been trained or processes enhanced, but that the perceived level of risk exposure has declined as a result.

Alignment of individual and organisational values will also require investment. This might be achieved through evaluations in recruitment processes for new employees but will also need to be tackled for individuals already in post. Quantitative indicators of alignment can be found in such things as staff turnover, sickness and retention rates. Qualitative indicators will be discerned in the myths and stories that pervade the organisation, the sense of coherence and collegiality that is sensed rather than directly measurable. Investment does not mean that 'beatings will continue until morale improves'. Value-enabling actors need to understand the organisational benefit of aligning interests and ensure that mechanisms are in place through which lack of alignment can be recognised and addressed, particularly by encouraging and enabling managers to 'model the way'.

That was all a bit thoughtful and thought provoking. In the next chapter, I shall try to put it into practice.

# 8

# MANAGING AUTONOMY

## Cases

With every pair of hands you hire you get a free brain.
Peter Drucker, *The Age of Discontinuity* (1969)

## Introduction

We did lot of thinking about autonomy in the previous chapter, explored the decision model for autonomy and considered the implications for enabling value. We shall now return to the ongoing case studies, apply the model and see what the implications are for each one. I have (Figure 8.1) consolidated the five diagrammatic elements of the model into a single diagram. This is informationally equivalent to the individual elements and allows us to see, holistically, each element in the context of the others.

## Fusion21

You will recall that Fusion21 has three value-generating elements: Procurement, Training and Employment Services (TES) and Consultancy. Each has a slightly different business model and while the guidance for determining appropriate autonomy in each are the same, there are differences in the outcomes. The rules have been applied and are shown in Figure 8.2. Different symbols are used for each of the elements in order to ease comprehension: the star is procurement, the heart is TES and the cloud is consultancy.

For Fusion21 as a whole, the procurement business model is relatively high value (it generates the greater part of the income) and high volume. It undertakes the majority of the work with in excess of 300 projects per annum. The process was developed in partnership with those who deliver it and, as far as practical, was codified into information systems. One element deals with the procurement

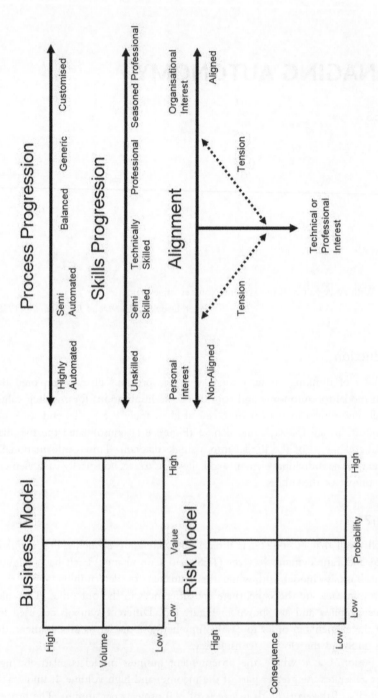

**FIGURE 8.1** Integrated decision model for autonomy

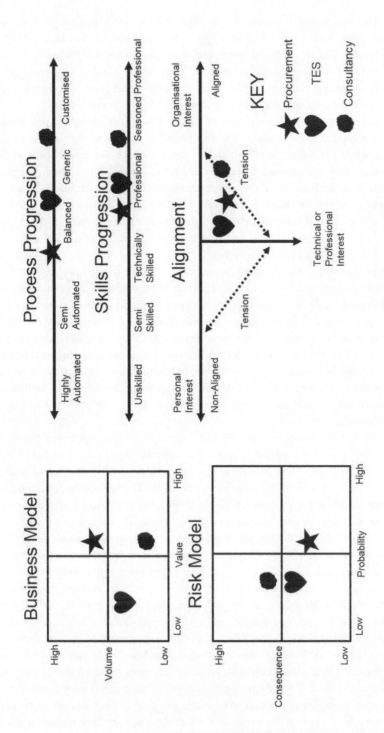

**FIGURE 8.2** Fusion21 autonomy

of materials and labour for projects, the other deals with the project process itself from inception to completion. The whole is more than semiautomated, giving it high reliability and repeatability, but it also relies heavily on the professional skills and knowledge of the procurement team. They are specialists, mainly quantity surveyors and project managers. On balance, procurement relies slightly more on skills than it does on process. There is a lot of judgement involved.

From a risk perspective, procurement can be thought of as higher probability but with relatively low consequences. The probability arises in the volume of the projects, while the consequences of failure are important but unlikely to be life threatening. The consequence of process or skill failure is likely to manifest itself in rectification work or loss of future opportunities. When we consider alignment, and looking across the team as a whole, they are most likely to be aligned to technical/professional interests first and organisational interests second. As professionals they have a duty to act in a manner consistent with professional standards first and organisational standards second.

The procurement team have no autonomy to change the business model; they are constrained to operate within it. They do need sufficient autonomy, within the constraints of the process that they designed (a higher level of autonomy), to exercise professional skills and judgement about how they do what they do. From the value-enabling perspective, we must ensure that they have sufficient process to deliver against the business model whilst maintaining and investing in the skills and knowledge necessary for the professional standards to be maintained. It would be appropriate to reflect on the degree of alignment between the technical/ professional interest and the organisational interest as a means of recognising and, if desirable, reducing tension.

Turning our attention to the TES team, we find a slightly different situation. The business model is very different – it has relatively low volume and relatively low value. The first of these is because it is 'batch based', a small number of intakes each year, each of which has multiple participants. The second because TES, to some extent, fulfils the purpose of Fusion21 (remember: 'Profits into People not into Pockets'). The desired outcome of the TES activity is employed people, not profit. The process is clear but more balanced; it is reliant on manual rather than automated processing, placing a higher emphasis on skill. It is therefore no surprise to find that the skills progression position is more professional than skilled technical. Quality delivery of the process, one which involves education, training and personal development, is highly reliant on the judgement and applied expertise of the staff. Considering the risk position it is low and low. The probability of failure is mitigated (through for example good classroom and workshop practice) and the consequences of process failure for Fusion21 are also likely to be low. There is a need to draw on the process but it is not dominant. Alignment is more balanced, though leaning towards the technical and organisational interests. What draws it back towards personal is that there is a perception that people working in that area do so because of the intrinsic reward of the work itself rather than the extrinsic reward of salary, professional recognition or standards. They do the work because they care.

Again, the TES team cannot change the business model and they were involved in defining their own process. Discretion is important here – the TES team are not dealing with physical artefacts but often with vulnerable people. It is easy in these circumstances for the process to get in the way of a good outcome. They need to have discretion, up to a point, to minimise the amount of process and emphasise the application of skills, knowledge and judgement. The limit is reached when there is insufficient process to make the whole thing viable. This is easily attained if there is failure to keep essential records about trainees, their skills and qualifications, or to sustain safe working practices in the workshops.

The value enablers need to be considering and investing in the skills and knowledge of this team and, in particular, developing mechanisms for capturing that and retaining it in the business – something often called knowledge management.

Consultancy is a small part of Fusion21. It is low-volume but relatively high-value business (the margins are very good). From a process perspective, it sits at the generic/customised end of the progression. Consultancy projects are characterised in this context as unique and complex, requiring a method to be developed for structuring a problem and then solving it. There must be a level of process, but that is at a level of principle. The real emphasis is on the skills where the focus is on seasoned professionals. The nature of the industry and the actors within it are such that the routine challenges can largely be solved by the clients within their own businesses. Where a consultancy project arises, it is because the problem or challenge is not tractable to the normal tools employed. Risk probability here is relatively low (assuming competent people), but consequences potentially high. These consequences are primarily reputational. If Fusion21 does a good job the clients will probably take the credit, if they do a bad job (or the client doesn't like the outcome) they will blame Fusion21. This is not uncommon.

From an alignment perspective, consultancy staff will largely align themselves to the organisational interest whilst leaning on professional/technical interest as the base of their capability. As employees they have chosen to exercise their skills within an organisational context rather than a self-employed one.

In terms of the value enablers, the critical issue will be the maintenance and development of problem-solving and consultancy skills and ensuring that the context continues to be conducive to maintaining the values alignment. Consultants can often 'model the way' for other, less-seasoned professionals. They should be encouraged to act as mentors in developing capability and need to be granted the autonomy that lets them do so.

## Southern Mill

You will remember we left Southern Mill as it was sold to its new owners. Nonetheless, we can apply the decision model to the organisation as we left it.

When we consider the model here, we shall apply it primarily to the core process of paper making. The business model is based on high volume and

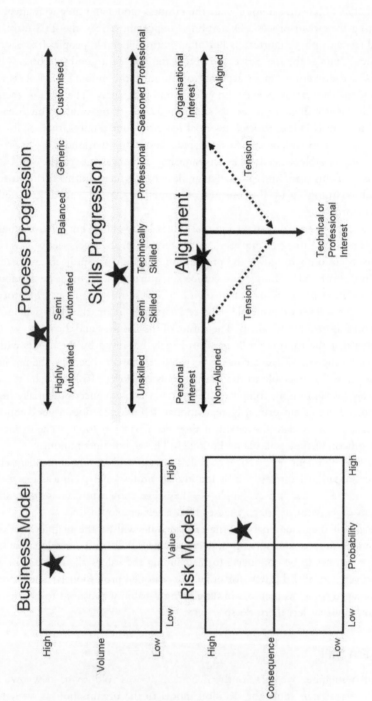

**FIGURE 8.3** Southern Mill autonomy

moderate value but operating in a high input cost environment where the key to profitability is reliability and throughput. That is not in our gift to change; it is a property of the global market itself, not Southern Mill or its owning parent.

When we consider process progression in Southern Mill, we find that it is both highly automated (paper making) and manual (paper conversion). The paper machine only works one way; productivity is primarily a function of the capability of the machine itself and its inherent technology. There is an undoubted level of technical skill required to make 'good' paper, but that is constrained by the limits of the machine. The operator can adjust speed, weight, volume and colour and, by setting the machine well, can ensure that good paper comes out, but that is it. They cannot change the process. On skills progression therefore the evaluation rests on a combination of semi-skilled and technically skilled people, applying those skills in machine set up and minding. Paper machines are big, fast and loud and have lots of dangerous rotating, heavy parts. They process prodigious quantities of water (the 'soup' going in to the front of the machine is about 97% water) and energy (energy is about 25% of the base cost of making the paper in this instance). They are easily capable of maiming or killing their operators.

Although the machines are well guarded and protected, paper making is a high-risk process. The consequences of failure to follow safe practices are high, even fatal. Alignment with organisational interests in this particular case were low, tending towards the personal end. This was a function of a number of circumstances. The mill had been in its location for several generations and employed more than one generation of several families, as well as several members of the same generation. It was seen as 'our mill', physically distant from its parent and the single largest employer in its community. Decisions were seen to be made by managers within the mill that were clearly in the interests of individuals rather more than they were the organisation.

In this case, autonomy was primarily constrained by the process technology employed. Skills development needed to focus on two things. First was working within the safe processes defined, i.e. individuals could not simply modify the core process for reasons of technology and safety. The second matter was to emphasise the development of semi-skilled and technically skilled people so that they would be able to reflect on their own performance and deliver improvement in those elements which were under their control.

Whilst the conversion process is less technologically constrained, it still had high risk. Handling large reels of paper (say five tonnes each) and using powered guillotines whilst manually inserting and extracting blocks of paper carried with it risk of injury. Conversion required greater autonomy in relation to process, and a number of innovations were conceived and implemented during our time there. The emphasis on skill development for the value enablers in this area was much more on process improvement than was possible on the paper machine itself.

## ChemCo

The research organisation is challenging. The business model is about producing new, performant molecules, not about generating short-term profits, and doing so using a process which was demonstrably adding potential value to the organisation over time. The business model has been characterised as high value, low volume. That contains a potential distortion. The successful output of the research process would be a small number of new products (three or four) which would go into the market and each would generate significant value. So, low volume. However, the process of getting to those three or four successful new products relied on a process called 'high-throughput screening', a research process for rapidly testing the basic performance characteristics of a high number (several hundred thousand) of molecules. Hence, it would be possible to argue that the business model has high volume. Judgement?

As regards process progression, assessment of the process suggests that it sits neatly in the balanced position. There is much process. It is essential as much for the 'scientific method' (which helps ensure the science is robust) as for the data capture essential to repeatability, regulatory approval and investment protection through patenting. Chemicals tend to require regulatory approval before they can be sold in the market, and that approval requires a mass of data about the chemical, its performance, side effects (especially if being applied to humans) and residual effects, such as leaching into groundwater if applied in agriculture or industry. The pull towards generic resides in the need for the researchers to be able to adapt and modify processes to accommodate the peculiarities of particular chemicals and, of course, to develop new methods, processes and tests.

The skills requirement is professional. Each individual needs to be working with a skill set, appropriate to the tasks and the nature of the matters being researched. Here we can see that skill dominates process. The risk is of researchers undertaking tasks 'because they can' rather than because they are desirable or necessary. There is a possibility that the researchers will feel that the process constrains them unnecessarily and that generates its own level of risk.

When we then look at the risk model, both probability and consequences are characterised as just on the low side but close to the centre. That is *my* judgement, others may think differently. Here, the organisation should be adopting (and monitoring) the use of 'good laboratory practice' as a means of mitigating risk and maintaining it in the 'low' zone.

Values alignment is an interesting one. Here it has been judged that the researcher will be inclined towards personal and technical/professional interest more than organisational. The evidence for this rests in recognising that progress in a research career is often a function of job hopping. Researchers move to employers where the research is relevant to their particular interest. Such moves often rely on publication of successful research or experiments, disseminated in academic or trade journals, written by the researchers themselves (even if on behalf of their employers). The incentives for researchers and the means of developing their careers often

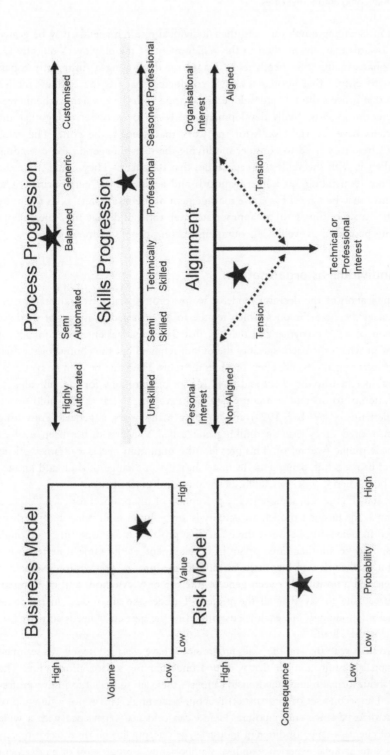

**FIGURE 8.4** Chemical research autonomy

subsist in changing employers, and their individual research agenda may be geared more towards that success than to the achievement of the employer's objectives.

Emphasis in this case needs to be placed on developing a sufficiently robust process to ensure that good research is conducted that fits the business model. Ideally, that process should be developed in concert with the researchers themselves; they are the experts. Skills development needs to focus on ensuring that the researchers have the right skills for the work that needs to be done. The value enablers here may need to consider modifying the research agenda and extending it to align it with the skills and capabilities that they have. They could make the task more demanding, set higher standards and achieve more performance. The alternative may be a need for active management of the researchers' skills to ensure that the mix continues to be appropriate over time, and that may mean both bringing people in as well as encouraging existing people to move on.

## The individual as organisation

The application of the decision model is to my 'professional' selves rather than the personal, as these are the ones which require to be managed. It is part of the legal definition of self-employment in the UK that the individual enters a 'contract for services' in which the client specifies the output required but the contractor specifies the means and methods and, often, provides the tools. There can be then no particular 'process' specified by the client and there is a lot of autonomy for the individual.

To attempt to operate as a consultant and have no process at all would smack of "dilettantism" (Weber, 1924) and so, over many years, a generic consulting process, rooted in cybernetic thinking and called VSMethod, has been evolved and made public (webref 6). This provides the minimum necessary framework to conduct projects but, being generic, draws heavily on a range of skills and knowledge about clients, processes, skills, behaviours and performance.

The star (Figure 8.5) represents my perception of my position for each element. Looking at the business model, my activity is low volume, high value. I am perhaps involved in delivering between three and five projects at any one time (although there should be another three or so 'in development' at the same time to ensure continuity of work and income). Turning to the 'process progression' element, I have selected a position between generic (the use of VSMethod) and customised. It is reasonable to say that all the projects I undertake are rooted in the same essential methodology, but each is customised to the particular needs and circumstances of the client.

Consistent with that, on the 'skills progression' I have classified myself as a seasoned professional. Justification for that is in two underpinning sets of information. The first is about formal training and qualifications – these are sufficient to justify 'professional'. The second set of information is about 'seasoning'. This is not a function of age but of experience and exposure. Here I can evidence experience with a wide range of clients, a range of different industries, private, public and third sector organisations, international experience and, very importantly, a progression of engagement

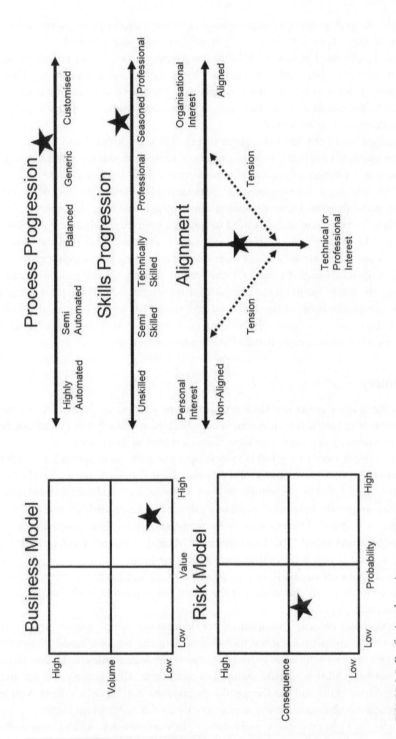

**FIGURE 8.5** Professional services autonomy

from small, local projects to large national and international projects over a long period of time. These can be regarded as sufficient to justify 'seasoned'.

Risk I have rated as low probability, low consequence (although close to the border on both). No work I undertake carries with it more than minimal risk of injury or death to me or others. Advice and guidance that I give is not insubstantial to the clients and can have significant business impact on finance, people and systems, so it is nontrivial.

Finally, I have considered alignment of personal, organisational and professional interest and here I am lucky. I am in a position where I can actively seek to manage and sustain a position where the tensions between these three things are resolved and I am able to act in a manner which maintains that position, but only over time. At any particular time I may be leaning more towards one than the others.

While 'no man is an island', I need to sustain a position in which my processes, skills and behaviours generate results and outputs that are of value to my various clients. I am in a position where a high level of autonomy seems appropriate and justified. To maintain that position, I must ensure that my generic process remains appropriate and fit for purpose. The focus of my attention in enabling value must be on the development of the skills and knowledge I bring to bear on the challenges faced by my clients. To be content, I need to maintain the alignment between my personal, organisational and professional selves.

## Summary

It was stated at the outset that there is no arithmetic solution or silver bullet to 'solve the problem' of how much autonomy is enough. It is, re-citing Fayol, a continuously shifting balance, a negotiation perhaps, always a matter of judgement.

Of course it would be possible to develop a complete prescription for (nearly) everything, to state in unequivocal terms the absolute boundaries to everybody's freedom. But, everyday something changes, everyday each individual is different, everyday somebody leaves and somebody joins, an old machine is removed, a new machine is installed. Do you *really* want to spend all your time modifying what one organisation called 'The Empowerment Manual'? And no, I am not joking; it was a manual which prescribed everybody's freedoms!

Think about starting with the core processes of the organisation (those processes which generate value) and assume at the outset full autonomy (with the potential for anarchy).

Then, proscribe only that minimal set of freedoms which would breach the values of the organisation or are inconsistent with the business model. Prescribe only those matters which are required by the technology employed. Define those skills and behaviours which are required to do the rest. Then actively manage and develop those skills and encourage the behaviours and create a culture where individuals are able to empower themselves to do the right things right.

Under the right conditions, enabled the right way, autonomy will manage itself.

# 9

# THE INFORMATION FACTORY

I fear the day technology will surpass our human interaction. The world will have
a generation of idiots.

Albert Einstein (Attributed)

## Introduction

In our progress towards the Intelligent Organisation we have established the need
for change in the way we use information and realise its value. The processes and
structures for generating and enabling value have been explored and the need to
sustain appropriate autonomy articulated. Making this work relies on changing the
way we structure and use information. If we want our people, processes and systems
to behave in an intelligent manner, then we need to provide the right information,
at the right time, in the right format to achieve it. That means we need a strategy
for information itself. I repeat, not an information technology strategy, not an
information systems strategy; an information strategy – there is a difference.

## Information strategy

An information system is not purposeful in its own right. It is purposeful only
to the extent that it enables the effectiveness of the rest of the organisation, i.e.
it meets customer expectations. Its performance and its value, in a broad sense, is
measured by the extent to which it fulfils that purpose.

### The data genie

*A small manufacturer has a highly complex product portfolio, several thousand possible
combinations, in a low-volume, small-batch-size factory. Their information systems consist
of non-networked, non-integrated SCADA (supervisory control and data acquisition) systems,*

*a stand-alone (and largely manual) manufacturing planning system and a stand-alone accounting system.*

*The business is out of control. Through the separate systems, the data genie has escaped from the lamp and is wreaking havoc. Data lacks integrity, is duplicated and triplicated – there are multiple possible 'right' answers to every question, all depending on which system is looked at and, importantly, who is answering the questions.*

Justifying investment in information systems gets progressively more difficult with each new generation. Gains through conventional thinking become more marginal, payback becomes harder to achieve; the dead weight of established practices, applications and data clog the organisational arteries. It would perhaps be mischievous to suggest that organisations with established information systems should abandon them on a wholesale basis and start again. It would not be wholly unreasonable though. It is my experience that some organisations are in such an informational mess that it might be the best thing to do.

The unconventional thinking of an information strategy needs to be rooted (Figure 9.1) in

- understanding the information needed for decisions;
- understanding the value of that information;
- determining what, if any, applications and hardware are needed;
- commissioning information projects.

The information strategy can be prioritised against appropriate criteria, for example: urgency, importance, economic value. The whole can then be measured in terms of information value and impact on business effectiveness and financial

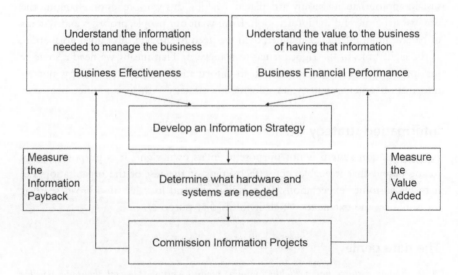

**FIGURE 9.1** Information strategy

performance. If an investment cannot be expressed in terms of its benefit to the organisation then, perhaps, it is not an investment!

The information needed, together with an assessment of existing applications, systems and technologies, will determine what, if any, further application(s) and hardware are needed, and they can be chosen accordingly. Completion of an information project is measured jointly by the delivery of the anticipated information and by the value added to the business.

It is critical to note that 'new-tech' tools are not necessarily the best answer. Technology can only solve a technology problem – *not* an information problem. The best answer to an information problem is 'right tech'. In one recent instance, the information was provided via a simple 'counter' display answering the key question: "how many have we produced?" In another, where the size and complexity of the site meant that simple counting was not quite so straightforward, white boards were used adjacent to each workstation, updated half-hourly with rolling results. It may have looked a little stone age, but the operators could see for themselves what was going on across the whole process and the supervisors' role became primarily the provision of information.

## The silent information system

*A habitual observer of organisations, I was sitting in the café lobby of a hotel in Kuala Lumpur between meetings, something I did several times over a few days.*

*The staff glided around the floor, never speaking to each other but seemingly always doing the right thing for each customer, always asking the right question. Intrigued I became determined to work out how they were doing this. They never spoke but were clearly communicating with each other. What was the information system that enabled this?*

*Paying careful attention, the solution quickly became apparent. Upon a new customer arriving in the café, the staff would approach the customer and ask for their order, and upon taking the order they would take the menu card and lay it down, signalling that the order had been taken.*

*Serving the drinks, they would pour roughly half the contents of a bottle of beer or a pot of tea, then place the bottle or pot beside the cup – a signal to the next member of staff to complete the pour when the glass was half empty.*

*Upon the second pour, the empty bottle or pot would be placed in the centre of the table, a signal to the next member of staff to offer another drink. If the offer was declined, the member of staff would remove the empty bottles or pots whilst the customer finished their drink – a signal to the next member of staff to present the bill which would be placed beside the evident host. The next member of staff would then accept the payment, by whatever means, and leave the paid bill in the centre of the table – a signal that this customer was leaving and had settled their account.*

*All of that done without a word being spoken, with no bureaucracy, no centrally managed process (although one was clearly being followed), no orders or instructions being given. Simply thoroughly trained, hard-working staff, doing the right thing because the process contained its own instructions. Genius!!*

## Solving the information challenge: the lean information system

If we want to be effective then we need to minimise data proliferation whilst maximising availability of information. That should make us think in terms of a 'lean information system' (LIS), one in which the decisions that need to be made at each point are understood and themselves generate demand for contextualised information. That determines what data needs to be captured, by which actors and processes within the system and for what purpose. This 'information-demand' approach to information is consistent with lean production (Dennis, 2007). It can be expected to have similar impact for organisational information as it has for manufacturers and service providers who have adopted it; reduced waste, greater operational efficiency, lower storage requirements, increased productivity. This thinking applies just as much to the data for value-enabling decisions as it does for value-generating decisions, and the two orthogonal views of the organisation will be sharing 'common' data, i.e. data which can be held once but used many times by different processes.

We can begin developing the lean information system by recognising that the information architecture must map isomorphically (Beer, 1966) to the organisation (Figure 9.2). The information architecture must be a direct function of the organisational architecture. Change in one demands equivalent change in the other, with all the implications for the technology and system layers (presentation, integration, applications, devices and network) and for the behaviours and skills of the users. This mapping must extend beyond the boundary of the organisation into the channels through which customers and organisation communicate. Unless the mapping between the organisation and the information is maintained, then one or the other, or quite probably both, will not work effectively.

When we map the information architecture to the organisational architecture we both simplify things and make them more complex. Simplicity arises from consistent application of the notion of the homeostat to the process, task and procedure levels which become very specific in the actual application. Complexity

Intelligent Organisation      Information Architecture

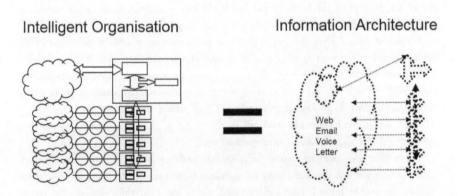

FIGURE 9.2 Mapping the organisation and information architecture

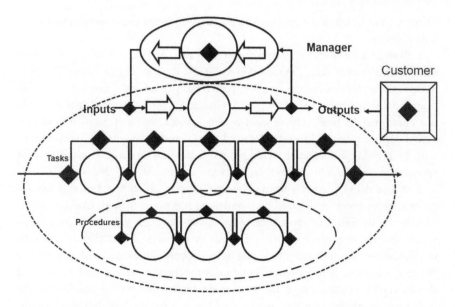

**FIGURE 9.3** Distributed decisions

arises in the decisions that we are now asking people to make, wherever they are in the organisation. Unlike conventional, functional decision making, we make explicit the complexity of such multiple criteria decisions and the need to meet multiple outcomes and constraints. Decision makers are asked to decide which input (or inputs) to modify to generate outputs closer to the desired goal. They do this in the context of all the other decisions being made in the organisation and its environment. Looking at Figure 9.3, we can see how decisions (the diamonds) are distributed throughout the organisation. Information is 'demanded' by the customer and that stimulates a chain of decisions horizontally and vertically through the organisation.

It is evident from this wide distribution that there will be a range of different information requirements and implications. Consistent with earlier discussion, we need to generate and distribute information both horizontally and vertically through the business.

## The information heartbeat

The provision of information is the key to self-regulation, and that works when the information in the system acts to damp error so that in 'going out of control' the system uses information to bring itself back under control. That saves the manager a job. Given the ability of technology to deliver fresh data, there is a need to damp the rate of its arrival and to synchronise it with the cycle time (the 'heartbeat') of the processes and decisions which it both informs and is informed by. Reporting and response then become consistent with each other and conform to the notion of using the process homeostat as both the organisational and regulatory device.

Failure to achieve this synchronisation increases the risk that what we respond to is "noise" rather than "signal" (Silver, 2012). Responding to "noise" leads to inappropriate actions which amplify rather than attenuate error and can risk "catastrophic collapse" (Beer, 1974). Our mental "hot" systems (Mischel, 2014), our emotional "selves", receive information first and respond intuitively to perceived opportunities and threats. We need to use process design and the synchronicity of arriving information with process outcomes to ensure that our 'cool' system, the rational 'self', is able to intervene and modify our responses.

Fast data delivery appeals to our "chimp" (Peters, 2012) but drives us towards correcting for every small variation. Sometimes it is better to wait. Good examples of this can be found in sport where the novice responds to every minor event; watch six-year olds playing soccer. Experts demonstrate much greater economy of effort, observing the pattern, reacting only to significant events (with significance being a matter of judgement, so sometimes they get it wrong) and positioning themselves in anticipation of the next event rather than in reaction to the last one. Snooker players take the current shot not just for the 'pot' but also to position the cue ball where it will be most useful next; drivers of rally cars (whilst appearing insanely busy from outside the car) demonstrate amazing economy of effort within it relative to the movement of the car – notably they are driving the car, it is not driving them. We must use information to ensure that we are driving the organisation and it is not driving us.

To do this we must design our decision models to get the right information, in the right format and language, at the right time. Then we can reflect it in our behaviours so that our human response can be dominant, not our chimp.

## Damping 'hot' response

*A healthcare organisation had an established unit whose task was to clean and sterilise surgical instruments ready for reuse. They handled about one million packs a week, with each pack containing between one and one hundred instruments and a contracted maximum eight-hour turnaround time for every pack. The essentially manual process was simple:*

> *Collect, Unpack, Check, Rinse, Wash, Check, Pack, Sterilise, Dispatch*

*Packs were received at irregular delivery intervals and batch sizes, a function of activity volume and availability of delivery staff. The staffing pattern had evolved over many years to accommodate the needs and preferences of individuals. This generated a typical queuing problem, both the flow of dirty packs and the staffing capacity had irregular, asynchronous heartbeats leading to pulses in the workload.*

*Unable to see the whole process because of the physical size of the facility and the incomplete information, supervisors undertook what Peters and Waterman (1982) called "management by walking around". Whilst this can have merit, in this instance they would observe a backlog occurring in one area and, hot response, call for staff from other areas to 'come NOW' and address it. Meanwhile, of course, the processing in the other areas would slow due to the lack of staff, and a backlog would start to arise there. The backlog in the first area would come under control and the staff, respecting the command and control ethos arising from the 'come NOW' style of management, would wait to be given fresh instructions to be sent to the next identified backlog.*

*The natural ebbs and flows were thereby amplified rather than damped. This caused frequent breaches of contracted turnaround times and, of course, a need to insert 'urgent' packs and fast track them drawing at least one, and often more, members of staff out of the standard workflow, increasing the workload on others, further increasing delays.*

*The challenge was addressed in five ways. First, we developed a process and data model of the whole system, allowing its status to be seen at any time, creating a context in which 'cool' decisions about staff allocation could be made. Second, we established priorities for different pack types, giving priority to bigger and rarer packs for neuro and cardiac surgery over the thousands of single instrument packs containing only one scalpel or pair of scissors. Third, we regularised the flow, initially establishing a 'heartbeat' for introducing packs into the flow which meant accepting that it was OK for the stock of dirty packs to ebb and flow. Fourth, we introduced a collection and delivery schedule, based on the planned hospital activity, to induce a regular heartbeat in the supply chain so that the frequency of deliveries became stable.*

*Fifth, over time and in consultation with the staff, we adapted shift patterns and staffing levels to balance against the anticipated flow of work. The outcome was that the contracted turnaround times were always met and overtime costs were reduced by £330k per annum (all but eliminated).*

## Design for decision: exploiting the model of self

If the information architecture is mapped to the organisation we know what decisions need to be made where. Managerial action can then be focused on deciding what to do to close the gap between the actual and desired performance rather than collecting and collating data. Doing that requires us to have a robust, rigorous understanding of our intentions, and that is the MoS embedded in the homeostats.

For many managers and in many situations, decisions can almost be regarded as programmatic and, given properly designed, constructed, authentic and useful informational 'models of self', they can indeed be so. Given a desired output, the manager should be able, with the right information, to determine which input(s) to change in order to close the gap. The algorithms of computer programmes are ideal where a good level of relative certainty exists. In those cases, we can design the application and reporting programmes to do what they are good at and free up the people to deal with relative uncertainty and do what they are good at, and that is making judgements.

With the organisational and informational architecture aligned, the key to reducing uncertainty (where possible) in decision making is to attenuate variety where possible and appropriate. Such attenuation can be applied to many business decisions by generating rules for reporting and decision models which rely on known and agreed assumptions and definitions of the meaning of data. Where these do not exist then the models themselves are inadequate.

Obtaining value from information relies on competent users, but now anybody with a PC and a spreadsheet can be a data analyst. But can they? What if they are using the 'wrong' data? What if they are using a 'wrong' tool, one not designed for the particular job, or a problem-solving model developed for a different purpose or making different underpinning assumptions (or even simply putting the decimal point in the wrong place)? What they will get is a perfectly correct, often beautifully presented and utterly wrong, right answer.

## Beware of geeks bearing GIFs

*Working at one time with a major logistics organisation we were developing a performance reporting and modelling tool. This tool took a data feed at the close of business each day (the network for their system could not deliver a live data feed) and through a series of algorithms, produced reports by shift, sector, line, infeed, outfeed, process and team covering work done, rework, failures and stoppages. It enabled the active balancing of workload with staffing level and was saving the client around £15k per 24-hour period, delivering real value to the business.*

*We decided to look at the pattern of activity over the course of a week to identify regularities (or irregularities) to enable further performance gains. The in-house data analyst was asked to take the raw dataset (about 1GB of data per day in 43 columns and about 500,000 lines) and represent the activity through the week as a time-series graph.*

*Very pleased with himself, the analyst arrived to present the results complete with a first interpretation of what they told him. They contained some surprising results; in particular, the workload peaked much earlier in each time series than we expected, with a dramatic mid-period slump followed by a second peak and a further slump. This needed further investigation and validation, but where to start? The results did not match our combined experience and expectations.*

*A difficult choice was made – perhaps if we reordered the data so that the days of the week were in order of occurrence, rather than sorted alphabetically . . .*

Nearly all established organisations use decision models, though often they will not be recognised as such. In functional structures they may well be inadequate or dysfunctional. Nonetheless, they provide 'rules' for decisions. Such models might embrace issues of performance (of individuals, teams, business units and divisions), investment payback, return on capital, presence (or absence) of staff, numbers on payroll, asset performance, reliability, quality, yield, revenue and a whole host of others considered important to any particular organisation. However, they are most frequently only brought together in a single place as a debate or discussion in the boardroom, rather than integrated with the workflow at the operational level. Similarly, because each of these elements is managed and measured separately, it is difficult to bring them all together into one coherent story.

There are a wide variety of sources from which decision models can be identified, all of which rely for full effectiveness on the operational definitions, i.e. structure and meaning (Oakland, 2003), of the underpinning data (values) being properly defined and the data itself being timely and accurate. While Mark Twain suggested that there are "lies, damned lies and statistics", if you want to be effective in your lies then refer to the work of Darrell Huff (1991) or read the work of Goldacre (2013) on the pharmaceutical industry. If on the other hand you would like your decision models to be rigorous, transparent, verifiable and useful, I suggest you draw inspiration from a more broadly based literature. Harper and Lim (1982) provide a sound insight to mathematical analysis of business problems through operational research while Knott (1991) gives a sound grounding in models for financial management (though the relevant professional bodies in this field provide the contemporary standard and statutory models to which the Finance Director will refer). Tennent and Friend (2005) provide a useful and well worked out set of tools for business modelling and demonstrate good use of computers for this purpose. Goodwin and Wright (2004) offer a range of methods for modelling decisions under conditions of uncertainty. Between these four sources the greater part of the business decision world can be addressed, although many others are available. All of these models should also be used to enable organisational learning (Senge, 1993) and knowledge management (Hislop, 2013). Like babies and bath water, we need to ensure that the models we use enable us to solve the problems we already have, to learn from our past errors and to carry new knowledge into our future – to provide feedforward information that allows us to anticipate error as well as feedback that allows us to self-regulate.

When we understand what decisions need to be made, the information needed for them and the data that underpins them, we can determine how to capture and store it – once.

We started to address the 'lean information system' (LIS) by identifying the decisions we need to make, developing the information needed to make them, establishing the decision models that we need and the data that is required to populate them. In this 'demand-led' world it is reasonable to question what other internal data needs to be held and what mechanisms we should use to archive (forget?) material that no longer has relevance to our decisions. One of the tasks of the managers throughout the organisation is to understand how the information architecture needs to evolve – that is *not* just a job for the IT crowd. This is necessary to ensure that the relevance of 'new' data is recognised, the relevance (or not) of 'old' data is understood and that the information architecture and its supporting systems are enabled to ensure adaptation of the whole.

## The information (systems) hierarchy

Most, if not all, established organisations, even those that are very small, have an information technology system comprised of five essential layers:

- Presentation: programmes used to display outputs;
- Integration: programmes which allow programmes to 'talk to each other' and share data;

- Applications: the programmes through which we work and in which data is structured and organised;
- Devices: mainframes, servers, PCs, tablets, smartphones and peripherals that physically store the data;
- Network: the telecommunications infrastructure that carries the data.

The top three layers are what we have been concerned with so far. Presentation and integration deal with the decisions we need to take, the process models we adopt and the data requirements that go with them. They constitute much of the Executive, Management or Business Information System and deal with the business process (or processes). Applications cover value generation (Customer Relationship Management, Sales Management and Enterprise Resource Planning) and value enabling (Asset Management, Human Resource Management, Procurement and Finance). These should be thought of as 'IS' and require data sharing between applications. Applications are typically functionally oriented and hold a set of data, data which may be required in other parts of the business. Unfortunately, this requirement is often met by developing and storing multiple similar datasets. In the Intelligent Organisation, we recognise that data can be used for multiple purposes and there must be only 'one source of the truth' within the organisation. That requires the development of master data sets (and their custodianship) which holds only one version of the present truth (and its history) and makes it available to all the applications that need it.

Organisations typically have one set of customers, one set of staff, one set of assets and one set of suppliers. Is it not better then to hold one set of data about each of these and make it available to all who need it within the organisation? A decision model for asset maintenance needs to draw on the shared data set (what assets have we got?) but addresses questions specific to the maintenance processes. The shared data set (what assets have we got?) is *also* relevant to the production system, but the decisions they are concerned with are about utilisation. So asset data must be stored once (to avoid duplication, error and decay) and contain everything necessary to allow it to be used for all legitimate purposes. This compares with the common practice of holding the base data in two separate systems – one for asset management, the other for production. Immediately, this latter situation occurs there is either unnecessary work to maintain synchronisation or they diverge, leading very rapidly to a situation where there are two versions of the truth and neither is authoritative.

The bottom two layers, devices and network, constitute the 'T' in IT. They are the information technologies which carry, store and distribute data and their job is just that – to carry the data around the network and deliver or store it as instructed.

Contemporary technology offers a plethora of devices which individuals might use to carry out their work. The LIS considers these devices from the viewpoint of the work the user needs to do with them, i.e. the decisions they will make, the processes they will operate or control, the data they will transmit and receive and the locations in which they are expected to work. These then drive the type of devices that are necessary, their size and data processing capability. There is little more entertaining when commuting, at least for the observer, than to see the frustration on the face of a fellow commuter trying to work on an unsuitable device. This embeds a further hidden inefficiency in the business as well as causing unnecessary frustration. It is unfair to blame that only on the provider; often the user should recognise the stupidity of the way they are trying to work – and where.

The information 'feedback' loop between the device and the organisation's network needs to be taken into account in application choice, device choice and network design. The network is the data-conveying capability of the organisation (its wiring diagram) and, to be effective, must have:

- sufficient access points (network nodes) that every user, customers included, who has a need can gain access, including those working remotely through virtual private networks or mobile telephony;
- sufficient capacity (bandwidth and speed) at each node and through the cables or wireless network to carry the volume and frequency of data;
- sufficient capacity to store and process the required data;
- sufficient resilience both in its internal and external connectivity to cope with service failures.

The LIS must accommodate all of this and, to be resilient, should have more capacity and connectivity than is likely to be needed for even peak demand. Given that networks, network switches and machines are low cost relative to the value of the work that is done on them, this is one area where redundant capacity adds more value than it does cost. Network failure because of poor connectivity or inadequate capacity simply slows down the work of the organisation and generates a flood of unnecessary activity, which adds no value.

## Long-distance printing

*One small organisation I worked with had outsourced technology provision with its servers for data and printing located at the outsourcer's data centre some 200 miles from the office itself.*

*With data travelling at the speed of light 200 miles is not a significant distance, but there were substantial delays in transmission and receipt of data, frequent service failures, failed print instructions and much retransmission of failed jobs.*

*A brief analysis of the situation revealed that the available capacity of the telecommunications lines and associated switchgear was inadequate for the volume of data being handled, which was far greater than had been comprehended. For example, for data and documents held remotely, any individual wishing to print a document would first open it on their desktop (involving the transmission of the document from the data server to their PC), they would then send the print instruction to the print server (which involved sending the document again), the print server would then send the document to the designated printer.*

*For the document to be printed it had to be transmitted three times across the network and with around 30 staff all engaged in this activity, it was no great surprise that the network was struggling and performance was poor.*

*The audible signs of this were the gripes and complaints of the staff affected, the invisible cost was all the time that was wasted either waiting for documents to load, for print jobs to complete or retransmitting instructions that had, for one reason or another, failed.*

## Aspirations to mediocrity

The primary focus of the lean information system is enabling the business processes, end to end; the end is the outcome for the customer. The process represents the workflow of the organisation which we need to understand and manage, because it is that which delivers value to the customer. It is only when we have grasped the whole that we can make sense of and meaningful assertions about the parts. This approach also enables us to capture data as a by-product of the work itself rather than as a series of partial, functional or siloed activities that we try to interrogate after the event through 'data mining'. Data mining is the attempt, after the fact, to reconstruct what happened; it is inevitably difficult, expensive and, more often than not, wrong. Its necessity means we have not built *in* to the system those elements of data that we subsequently want to take *out*. Capturing data as a part of the workflow is precise, effective and free.

When undertaking this work in practice, it is important that we design and build the information systems around the process for the particular organisation, its customers, its people (especially their skills and behaviour), its culture and its needs. It is increasingly common to adopt 'best practice' from another organisation. Often that practice isn't actually very 'best', does not suit the particular circumstances and needs of *this* organisation and, a little like benchmarking in the quality arena, is often an aspiration to mediocrity. Being 'as good as' or 'good enough' is not good enough.

Nobody knows the process better than the people who do it, so they must be fully engaged in documenting, reviewing and improving its design. Nobody is in a better position to improve work than the people who spend their days variously baffled, frustrated and enraged by the 'stupid way we do things around here'. Appropriately engaged people in well-designed consultations will reveal not just the obvious but the hidden, subtle and nuanced ways of working that can really enhance the process. In the Intelligent Organisation, the people who do the work are largely self-regulating; they must then be engaged in specifying the necessary inputs, outputs and outcomes and in developing the tools that will help them to be more effective.

## Summary

We have explored the notion of a lean information system (LIS), a radical departure from the organisational norm. The Intelligent Organisation pulls through the LIS that data which it needs to enable its decision makers, to support process control and improvement and, most critically, to meet its customer outcomes. It eliminates waste and duplication through its architecture.

In the next chapter we shall consider how this can work in practice.

# 10

# THE INFORMATION FACTORY

## Cases

It's possible for good people, in perversely designed systems, to casually perpetrate acts of great harm.

Ben Goldacre, *Bad Pharma* (2013)

## Introduction

In the last chapter, a lean information system (LIS) was proposed to support the Intelligent Organisation. In this chapter the challenges, benefits and pitfalls are considered and the focus is on the provision of information for decisions. We are only looking at Fusion21 in this chapter, but you will recall that in Chapters 4 and 6 the studies were concerned with the use of information. They may be worth revisiting at this point.

## Fusion21: deal with things as they are!

We revisit Fusion21 to look at the development of the lean information system that supports it. The organisational representations remind us that the information architecture must reflect the organisational architecture (Figures 10.1 and 10.2); they are alternative views of the same thing.

It would of course be wonderful to tell the story of the development of this LIS in the delightfully linear fashion proposed in the previous chapter, starting with a strategy and working from that. Life however is not like that.

The initial invitation to work with Fusion21 arose when its growth exceeded the capacity of the supporting technology infrastructure. Presenting symptoms were low quality and availability of data, technology underperformance and excessive costs. The IT (the network and devices) could no longer handle the volume of data traffic generated by the growing business going through the IS (applications,

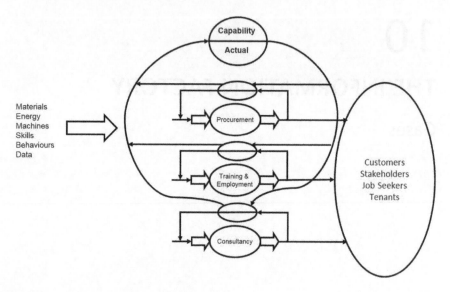

**FIGURE 10.1** Fusion21 processes

data integration, presentation). The consequence was frequent service failures, delays and disruptions. The 'outsourced' provision of the whole system appeared expensive relative to open market costs and supplier service was slow causing further disruption.

Working with the 'Head of Business Improvement' (an enabling role), the performance of the whole system was reviewed. While the organisation had grown, from 3 people at the outset to around 25 at that point, the overall information system had not grown with it. Costs had grown disproportionately to both volume and performance; information value at Fusion21 was deteriorating.

Exploration continued, seeking to understand how data was being captured, held and used for decisions.

After establishing its initial Procurement activity, Fusion21 through organic growth, both generating and reacting to opportunities, had developed additional lines of business (Training and Employment Services, Consultancy). Data storage reflected this; data was held in and drawn from small functional 'pots' throughout the organisation. These represented the narrow interest of particular individuals or tasks. They could not be interrogated in a business-wide or systemic manner. Much data was held in spreadsheets which were not systematically maintained, partly because of culture, partly because of underdeveloped processes. The consequence was periodically made evident when the need to report completed projects, invoice clients and settle suppliers' accounts caused major difficulties. Each time, there was a mass of work to be done to update records and generate the required information spreadsheets. Errors and omissions were frequent.

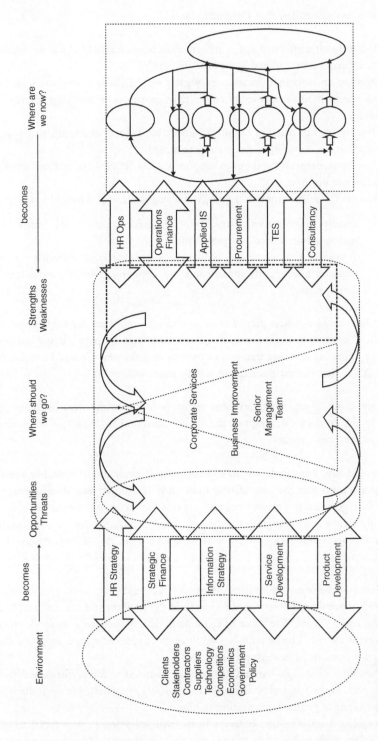

**FIGURE 10.2** Fusion21 value-enabling activities

It was recommended that Fusion21 should:

- Recognise that effective use of information was essential if it was to sustain its value proposition in 'intelligent procurement';
- Develop an information strategy which would allow it to sustain its leading position and improve its competitive position by working smarter, not harder;
- Develop an information architecture suitable for the emerging shape of the organisation, consolidate disparate data records;
- Develop information systems to support process delivery, control and reporting across the business;
- Address the information technology challenges through a hybrid strategy:
  - insource those activities that Fusion21 could do better itself (information management, device procurement);
  - outsource those activities which required specialist expertise or were required infrequently (broadband and network provision, server and PC maintenance).

A value-based business plan was presented and approved for implementation. Reflecting continued aspirations for growth, the business payback was addressed through 'reducing cost per transaction over time' following Coases' Law (Lorenzo et al., 2011) that companies expand to the point where:

the costs of organising an extra transaction within the firm becomes equal to the costs of carrying out the same transaction by means of an exchange in the open market.

It would have been foolhardy to seek an absolute reduction in costs, but a relative reduction means that the cost of operation grew at a slower rate than the increase in revenue generating a greater margin. Such is the value of information.

With a new understanding of the information requirements of the business, the prevailing technological constraints were addressed. A plan was designed and implemented to

- Enhance the wired and wireless networks to provide sufficient capacity to cope with more than the anticipated growth of the business and the frequent visitor and client events. The value of redundant capacity in such a network far outweighs its cost. The benefit showed through in reduced system-imposed delays and downtime increasing productivity;
- Provide a new high-bandwidth internet connection for performance with a second, lower bandwidth line sourced entirely separately, giving resilience in the event of primary connection failure;
- Establish a small in-house 'server farm' (mail, data and print servers) to bring all data within the walls of the organisation supported by procurement of

an 'online' data backup service. This ensures both local control and business continuity.

- Procure user-specific replacement devices against a rolling replacement plan.

Investment in training and education of staff in the use of the new network and systems soon saw initial challenges and difficulties overcome, and the previous complaints about connectivity and delay fell silent.

## A lean information system for generating value

The starting point for the information strategy was to determine what decisions needed to be made throughout the business and what information was required to enable them. These decisions ranged from Board-level decisions about strategy, business performance, investment and reporting social return on investment (non-financial contributions consistent with the social objectives of the organisation) to operational decisions about delivery of outcomes through processes, tasks and procedures.

The company had already made a substantial long-term investment in a 'supplier and contractor' costing system to support its intelligent procurement activity. This system was embedded and working well but only supported the procurement process and only dealt with one critical stage in it. It matched client requirements through house archetypes to produce indicative project specifications and costings prior to on-site survey. This system made excellent use of the notion of a MoS, the various housing archetypes being such models. The IS development needed to capitalise on the established investment, not replace it. This placed a small and appropriate but significant constraint on the project.

In addition to the intelligent procurement system, a number of other areas were identified for which data was being stored in multiple databases and spreadsheets. Inevitably these were different in structure and content (even when being used for similar purposes) and were under the stewardship of individuals. This generated significant risk when individuals changed roles or moved on from the organisation.

Fusion21 now understood that knowing what, knowing how and knowing why made information its most valuable resource. Knowledge management was impossible unless information was embedded in the system itself. It could not be left solely at individual discretion. The company needed to use intelligently designed models to ensure sustainability. 'Brute force' reporting, or throwing resources at a data problem, would continue to risk loss of knowledge.

The next step was to map the data flow across the organisation. This outcome-focused flow was developed through 'brown paper' process mapping workshops. They involved staff from each team for all core processes from beginning to end. We established that any one individual might engage with Fusion21 many times. Someone working in the social housing sector might be a customer of all three of the core business processes at different times. They might encounter Fusion21 as a housing officer with one registered social landlord (RSL) and reappear in a new role with another. Trainees participating in one training course with TES were likely to appear in others funded by different agencies. Consultancy clients were already likely to be clients for TES or procurement. On the procurement side there were clients, contractors (labour) and suppliers (parts) engaged on each project, all employing trainees. The relationship of any one individual with Fusion21 was likely to be complex. The company needed to be able to track those relationships, not only to ensure continuity but also to be able to understand how the relationship was evolving and adding value.

The output of this activity was a data flow diagram (DFD) (Figure 10.3) which shows how the data is pulled across the organisation from contact to business process to output (reporting).

In the top-left corner (Sales Administration Process), contact data is captured. This contact data supports activities such as prospecting, networking, key account management, framework management and relationship building.

Data is drawn from that source to inform the sales process (VSProspects). This presents the data as a sales pipeline with opportunities contextualised to the requirements of the individuals concerned. The 'sales' staff are thereby provided with information that lets them decide which product or service to target at each individual and the system tracks progress towards a 'sale'.

When the sale process has moved to 'precontract' (a task within the process), the data is available to the relevant delivery process, whether that be TES, procurement or consultancy. Each of these processes has a 'tracker' built in, allowing the staff to both draw on and add to current data about individuals, companies, projects, products and services. Simply by doing their job the staff are capturing the data to inform later decisions.

It is often difficult to judge in professional organisations 'how much process is enough'. In this case we had confidence in the answer because

- the people actually doing the work thought there was too much process;
- the people managing them thought there was not enough.

The process flows represent only a part of the work. For all three core processes, the work draws on the professional knowledge, skill, relationship capability and judgement of the quantity surveyors, project managers, trainers, educators and consultants employed to do it. These capabilities needed to be identified, codified and managed somewhere outside the core workflow. At present this is handled manually to match and develop the skills and competencies required for any process role to the skills and competencies claimed by staff members, verified through evidence of qualification and demonstrated capability. It is reviewed through 1–2–1 discussions and development-focused appraisals. In a larger organisation, or should it become necessary in Fusion21, the information element of this could be integrated to the overall data structure.

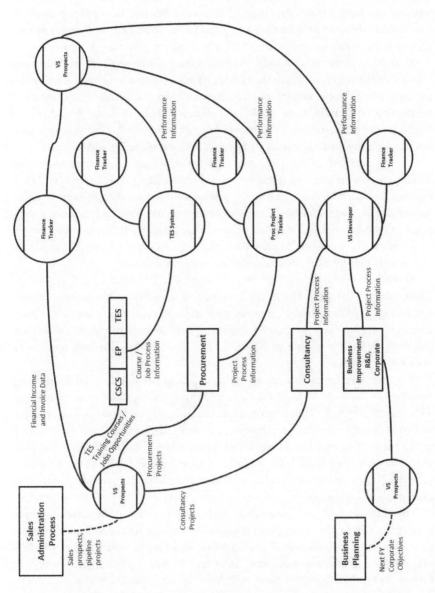

**FIGURE 10.3** Fusion21 data flow

Queries built into the core processes provide information to the 'Finance Tracker' informing the finance team about what projects, products and services are at each stage of the pipeline and what revenue and costs can be expected and when. Importantly, the core process generates the triggers for the dispatch of invoices to clients. This integration eliminates a number of reporting activities that would otherwise be necessary and provides an audit loop connecting process activity to its financial consequence. The 'on-cost' of reporting is zero.

As each core process is updated, the data is immediately available to the reporting tool (VSManager) in which the 'models of self' required to manage the business are embedded. These require no 'interrogation', no 'data mining', no arbitrary connecting or simulation of results; the data is simply available to individuals, teams, processes, finance and the whole business. The results also inform value-enabling activity such as resource planning, business planning and so on.

The development of the DFD provided the information necessary to develop an information architecture (Figure 10.4). Understanding how and where data is captured and used by the organisation enabled an understanding of how it should be stored and made available. This is 'one view of the truth'; all data being captured and stored once but available for use many times for different requirements. This reflects the notion of 'master data management', a powerful and important idea which is sadly not adhered to by many organisations.

At the root of this diagram are two elements. The first are the 'core data' tables. These contain the data which, for Fusion21, is universal. This includes clients, contractors, suppliers, funders, trainees, staff and addresses. Complementing those tables are those which are process specific. These include products and services and each element is unique to a particular process; its data does not need to be available to others.

The next level represents the operating (value-generating and value-enabling) processes of the business, from sales administration through procurement projects, TES, consultancy to business improvement, research and development. Each embedded MoS is a specific instance, drawing on the underlying data and presenting it in the form of an end-to-end workflow. These provide the staff with a complete record of each project, guidance towards the next steps and, with time cycles built in, alerts to any delays or overdue activities. It enables them to self-regulate, to manage their own work.

The final level of the information architecture is that of reporting. This is both straightforward and extensive. Reports are available for individuals to regulate their own work, for team-level management, and for the business as a whole at two levels of granularity (executive team and Board). Other reports extend to, though not exhaustively, customer outcome, quality, efficiency, cost, customer-relationship management, key account management, marketing, business performance and social value.

All the data required to generate the reports is captured in the system just by doing the work. The biggest challenge was to design and build the data queries that construct the different 'models of self'. It is not good enough to say 'we did

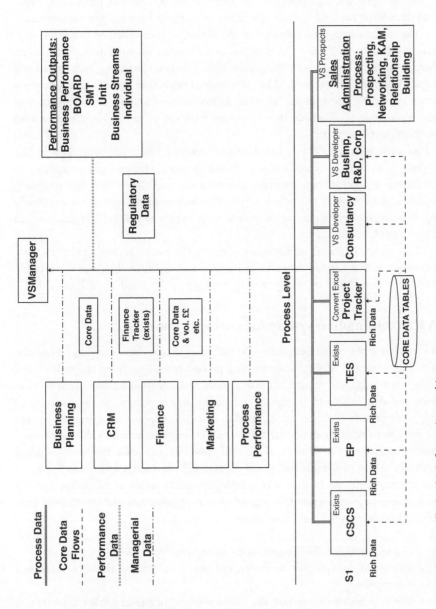

**FIGURE 10.4** Fusion21 information architecture

*this*'; what is required is to be able to say 'we *did* this, you wanted *that*, *here* is the difference', and to follow that up by explaining what has, is or will be done to improve performance through change in process, skills or standards. This approach is fast and effective in operation, because it relies not on fast processing speeds and document retrieval but on rich interconnectivity between the various data.

The staff, having been involved in the design of the workflow processes, were also involved in the design of the numerous reports required from the system. Members of each team were trained in report design, enhancing and embedding capability in the organisation. They determined what they wanted to know, when they wanted to know it and in what format of presentation and everyone had the opportunity to be involved in the design from the newest and least experienced to the Chief Executive.

As each element of the system was developed, from the workflow to the reporting, all those affected by the particular element were engaged in testing and evaluating it against their evolving requirements and the system was modified, updated and edited to meet their needs. The lean information system was developed through the integration of people with their process and the information they needed.

This makes it a lean information system for the user as well. They are only presented with information which is relevant and useful to their needs, only able to address those parts of the system appropriate to the conduct of their duties.

## A lean information system for enabling value

So much for the value-generating IS, but what about value enabling? Here the challenge changes. The value-generating process relies heavily on the professional skills, knowledge and judgement provided by individuals, but those are applied to processes which have to be repeatable, reliable and responsive to the demands of the customers. It is in this standardisation that consistency and coherence emerge in the system which reduces variability and, in doing so, provides the process and cost efficiency that is valuable to the end customer. However, the value-enabling activities, whilst they must have good process and consistency (particularly around the appointment and treatment of people) are much softer in this respect, that is to say they do not have the 'heartbeat'-driven regularity of the operational processes. Instead they address three needs:

- The requirements for support of the operational processes;
- The need to respond to emerging requirements of the organisational environment;
- The requirement to sustain the identity of the organisation, for it to remain true to its identity (the purpose and values it espouses).

This is difficult, complex, evolving, shifting over time. We did not therefore even attempt to build the complete information system that might be required (though that could be fun). It is of course human activity, wisdom, experience and judgement that is applied, and the challenge for Fusion21 was to determine what information those involved in the value-enabling activities needed in order to be effective.

The first part of this was already embedded in the reporting structure of the operational LIS. Report production was automated so that aggregated data about the overall work of each process was available to the appropriate people.

The support firstly ensured that the operational teams have available to them the requisite resources for their tasks, and the most significant of these is people. Fusion21 chose to deal with this through five elements:

- A 'model' establishment;
- Job descriptions codifying skills, competencies and experience;
- Individual reviews;
- Appraisals;
- Training and development.

While the LIS could tell them how *much* of a particular skill or knowledge set is being used, the HR processes enable them to understand how *well* it is being used, with the reviews and appraisals generating as their outcome the future training needs. Internal resources are used to cross-train and share knowledge amongst team staff, whilst Managers and Senior Managers meet regularly to bring together knowledge about the whole business, its performance, needs and aspirations. These meetings and discussions provide the basis of the response to the emerging demands of the environment. That is, they bring together the people who best know what the customers want to buy, both now and in the future, and how to provide it.

There is inevitably a danger in these circumstances that Senior Managers, Directors and CEOs will get their hobby horses from the cupboard, put on their bee-filled bonnets and whip into submission anyone who has the temerity to challenge them. Rather than this, we experimented with the notion of 'the future you are currently in' (Ackoff, 1981). This is the approach that uses the information in the LIS to create a LIS:Sim (lean information system: simulator). This simulation replicates the underlying LIS and allows, by the addition of adjustable parameters of volumes process, skill, finance, customers and so on, the impact of changes to be assessed in terms of the impact on the 'current capability'. This is set out in Figure 10.5 and essentially revolves around the repeated asking of one question: What if . . .

- the volume increases or decreases?
- the value of contracts changes?
- we add or remove staff?
- we change the skills applied?
- we change the process?
- we change the products?

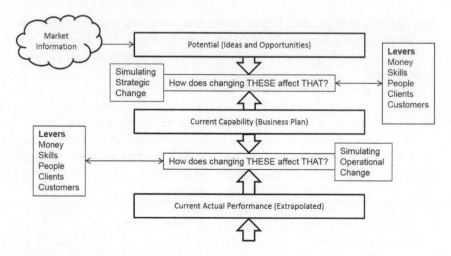

**FIGURE 10.5** Fusion21 whole organisation adaptation

Each of these simulations generates a different 'future' for the organisation and those responsible exercise judgement in choosing the future they want. And, very importantly, that is done using facts about the current state of the organisation not guesses about the future. This allows the debate about change to be set in relatively objective terms; it becomes about things and processes, not about people. It creates a context in which, rather than individuals confronting each other across a table, they can jointly confront the problem and jointly explore the impact and consequences of any particular proposal (or indeed multiple proposals). The debate is not about winning or losing for the individuals, but about the benefit or risk to the business from a particular proposal.

Is this a perfect approach? Probably not. Does it deliver benefits? Yes. In the particular circumstances described, but also with a number of other clients, this thinking has responded to the needs and situation as it is, not as we might like it to be. The sophistication of the simulation is partly about the data and information that is available, partly about the complexity of the debate – it is after all simply a model – and as we all recall, "a model is neither true nor false, it is more or less useful" (Beer, 1985).

## Nurturing identity

Finally there is the requirement to sustain the identity of the organisation, to keep it true to itself. This is very useful because the identity can be expressed as the purpose of the organisation, the reason it exists – and *that* is rooted in answering the question:

What is it we do that is of value to our customers?

We have already established that Fusion21, under the strapline, "Pounds into People, not into Pockets" is an organisation that is built around efficiency in social housing procurement to generate surpluses that regenerate jobs. Resolving any tension between the tendency of those generating value to want to 'do things differently' and those enabling value to want to 'do different things' is easy. The question becomes:

> Which of these choices best helps us fulfil our purpose, now and over time? We will do that one then.

And as for value? The cumulative net gain arising from the application of the LIS in this information-intensive business is around £500,000 against a turnover of around £5m (a turnover increase of about 33%), while staff numbers have increased by only 15%. Proportionately, information is enabling more to be done for less.

## Summary

This chapter has shown how the idea of the lean information system, developed in the previous chapter, has been applied in one particular context. While the scale of the challenge in this instance is moderate because the subject is a small organisation with limited complexity, there can be no doubt that the ideas can be applied to much larger and more complex situations.

The first challenge will be to embrace the essential thinking of aligning the information and organisational architectures. The second challenge will be to identify what decisions need to be made throughout the organisation and to engender the autonomy necessary to make such decision making legitimate. The third challenge will be to design the information systems so that the information flows to where it is needed.

# 11

# MANAGING PERFORMANCE

The ultimate result of shielding men from the effects of folly, is to fill the world with fools.

Spencer (Cited in Malachowski, 2001)

## Introduction

We start this chapter by briefly considering the conventional means of managing organisational performance and its limitations. We then explore what performance means for the Intelligent Organisation and the different ways it needs to be considered. The chapter introduces Beer's "potentiometer" as a framework through which disparate measures can be reconciled and synthesised into a coherent view of the performance of the whole organisation.

### If you always do . . .

. . . what you have always done, you will always get what you have always got.

*Variously attributed to Mark Twain, Henry Ford,*
*Albert Einstein, Anthony Robbins or 'anon'*

Bizarre as it may seem, this is how we typically manage our organisations. The common measures and questions tend to be:

**Measure:**
- Cost and/or income:
- Output volume:
- Conformance to specification:

**Question:**
'did we make budget?'
'did we make target?'
'were they good enough?'

- Customer Satisfaction:       'how many complaints?'
- Employee Satisfaction;       'how many complaints?'
- Health and Safety:           'any reportable incidents?'
- Environmental Impact:        'were we within the legal limits?'

I have perhaps been a little harsh, but not very. Even where these measures and many others are brought together in something like a "balanced scorecard" (Kaplan & Norton, 1992), notionally aligned to the corporate vision and strategy and informing the future, they tend to be dealt with

- Retrospectively – What happened?
- Functionally – Where did it happen?
- Judicially – Who is to blame?
- Independently – The effect of each on the others is not considered.

OK, now I am being harsh, that would be to look backwards to see the future. Surely nobody would do that? Except, in many organisations, performance reporting is about

- Process compliance;
- Conformance (budget, volume, safety, quality);
- Fault finding and blame;
- Functional, partial, siloed views of actions rather than outputs or outcomes.

Performance management is usually looking inward and backward, it also needs to be looking outward and forward. Where we are going is, at least, as important as where we have been.

For many organisations there is a whole internal industry concerned with regular reporting. Driven by a periodic management meeting timetable, it is often dedicated to obfuscation; disguising the errors made in the last period, generating excuses, displacing blame, making "*my* figures" look as good as they can. The whole suite of associated activities often adds cost rather than value. This approach directs effort towards justifying the past and draws it away from modifying the future. It is designed to 'hold people to account' rather than realising the desired customer outcome. Targets and objectives are often relatively arbitrary . . .

*last year's budget plus 3% for growth minus 2% for efficiency improvement*

. . . and uninformed by the capability of the organisation or customers' wants. The whole panoply can be a sham. It demands that often meaningless reports be generated, received and reviewed. It provides an audit trail for post-hoc justification of decisions without actually improving the outcome. It can be the worst form of managerialism (webref 7), creating the illusion of control and accountability whilst adding only waste to the organisation.

Improvement comes not from hiding, disguising, justifying, explaining or rewriting history, but from changing the things that cause the result. That means improving the processes, skills, behaviours and information that generate the outcomes for customers.

## Cheaper not to bother

*The marketing department of an organisation in the travel industry decided to promote leisure travel between two of its key locations by offering a limited number of low-priced tickets for journeys during the school holidays. The aim was to temporarily boost traveller volume and therefore revenue in a traditionally quiet period. The campaign was duly devised and executed. The promotion was a great success, attracting around 30,000 additional travellers at £10 per head and delivering additional revenue of about £300k, an increase of 1% in monthly revenue with a promotional cost of advertising of only £15k – one-twentieth of the revenue.*

*The Marketing Director exultantly reported this great success to the next executive meeting to great applause until the Finance Director asked how the operational cost of selling the tickets had been factored in. It was rapidly established that it had not been and it was realised that at a sales cost of £12.50 per ticket, the successful promotion had cost the company £375k plus the promotional cost of £15k – a total of £390k.*

*Net, this successful promotion, based on an inadequate model, had cost the company £90k. It would have been cheaper not to bother.*

Think about your organisation – how is performance managed?

- Lots of people working hard compiling reports;
- Many 'business systems', but all your reports are in hand-built spreadsheets and carefully written documents (even if they are largely 'cut and paste' from last month);
- Inconsistencies from period to period;
- Activity volumes apparently erratic and uncontrollable;
- Inexplicable errors;
- Managing is disconnected from doing.

You are not alone!

## Not solving quality

*Arriving one day at the premises of a regular client, I was greeted with some surprise by the receptionist who was clearly not expecting me:*

*"They are all very busy today, John."*

*Explaining that I had a number of meetings organised, she signed me in and I proceeded to the first appointment. Knocking on the open door, I could see the pile of work spread across the desk.*

*"Hello Graham, busy? What are you up to?"*

*(You have to start the conversation somewhere.)*

*"Hi John, sorry, can't see you today; we will have to reschedule. Should have let you know."*

*"Big problem?"*

*(Here I am assuming the lid has blown off the chlorination plant or some similar disaster.)*

*"Yes, monthly quality meeting tomorrow, auditor is in, need to make sure I have resolved all the nonconformances for the last month so I keep out of trouble with Gary."*

*"Oh."*

*"Yes, will take me all day, need to speak to every customer for every out-of-specification order to get them to sign off the variance to specification as acceptable, so that all the 'out of specs' become 'in specs' for this month."*

*"Oh!" (Somewhat taken aback.) "Why were they out of spec, process problem?"*

*"They are not really, the sales department has agreed to a specification with the customer purchasing department which is far tighter than they need for their process and, frankly, far tighter than our process can reliably produce."*

*"OK, so the contract is being renegotiated to the specification that can be produced?"*

*"No, we do this every month. Complete waste of time but it keeps the quality people off our backs."*

*"Is there a plan to improve the production process and meet the specification?"*

*"No, no time for that."*

*"OK, next time Graham, bye."*

*The conversation with the Quality Manager was much more relaxed. He was after all confident that at the audit the following day there would be no nonconformances and no follow-up actions.*

We often manage, and I have tested this in a host of organisations over many years, through a focus on 'reducing costs' or 'reducing quality issues'. That is pointless; the costs or issues just bounce back when we take the pressure off; it is 'flavor-of-the-month management':

> 'Don't worry about this initiative, keep your head down and ignore it, it will be something else next month.'

There are constraints on performance. Directors have an absolute, legal obligation to maximise the return to shareholders or the surplus in not-for-profit organisations or to work within budgets for the public sector. There has to be accountability. Effective control *and* improvement requires reporting at a number of levels of organisation. The two objectives of maximum return and minimum cost are not inconsistent. While much depends on how return and cost are defined, performance is a function of the purpose of the organisation. That purpose is achieved by delivering the outcome valued by the customer and coexistence with other stakeholders and is likely to have multiple dimensions. Fulfilment of the outcomes required by the customer will enable the survival of the organisation itself.

## Organisational adaptedness: the capability for survival

Organisational survival is a function of total adaptedness; the extent to which the organisation is capable of survival in its changing environment, its ecosystem. Adaptedness means meeting the needs of all stakeholders, including (but not exhaustively) customers, beneficiaries, employees and funders (shareholders, financiers, grant makers, government), meeting regulatory requirements and societal expectations (environment, quality, wider society). Integration and synthesis of performance measures allows the Intelligent Organisation to do that.

Performance, that is, effectiveness, is measured by the extent to which an organisation fulfils its purpose. It cannot be meaningfully expressed through a single measure such as profitability, but requires a synthesis of metrics suited to the expectations of the organisation's stakeholders.

Sustainable performance is not then one-dimensional but multi-dimensional, with dynamic interdependence between the dimensions. Short-term maximisation of any one dimension may impart harm to another which, in the longer term, may damage the organisation. For example, profit maximisation through price rises or reduced product quality may both damage reputation and inhibit future demand. Either approach creates an opportunity for competitors. Poor environmental citizenship or poor staff treatment may lead either to loss of revenue or, more immediately, to loss of good staff. Each of these carry existential risk.

Achieving an integrated view of performance in the context of purpose is critical to long-term survival. We must understand, represent and manage organisational performance through a dynamic system with understood limits to each dimension; a performance envelope. Information must be provided at an appropriate rate to allow corrective decisions to be made, and each dimension must be managed simultaneously in the context of the others to ensure adaptedness is achieved at two levels of consideration:

Operational (value generation);
Strategic (value enabling);

and with reference to two time frames:

Managing the present;
Creating the future.

Figure 11.1 symbolises how a number of arbitrarily chosen dimensions interact with each other and synthesise to deliver organisational performance, and that performance is measured by the extent to which performance does, or does not, equal the espoused purpose of the organisation. We cannot deal with these dimensions individually but must explicitly recognise their interactions and their interdependence. Changing any one will have an impact (positive or negative) on the whole.

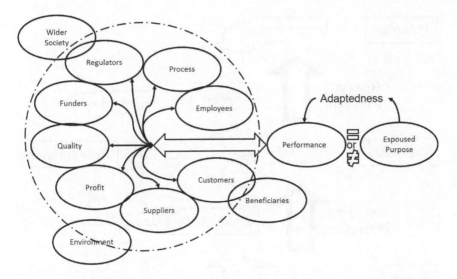

**FIGURE 11.1** Dynamic interaction

That sounds quite a task, but we have encountered it before in the homeostat. While that dealt with self-regulation (performance management) at the level of process, we are now considering it at the level of the whole organisation. This requires a real comprehension of the total value exchange between the organisation and its environment.

## Realising potential

To deal with this rather challenging scenario (synthesis of two levels of organisation and two time frames) we need to embrace its complexity and find a way to handle it, rather than, as we have historically done, fragment it into notionally manageable functional elements. The mechanism through which it is proposed we do this is Beer's potentiometer (Figure 11.2).

This breaks down as follows:

| | |
|---|---|
| Potential: | a formal statement of what the process could do if known constraints were removed or lifted; |
| Capability: | a formal statement of the current capability of any process, i.e. what it is capable of producing; |
| Actual: | a statement of what it actually did (at the last iteration or cycle); |
| Productivity: | actual performance divided by capability, the gap between output and capability; |
| Latency: | capability divided by potential, the gap between capability and possibility; |
| Effectiveness: | productivity multiplied by latency (or potential divided by actual); the performance of the whole organisation. |

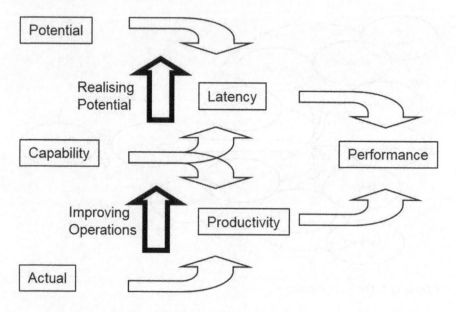

**FIGURE 11.2** The potentiometer (adapted from Beer, 1985)

Productivity (or efficiency) measures the extent to which the resources (of all types) applied in any particular process have been used. If the ratio is 1:1, then the resources used in this process were fully utilised with no waste or inefficiency; if the ratio is 0.5:1, then only half the resources have been utilised. The gap between 'capability' and 'actual' performance is the basis for managerial action; it defines the scope for improvement.

Latency measures the extent to which, by removing limitations or constraints on certain aspects of the process, capability could be increased. Again, a ratio of 1:1 implies that the capability of the process cannot be improved. Any gap between current capability and potential is a measure of what else could be done.

The use of ratios (as opposed to real numbers) in the potentiometer allows us to make meaningful comparisons of process performance for things which would otherwise look incommensurable. They let us meaningfully compare unlike things, such as the productivity of a process plant with that of a quality assurance process or services with manufacturing. This is expressed not in terms of their profitability but by the extent to which they utilise their resources to achieve their objectives. There are, of course, always 'real numbers' underlying the ratios, but these can be distorting or misleading when what we are trying to understand is the scope for improvement. That is what the responsible manager can take action upon.

The productivity gap (the difference between actual performance and capability) is, in general, the responsibility of the managers running value-generating processes. They are charged with 'doing things right' and their focus is managing the present, meeting the needs of current customers and working in the first of the two time frames.

The latency gap (the difference between capability and potential) is, in general, the responsibility of the managers running value-enabling processes. They are charged with 'doing right things' and their focus is on strategic change of the organisation to meet anticipated and future needs of customers and other stakeholders.

When there are tensions between these two perspectives, and there will be, reference is made back to the purpose of the organisation, its identity, to resolve it. This you will remember was presented as the 'trialogue' in Chapter 5 and the 'lean information system for enabling value' in Chapter 10.

We can now think about dynamic interaction (Figure 11.1) as a network of connected potentiometers, each representing a particular dimension of performance (Figure 11.3).

The potentiometer provides the basis for performance management of the whole organisation simultaneously in multiple dimensions. As well as allowing us to manage the present, it allows us to simulate the impact of possible changes and understand the critical issue of interdependence. It allows us to understand the bottlenecks and limitations of the whole organisation and direct our improvement efforts to the most beneficial points.

The potentiometer compiles into aggregate forms. Aggregated vertically it offers an integrated view of the performance of the organisation from the self-regulating individual through every process level to the boardroom. It offers disaggregated views of individual procedures, tasks and processes and their aggregation through process management. Aggregated horizontally it addresses interdependent processes, for example where the 'sales' process and the 'delivery' process for a product or service are dependent upon each other (think about the flow diagram used for Fusion21). Most importantly, it provides the basis of managing over time. It is not simply retrospective but, because of the way the data is compiled, provides the basis for understanding "the future we are currently in" (Ackoff, 1981) and taking pre-emptive action which changes that future.

Within the performance envelope, the organisation can adapt itself over time to further develop in both size (physiological growth) and smartness (psychological growth). What we must do is embed within each homeostat a potentiometer for each critical parameter of its performance. We can then use the information generated to enable managerial decisions about improvement of the parts, as well as integrating them to understand the performance of the whole. This sounds more complicated in theory than it is in practice. Simplicity arises from the universal structure that we have already adopted – a process governed by an information loop which enables self-correction, the homeostat. Because the homeostat structure is adopted for all processes, it is both possible and essential to aggregate the information from each at higher levels of organisation to generate performance information for the organisation as a whole in a consistent, coherent manner. This approach provides information about efficiency, latency and effectiveness to every responsible person and does so in a shared language.

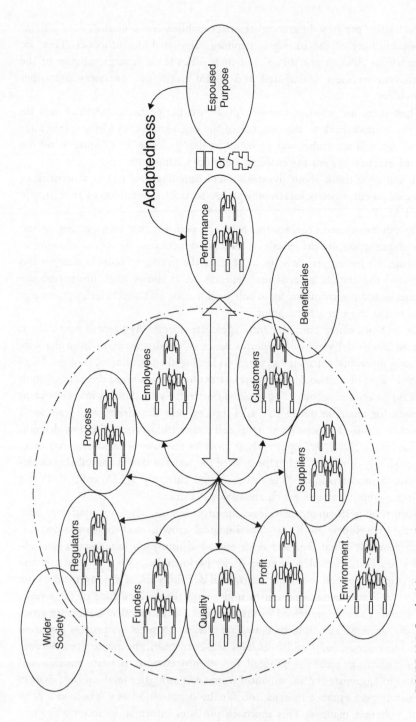

**FIGURE 11.3** Synthesising potentiometers

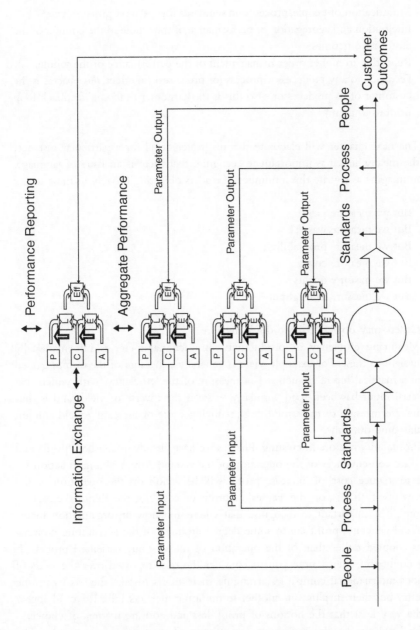

**FIGURE 11.4** Aggregating potentiometers

Figure 11.4 shows this structure brought together. Monitoring of output against 'standards', 'process' and 'people' is fed back into the potentiometer, enabling

- Modification of people, process and standards for the next process cycle;
- Integration and aggregation of performance of the whole in the context of the customer outcomes;
- Reporting to higher order management of the performance of the whole;
- Feedback to any predecessor process (or processes) (in effect, *this* process is the customer of its predecessor – so this is the 'customer outcome' feedback loop from us to them).

The next chapter will elaborate this in greater detail for a particular instance. In the meanwhile, it is important to recognise that there is an issue of language. I can imagine as I write this a number of readers objecting broadly in these terms:

- But we measure yield;
- But we measure waste;
- But we measure profitability;
- But we measure costs;
- But we measure quality;
- But we measure throughput.

Others may object, 'but we don't measure . . .'

Measuring efficiency or productivity on each parameter is informationally equivalent to these. For example, yield is generally a measure of the output gained from a material input, as such it is a measure of the 'efficiency' with which that material input has been used. Similarly, waste is the inverse of yield (and is thus an inverse measure of the same thing); reducing waste or increasing yield amount to the same outcome.

Profitability is more interesting. First, as we have already established, 'profit' and 'loss' are consequences of the operation of the system. Any meaningful action we take to 'reduce cost' or 'increase profit' will be action on the operation of the process itself; that is, on the 'causes' of profit or cost, not the things themselves. Second, it is important to recognise that where and how an organisation incurs cost and generates profit are to some degree products of the accounting conventions adopted rather than of the operation of the customer-oriented process. If you doubt this, then I urge you to consider the tales reported over the years of various international companies arranging their affairs to take their costs in one country but their surpluses in another to minimise their tax bills. It would appear at the very least that the notions of profit, loss and cost are matters of choice.

So, I will not be precious about particular words, and nor should you be. The essence of what we need to achieve is to understand, in the broadest sense, those parameters that need to be monitored in order to understand how the organisation can perform within its envelope and take action on them to close the gap between what is desired (potential), what is currently possible (capability) and what is happening (actual).

## What is the role of the manager?

In the Intelligent Organisation, management is enabling, not controlling, because control has been built into the system itself. The manager is released to add value by acting as a transducer (Beer, 1985), bearing information about requirements across the internal boundaries of the organisation, translating the language into that of the receiving party and gaining feedback to ensure the message has been understood. The manager provides resources and holds the recipient to account for the use of those resources, but measured against the achievement of the intended outcome and *not* the input or output variables. This demands that any self-regulating individual asked to generate an outcome *must* be granted the autonomy to do so. One of the resources the manager will be responsible for is people. It is their task to motivate, train, coach and enable those people to perform their tasks – and if the manager is not bogged down in generating fanciful excuses for *their* manager, then they will have time to do this.

One critical aspect to consider is the distinction that must be drawn between the managers' roles of

* looking into the process: resource provision, coach, technical expert;
* looking out of the process: transducer.

These roles require different behaviours, perhaps different languages and, of course, require the manager to understand their role in the whole organisation, its expectations, opportunities and constraints. Very often, particularly in operational management roles such as team leader, foreman and charge hand but seen quite often in the 'C suite' [the executive offices of the organisation], is the tendency of the manager to play technical expert, to demonstrate his or her competence at the job itself, usually by nudging aside the incumbent and saying:

'I'll show you how it should be done!'

Great care needs to be taken here to distinguish roles. It *may* be part of the manager's role to provide some technical expertise to others in the process, perhaps on the difficult or rarer tasks – but when providing that expertise, they are doing so as 'expert' not as manager; the behaviour and approaches are different.

Similarly, when showing someone what should be done, are they simply doing it for them or are they teaching them how it should be done? Quite often they are doing it for them so that far from living up to the role of manager as coach, they are simply denying the individual the opportunity to learn.

It is critical to the Intelligent Organisation that the skills, competences, behaviours and values required for its success are understood, codified and captured in such a manner that it is possible to both apply them and manage them. The process-related aspects of this are generally quite straightforward and can be developed in the course of process design and, in particular, the principles for designing in autonomy discussed earlier.

Once we know the constraints that mechanisation or automation of the process may impose on individual autonomy, it is possible to be precise about the technical skills and knowledge that the individual must provide. That is, we can make a formal statement about the technical capabilities required by those carrying out any specific task or tasks and we can objectively test the skills of any individual and compare them with those required.

Dealing with the behavioural dimension is rather more challenging. Whilst it is possible to make a statement of the values to which those in the organisation should adhere, it is very much harder to generate a fully objective 'test' of whether or not they are adhered to on an ongoing basis. There are, of course, a whole battery of psychometric evaluation tools available such as Myers-Briggs Type Indicator, Rorschach Inkblot Method, Strengths Deployment Inventory, Occupational Personality Quotient and Belbin Team Roles. All of these have been developed, polished, redeveloped, tested on large populations and found by many to give reasonably reliable indicators of likely performance. However Murphy (2005) questions their overall validity. It is certainly the case that individuals familiar with such tests, their underlying logic and assumptions and the behavioural attributes sought by a particular employer, are perfectly capable of 'beating the test' from time to time.

The role of the manager in managing performance then is to gather appropriate, objective information about what is actually happening and to have appropriate and meaningful information about the gap between the knowledge and skills required for a task and those available to any particular individual. He or she can then exercise judgement about the best form of action to close that gap, whether that be training, coaching, instructing or, in the limiting case, encouraging the individual to think about their own future.

While that sounds perhaps a little harsh, an individual who is not competent in a particular role, who lacks the skills or training, is unlikely to be content in it. That lack of contentment is likely to show through in one or more ways. It may simply show in symptoms such as poor productivity, high sickness or absence rate, poor timekeeping or some other characteristic. The responsibility of the manager is *not* to act on the symptom but to understand and address the underlying cause(s) of that symptom and take action to correct it.

Capturing and presenting the data in the form proposed has generated information for decision making which not only locates the challenge for the value-generating process but also for the HR value-enabling process on which it relies. With the principles from the examples applied to all processes, meaningful action can be taken by the relevant managers to close the gaps. The whole thing is presented in a form which enables that action, rather than seeking to either blame individuals or generate meaningless encouragement, incentives or admonishments.

The outcome, rooted in a rigorous understanding of the process and the data that supports it, gives an objective view of both the driver of performance and the adaptive action required to correct it – and the informational logic can be applied to every value-generating and value enabling process for the whole organisation. It becomes then a cybernetic organisation, one in which self-regulation, adaptation and change are built into the decision-making architecture, where going 'out of control' provides its own corrective action to come back 'in control'.

## Summary

This chapter has introduced a very different way of measuring and managing the performance of organisations in a systemic manner. It attempts to embrace all of the dimensions of performance through a unifying framework and will undoubtedly pose challenges to any organisation that attempts to put it into practice.

In the next chapter, we shall do just that and see how it all fits together.

# 12

# MANAGING PERFORMANCE

## Case

And have the wisdom to balance compassion and challenge . . .
. . . to rise above the fester of small mediocrities.

John O'Donohue, *Benedictus* (2007)

## Introduction

All that has been elaborated so far relies on appreciating the Intelligent Organisation as a dynamic system. That is as richly interdependent, interrelated and interactive with the desired customer outcomes generating value and drawing on the delivery and value-enabling processes. Overall, recognising the Intelligent Organisation in this way, appreciating its interdependencies, allows us to understand how, using meaningful information, we can manage its performance. This dynamic, process-oriented approach enables a much richer understanding of the business than is possible from traditional, functionally oriented reporting.

This chapter considers managing performance for a train operating business. It draws together all those aspects of Intelligent Organisation – structure, information, autonomy that we have already discussed – it brings the whole to life.

## Recent history of the UK railway

In the UK, the railway was denationalised in the 1990s, and what had been a single integrated business was reorganised into a series of separate functional parts:

- Infrastructure: Responsible for the track, control systems, major stations;
- Train Operators: Responsible for passenger and cargo services;
- RoSCOs: Owners of rail vehicles, typically leasing them to the train operators;

- Government: Responsible for overall governance, regulation, system management and performance.

This case study is concerned with a franchised passenger train operator. 'Line of route'–based franchises are open to any organisation to bid for (qualification being a combination of competence and money) and most are run by organisations already established in the transport sector. While the apparent intent in privatisation was perhaps to introduce competition into the railway and improve financial performance, it was and remains the case that the rail industry as a whole requires substantial subsidy both for investment in its future and for the provision of low-revenue, high-cost services. This is common to mass public transport systems globally which fund their own debt.

Prior to privatisation whilst safety standards were, and at the time of writing remain, very high, customer satisfaction was low, passenger numbers were declining and there was a continuing history of poor industrial relations. It is fair to say that since the privatisation process, there has been a substantial increase in passenger numbers (although satisfaction shows significant variance), a much more settled industrial relations environment and massive investment in the network and vehicles, not least to respond to major incidents but also to increase capacity on the railway.

## A question of purpose

To understand how to manage performance we must first comprehend the purpose of the organisation; without clarity of purpose, performance management is meaningless. A purpose is the reason the organisation exists, the customer need it seeks to fulfil, the customer outcome it aims to satisfy. In customer terms, profit is not meaningful as it is an internal measure important to the owners of the capital invested in the business rather than the customers.

We cannot and will not ignore profit. It is fundamental that investment and growth are only possible when there is an excess of income over expenditure; that is inherent in the arithmetic, not a political statement! However, the Intelligent Organisation pursues survival in the long term and that depends on retaining existing and attracting new customers, something with which a focus on short-term profit maximisation may conflict. Consider a passenger train operator from the customer's perspective; we can suggest that the purpose is to provide customer journeys, i.e. to move people between locations on the network.

The government is also a stakeholder in this instance. While it necessarily has an interest in the delivery of the journey (the passenger outcome), it would be reasonable to think that it also has an interest in other outcomes which would include financial performance (reducing levels of subsidy or receiving a premium from the franchisee), and both passengers and government are interested in safety. We can therefore suggest that the desired outcomes, embracing both passengers and government, are

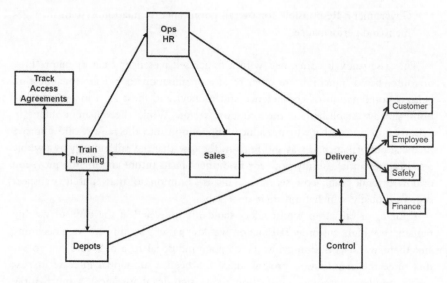

**FIGURE 12.1** Train operating company

- Customer Satisfaction;
- Employee Satisfaction;
- Safety;
- Financial Performance.

The train operator then has four outcomes to meet in fulfilling its purpose. It relies on a set of interacting and interdependent processes to achieve these as set out in Figure 12.1.

Customer Satisfaction, Employee Satisfaction, Safety and Finance are all dependent upon Delivery, which in turn relies on real-time Control. That is a higher order function which interacts with all the other operators attempting to deliver services on the same parts of the railway. Delivery also requires Depots to deliver trains and Sales to deliver passengers and all require to be populated by Operational HR. Delivery and Depots generate demand on Train Planning (making potential journeys available), which in turn depends on the Track Access Agreement. HR Operations also depends on Train Planning for the information about the required crew population.

The Track Access Agreement sets out the contract with the infrastructure operator (and franchisor) to run the particular timetable at any given point in time. Successful operation of the business, the achievement of desired outcomes, is dependent upon effective information sharing between these multiple dynamic processes. Feedback information about how well the business met its objectives emerges naturally from this. Track Access Agreements, which grant permission to run the services, also provide the fundamental, feedforward information needed to plan the business, in them rests one key element of the ability to create the future.

From both an organisational and informational perspective, once the Track Access Agreement has been negotiated (an enabling activity) thereby creating the timetable, it is possible to derive many characteristics of the organisation:

- The number and mix of rail vehicles required;
- The maintenance schedule for those vehicles;
- The likely need and timing of vehicle parts;
- The number of engineers required, their skills and their work patterns;
- The train crew requirements to run the services, their skills and their work patterns;
- The number of tickets that could be sold and the potential revenues of the business, i.e. the potential passenger volume;
- The staffing requirements for the ticket-selling operations, train dispatch and so on;
- The training and development requirements for all staff;
- The requirements from the on-board catering service.

In addition to this set of interactions, the organisation also has to deal with data and information flows to and from external organisations. In the case of the railway, that includes regulators, passengers, infrastructure operators, suppliers (e.g. energy, catering and vehicles) and, of course, other train operators and other forms of transport (alternative ways of completing the same journey). To design an organisation that not only fails to embrace this complexity but also fails to deal with the data generated by it, is to design for failure.

The particular franchisee with which this study is concerned was attempting to achieve two things in parallel. Apart from managing the business to fulfil the existing franchise performance criteria, they were also considering what form the organisation should take in order for them to be successful in acquiring one or more other franchises.

The established organisation chart, in use at the time and approved by the regulator for safety purposes, is shown as Figure 12.2. The headline functional split was between

- Production: maintaining, preparing, driving and controlling trains;
- Operations: on-board ticket sales, catering, stations, facilities management;
- Marketing: brand management, yield management, online ticket sales, public relations, customer compensation;
- Projects: projects concerned with vehicles, information systems, station developments and project finance;
- Financial Management: corporate bookkeeping and accounting;
- Human Resource Management: recruitment, payroll, industrial relations, operational information systems and operational HR management.

This tells us who to reward for success (the people at the top) and blame for failure (the people at the bottom, obviously), but little or nothing of how the

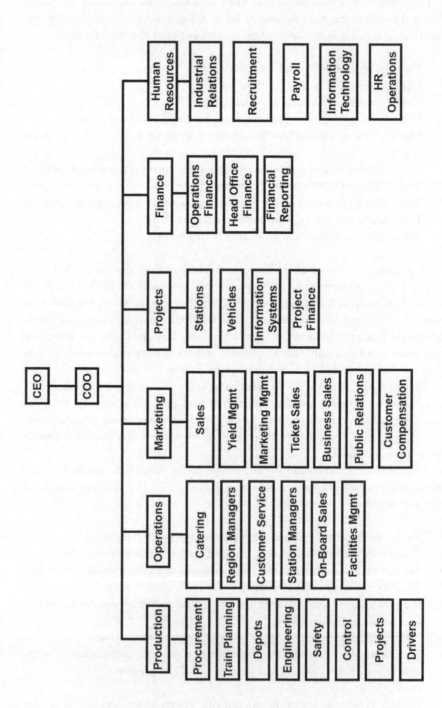

FIGURE 12.2 Train operating company hierarchy

**FIGURE 12.3** Operational services

organisation actually worked or of how its performance might be improved. It is particularly difficult to imagine how adding a further franchise could be accommodated without the sort of substantial disruption and change programme so endemic in modern organisations.

Adopting the principles of design of the Intelligent Organisation, it was considered best to redesign the organisation backwards from the customer. We could create a fresh organisation that would be more effectively run with a single franchise (effectiveness being expressed through the measures already established) whilst also able to accommodate one or more additional franchises within the same structure.

Figure 12.3 identifies the starting point for this redesign. With multiple stakeholders (passengers, government, safety regulators, shareholders), it was not possible to hold a single outcome as more important than the others; the organisation had to meet all four expectations. The delivery process that ultimately did this was identified as 'Operational Services', the operation of the rail services themselves via the timetable, vehicles and crews. It was in the day-to-day activity of the organisation that the company could meet performance expectations.

These Operational Services depended upon the effectiveness of two other processes, Ticket Sales and Train Production. While it could be argued that these are enabling processes, it was considered that they were purposeful in their own right (the activities could be 'outsourced' from the franchise so they were, in principle, capable of independent existence) and were therefore a purposeful part of the system. The purpose of the Ticket Sales process was considered as delivering the optimum mix of passenger loading against ticket revenue. The purpose of Train Production was to deliver 'Perfect Trains' (a performance standard) to the

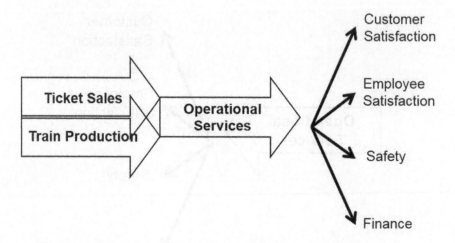

**FIGURE 12.4** Operational services with sales and production

right station and right platform at the right time to fulfil the Operational Services (Figure 12.4).

These three processes had to be largely self-managing for a number of reasons. The many sets of rail vehicles providing hundreds of timetabled journeys per day were serviced and maintained at multiple locations along the route. Prospective passengers could purchase tickets from hundreds of locations including stations and travel agents or online. Crews could join and leave services at multiple crew depots along the route and the overall 'line of route' covered hundreds of miles in each direction with multiple stopping points for collection and delivering of passengers. Passengers' secondary requirements for catering, ablutions, newspapers, internet access and so on could only be fulfilled on the moving rail vehicle. Centralised management was neither desirable nor practical at the operational level. Figure 12.5 shows the core processes with their embedded local management, local homeostats.

It became very clear that Operational Services could only succeed if both Ticket Sales and Train Production succeeded; the dependence was absolute. Any limitation in their performance would immediately inhibit the performance of operations. This demanded a sharp focus on both process capability and the requisite skills and behaviours of the staff and gave meaning and weight to the measurement of performance, all good reasons for not outsourcing the challenge but keeping it within the organisation where it could be managed effectively.

Whilst the organisation as so far designed required significant distributed autonomy if it was to succeed, it was nonetheless evident that a number of enabling processes needed to be carried out on behalf of the whole. Remember the justification for the existence of any part of the Intelligent Organisation not directly delivering products and services to customers is the extent to which that part enables its continued operation, adaptation and survival.

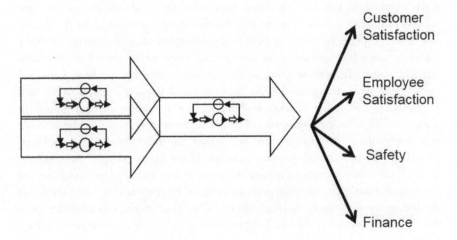

**FIGURE 12.5** Embedded homeostats

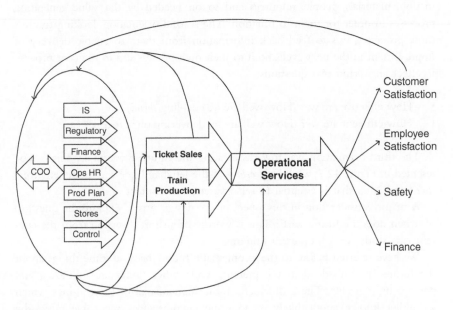

**FIGURE 12.6** Managing the present

This was the case with our subject organisation with enabling functions covering Information Services, Regulatory Management, Financial Management, Operational Human Resource Management, Production Planning (the scheduling of maintenance for rail vehicles), Stores (supply chain management of all consumables) and Control (the real-time management of rail vehicles in traffic).

Figure 12.6 shows the alignment of the enabling functions with the core processes. This required the redesign of these activities to focus on the value they were enabling in the core processes, how what they did contributed to their success and deriving from that the performance standards required for the future. It will not surprise the reader to hear that the simple realignment of the enabling activities around contribution to success and value added provided substantial efficiency and effectiveness gains, which translated into reduced headcount and costs. They were doing more with less. Of equal importance is that the oval (Figure 12.6) containing all those enabling services represents their integration in a form which relies on appropriate flows of information (the black line arrows). It is not setting an alternative view of a power hierarchy but rather an order of precedence in operational decision making, driven by the output requirements which 'pull' other decisions through the system. The enabling processes are not 'more important' than the core processes, even if the people that carry them out are sitting on nice chairs in Head Office rather than in the service office on a rail vehicle. They are all of equal importance, as failure in any one aspect means failure for the whole.

The first orientation of the enabling processes was the provision of the information, materials, people, resources and so on needed by the value-generating processes in order for them to function. The second orientation, looking towards those processes, was to feed back information from them to enable delivery of improvement in the next cycle, both to their own process and to the core process, in effect answering two questions:

- How effective are we? (How well are *we* enabling *them*?)
- How efficient are we? (How well are *we* delivering our process?)

The third orientation was towards creating the future. Structurally this is represented in Figure 12.7, which represents at the left-hand side the model environment and MoS that is essential to self-awareness in context.

A major consideration in this aspect of the design was to explore the question of 'when does the future start'? This is worthy of a short diversion from the current case study for a little extra thinking.

We have referred before to the 'problematic future' because some things about the future are embedded in the present, while other things are unknown and perhaps unknowable. The problematic future contains all of those things which are either known about, likely or, in some circumstances, inevitable given the current position. Each of those things will have a level of probability, from absolute certainty to likely to possible. The problematic future is concerned with exploring the unknown and reducing the unknowable. In 'managing the present', the organisation needs to be able to address all those things which are in the 'known' future, to have the capability to adapt and change and either control those things or, more commonly, seek to influence them in a manner which provides a positive outcome (one which is supportive of the objectives). In creating the future, the Intelligent Organisation needs to assess the opportunities and threats arising in its environment, consider its strengths and weaknesses in relation to them and propose

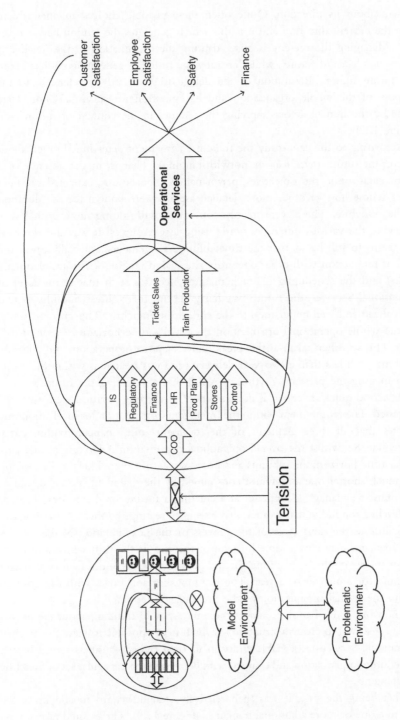

**FIGURE 12.7** Creating the future

choices about its direction. Quite often these possible choices are inconsistent with the current direction and it is this which generates the tension between the two. 'Managing the present' is busy adapting the organisation to the (relatively) short-term 'current future', whilst 'creating the future' is generating choices about the 'future future'. Resolution of the debate is generated by reference to the purpose of the whole organisation and its aspiration for survival. Choices are made by the human actors, applying their values in the context of the mission (Figure 12.8).

Returning to the case study, the franchise agreement determined much about its current future (*force majeure* notwithstanding). That is, in the absence of a major catastrophe the objectives, performance expectations, expected revenues and a whole host of other more detailed aspects were known for the duration of the franchise. These were mainly concerned with 'doing more with less' – achieving the various outcomes while using less resources. It was also the case, and seems to still be so, that the timetabling arrangements, especially given the level of interaction with other operators, the shared facilities (stations, platforms, tracks) and the scheduling of track maintenance was such that at the level of Operational Services, the future was fairly certain for eighteen months to two years ahead and well understood to the end of the franchise. The 'current future' for the whole operational organisation then had a time horizon of around two years. This was then taken as the 'breakpoint' for process operations and control– anything with less than a two-year delivery time was treated as within the scope of 'managing the present', anything beyond that as 'creating the future'.

A second quick diversion is desirable here, as there is a critical element to be addressed. The requirement within the Intelligent Organisation for local autonomy dictates that all three elements of the 'trialogue' must happen within every homeostat. So, whilst the overall operational organisation is looking at one particular time horizon, the subunits and processes within it are likely to be looking at a much shorter one and, whilst constrained by the shared 'mission and values', they must be managing a present and creating a future for themselves. That, at the level of the individual worker, may mean a 'creating the future' time horizon of as little as the next cycle of the process or the next iteration of the task. A shift manager may have a time horizon of the end of the shift whilst a production manager might be planning for the next few weeks and a factory manager planning for a quarter or a year. The planning horizon varies with the position within the overall organisation of the particular function.

The work so far had delivered a whole new way of thinking about the organisation. It served to create a structure in which it was possible to view the original Operational Services as a viable entity in its own right, a business served by the higher order organisation and charged with delivering the particular set of franchise requirements.

That being the case, it was then relatively straightforward to add in to the structure one or more additional franchises (Figure 12.9). These could take advantage of the established enabling structure of the whole organisation whilst

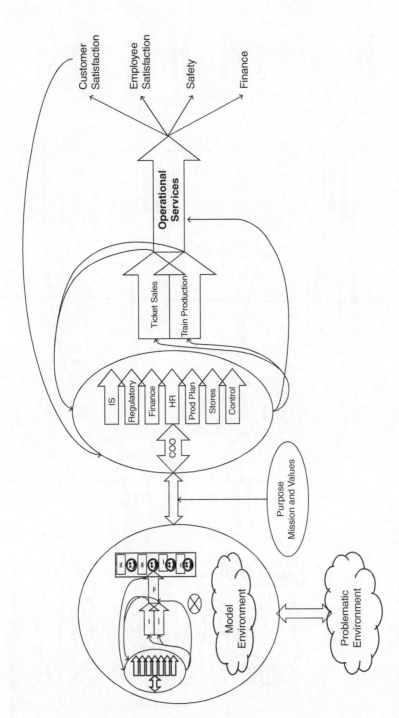

**FIGURE 12.8** The whole organisation

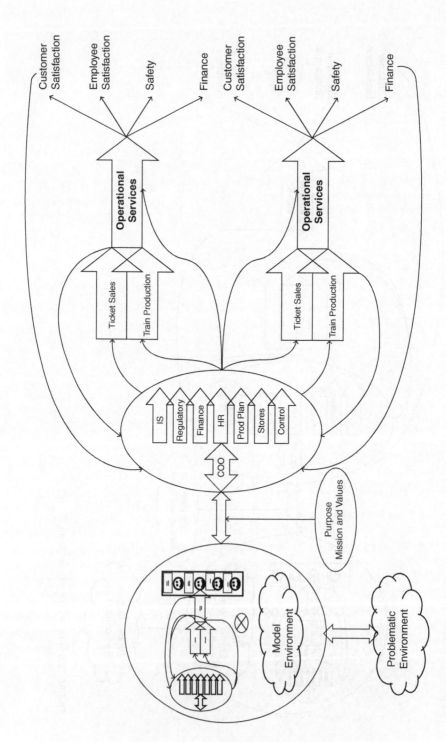

**FIGURE 12.9** Multi-organisation

replicating the service delivery structure of the original franchise. By thoughtful design, the Intelligent Organisation offered a 'plug and play' solution to the issue of merger or acquisition, minimised the disruption and risk to the whole from the performance of one part whilst at the same time providing significant benefits from integration.

In terms of business impact, the redesigned structure enabled a substantial step reduction in the number of managers employed in the business. It delivered savings of several million pounds per annum whilst eliminating a number of other activities which were not adding value, thereby generating further savings. Meanwhile revenue, driven principally by growth in GDP (an environmental effect), was increasing. For those enabling activities which were continued, it became possible for the first time to measure the value of their contribution to the success of the whole and hold individuals to account for their performance. As just one example, it was determined through analysis that the law of diminishing returns was applicable to the marketing activity of the organisation and that a substantial, around 30%, reduction in marketing expenditure would have no discernible negative impact on either ticket sales or brand awareness. Duly implemented, this proved to be the case.

## Information for performance management

The train operator was, at the outset, managed through traditional, functional reporting with all of the limitations already explored. Given the multiple interacting processes and the need for 'creating the future' within each one, there was a requirement for a redesign of the information system to support performance management. Most critically, there was a need to ensure that there was organisational closure. Closure is achieved by consistency between purpose, creating the future and managing the present being pulled through operations by the four objectives. It was believed that this informational and organisational closure could be delivered through measurement of performance against outcomes, with the results being fed back to the overall organisation.

Having considered how the process structure fitted together, it was right that the information architecture reflected the organisational architecture. As you read this, it is also important to separate the structure of the information flow from the specific data that flows through that structure, that data being potentially highly variable. This is an important distinction as it enables great simplification of the information systems.

The organisation now understood the outcomes it needed to fulfil to continue in existence (Figure 12.10). The specific measures for each are not important in this discussion, what is important is that they defined the requirements for Train Planning. The outcomes defined what services were to be offered and to what standard. These in turn defined what timetable was required and enabled the negotiation of Track Access Agreements (TAA). The TAA are constrained by the existence of competing services for the same permanent way. We can see here

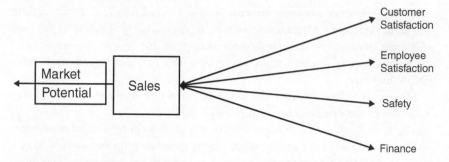

**FIGURE 12.10** Information flow

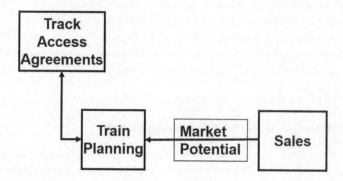

**FIGURE 12.11** Track access

the first homeostat appeared (Figure 12.11). The outcome of the negotiation of the TAA defined the capacity (the number of services and passengers) of the business and therefore what could be offered compared to those which were initially desired. In this case, the modifying action was to balance the services requested against those made available.

The result of that negotiation acted as a constraint on the resulting performance of the business – it limited income because it determined how many services could be offered, at what times and the number of seats. It also determined the level of customer satisfaction that could be achieved, as it was not possible to run all the services that the customers had asked for.

The TAA had the effect of determining what timetables were required which, in turn, defined the process requirements of the train depots to meet the service requirements and to work within the safety regulations:

- How many vehicles were needed;
- What mix of locomotives and carriages;
- What level of maintenance needed to be provided in which locations;
- Timing.

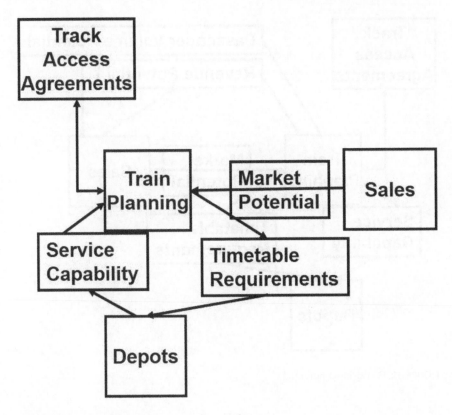

**FIGURE 12.12** Aligning outcomes and capability

Each rail vehicle is subject to periodic examination and maintenance which depends on its duty cycle, and that is determined by the TAA and the timetable for the particular vehicle. The TAA also determined the potential volume of ticket sales – by route, timetabled service and class. That information looped back to inform ticket pricing, revenue potential and capacity management. Altogether (Figure 12.12), that aligned the business objectives with overall capability; it became possible to understand 'the future we are currently in' – at least for the life of the TAA and its consequences.

Directly arising from that 'known' future, the HR function (Figure 12.13) could quantify with sufficient accuracy the numbers of staff – by role, grade and location – needed to run the services. They could then focus on fulfilling their obligations by providing the right people with the right skills and the right values. These were also informed by the understanding of the desired outcomes of customer satisfaction and employee satisfaction that started the process. Meanwhile, those responsible for the Depots processes had the information to develop their staffing and scheduling arrangements and to develop the parts management and supply chain processes needed to underpin their operation, and they could do so

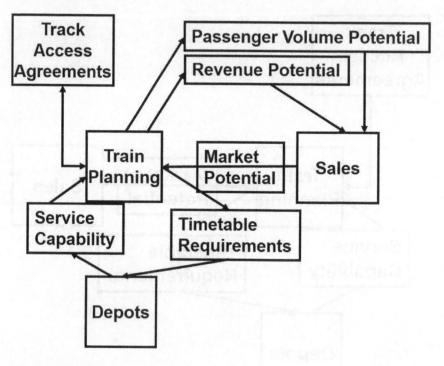

**FIGURE 12.13** Business potential

with reasonable certainty for the life of the franchise. Performance standards were also established to ensure the production of 'Perfect Trains' and their provision to the right place at the right time.

Ticket sales, staffing and vehicles (Figure 12.14) could now all be brought back together. They could be synchronised with the timetable requirements to deliver services to standards set in accordance with the initial objectives for the business. Performance could be managed both in real time (Control) and through Audit, generating feedback about how well the four objectives were being met.

With an understanding of the contribution of each process to the success of the whole, the determination (through the logical flow of the organisation backwards from the customer) of performance expectations and standards, then the measurement and evaluation of performance, became straightforward. Managers responsible for each process could both modify their own processes (remember – standards, skills, behaviours, process, task and procedure) to better fulfil their objectives whilst cascading appropriate performance measures to the task level. Enabling management, responsible for the whole organisation, could observe its performance against the objectives and, using their understanding of the process dependencies within the organisation, determine what modifying decisions for improvement were possible.

This was enabled by the redesign of the information system to ensure that the right information was in the right place at the right time and in the right format

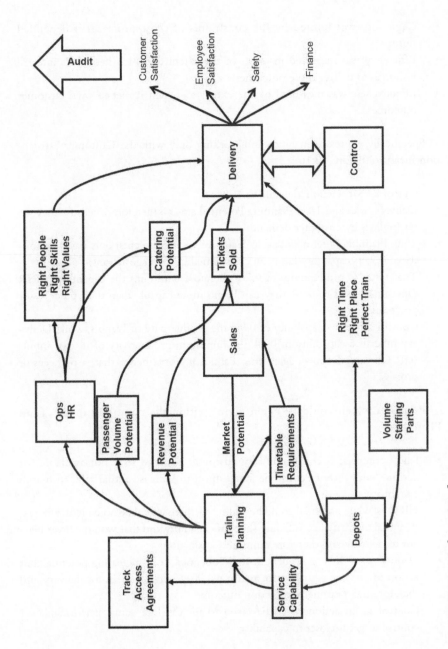

FIGURE 12.14 Information flows

to enable that to take place. The whole was presented through a series of linked potentiometers (Figure 12.15). For each of these:

- Capability was limited by the constraints of those processes it depended upon;
- Efficiency was measured in terms of the extent to which it used its internal resources to deliver those outcomes;
- Effectiveness was measured by the extent to which it met its own customer outcomes.

Specifically, expressed in ratios and working only with the Customer Satisfaction measure (Figure 12.16):

- Customer Satisfaction 'demand' is 1;
- Delivery, Sales and Train Planning Potential are also therefore 1 because they are set (pulled) by customer demand;
- Train Planning (after negotiating Track Access Agreements) only has a capability of 0.9, its capability has been constrained in the negotiations;
- That result (a productivity of 0.78) therefore constrains the capability of HR Ops and Depots to 0.78, they can be no more capable than their predecessor processes;
- Control inherits a capability of 0.90, the productivity of Depots, while Delivery inherits a capability of 0.64, the minimum productivity of its two inputs (HR Ops and Depots), again they cannot perform better than a predecessor process.

Processes which could be acted upon (within the constraint of the Train Plan) are:

- Sales: potential is constrained by customer demand so is not available for action. Sales activity could be acted upon to increase actual sales to match capability;
- HR Ops: while potential could be addressed, there would be no benefit, whereas its actual performance is falling short of capability and that would deliver benefit to delivery and therefore customer satisfaction;
- Depots: again there is no benefit to be obtained from increasing potential, but action to increase actual performance would generate benefit for delivery and therefore the customer satisfaction outcome;
- Control: again action could be taken to increase the actual performance of control to get it closer to capability.

In terms of improvement, the interesting outcome is that an 'improvement' to an internal process that does not lead to an improved outcome for the customer (more reliable trains, lower cost, faster journey times) adds no value to the whole.

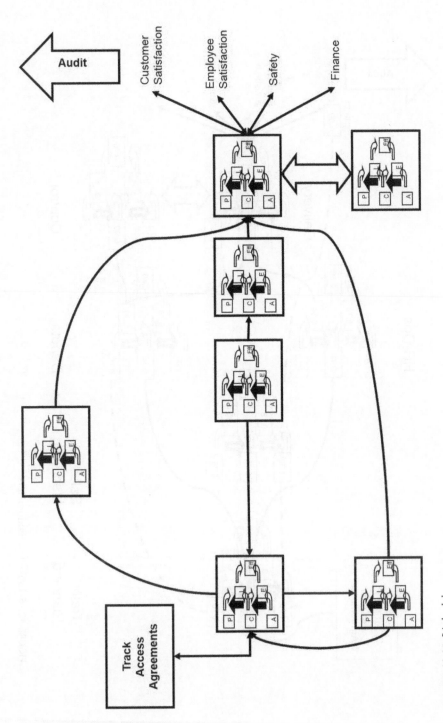

**FIGURE 12.15** Linked homeostats

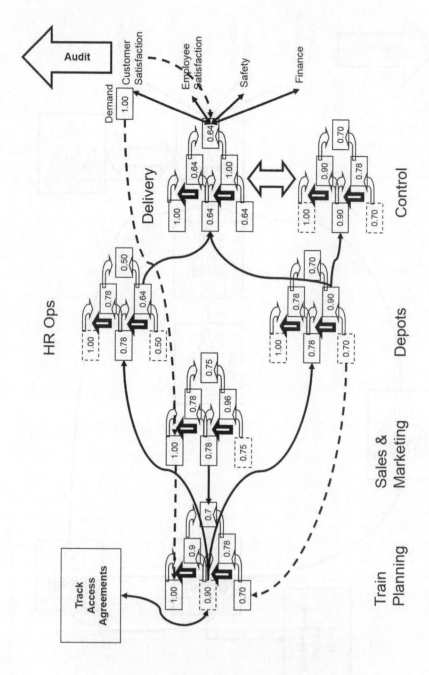

**FIGURE 12.16** Linked potentiometers

## If: then: it all depends

The solution revealed in the foregoing pages was not, of course, the only possibility, but it was the one that best fitted the organisation to the achievement of its objectives whilst being consistent with the underpinning thinking and theory of organisations. A number of alternative designs were developed and discussed, but none fitted the situation so well nor answered all of the questions so adequately.

Just in case you are thinking 'ahh, but, that has set it all in stone, it is just deterministic central planning, that is bound to fail' (or words to that effect), then stop and read again. The whole structure and all of its information flows are dependent on the objectives which, in this particular case, are given to the organisation and everything flows from their interpretation. They tell us what is important about this particular railway, in the particular set of circumstances that pertained at the time and in the then-prevailing political, social and economic context. If the franchisor (the government in this case) decided that, say, safety was less important than moving as many people as possible as fast as possible or that financial performance was unimportant, then a different solution might apply, but probably not at the overall process level; the structure would probably be the same. What would be different would be the performance measurement, the content of process control, the balance of effort (less focus on 'ticket sales' and more focus on capacity management). There is a level at which, reflecting Joan Woodward (1965), the process structure can be optimal. There can be a 'best' shape for the organisation – and that is rarely a pure hierarchical, siloed form.

## Summary

This chapter has provided an overview of the application of the potentiometer as a device for enabling the management of performance. Of particular importance is the ability to use it as a unifying framework through which disparate aspects of the performance of the organisation can both be presented in a uniform language and compared. Coupled to that, it has shown how the performance of interdependent elements, brought to life through the information system, can be reviewed and used to apply improvement effort to the right part of the organisation at the right time.

# 13

# THE INTELLIGENT ORGANISATION AND PUBLIC SERVICES

> Every time Whitehall has made the case for technological innovation on the grounds of efficiency, it has ended up costing more not less.
>
> *Daily Telegraph*, 30th September 2011

## Introduction

While the ideas in this book are relevant to all organisations, this chapter takes a look at the particular challenges faced by the public sector. Case studies are included which look at infrastructure, transport and health in particular.

There are four key areas that distinguish public service from private sector organisations in general. The first is that they do not enjoy the same degree of self-determination (autonomy), their purpose is given to them by government which also controls their budget. Second, the focus of activity often appears to be on output (compliance to process) not outcome (satisfied customers). Third, with their age and size, to achieve change a lot of organisational inertia has to be overcome. Even the youngest government services such as healthcare and education are decades old, while diplomacy and defence go back hundreds of years, and incentive systems (extrinsic and intrinsic rewards) are typically geared towards administrative compliance rather than innovation or leadership. Finally, such organisations are either information driven or information enabled, sometimes both, but government (at least in the UK) has a long history of less than successful IT projects.

## A question of purpose: revisited

Public sector organisations are in a different survival situation than the private sector. First, while funding levels vary over time and budgets may be over- or underspent, they do not cease trading or retain a surplus, they are not motivated to perform by profit; they are constrained to perform within budget. Second, the services they provide will, for the most part, continue to be provided regardless of performance (or indeed budgets); they are persistent and protected, although 'rationing' of some services does occur. Third, they have (at least) two distinct and discrete 'customers' to serve, the public (who receive the services) and the government (which funds them through taxation of individuals and corporations). Although individual senior employees may be removed from office, the organisations themselves are invulnerable to the ultimate failure of bankruptcy; they do not have to 'adapt to survive'. The price of their protections is that they do not enjoy power of self-determination (autonomy) equivalent to the private sector. They cannot choose to 'grow the business' to the same extent nor can they decide that the resources which they receive would be more productively employed in pursuing different goals; they operate to fulfil the tasks allocated to them. They are protected but constrained, functioning on decision cycles largely dictated by elections and budgets.

Whilst independent organisations are, ultimately, governed by their shareholders, represented by the Board, every public sector organisation is subject to a sociopolitical level of governance. The government, whether national or local and by virtue of its mandate, determines organisational purpose and performance expectations. Public sector organisations often have very broadly drawn purposes, making it difficult either to know what constitutes good performance or indeed, how much of a particular service is 'enough' – regardless of the political drivers. While governments are criticised for attempting to set standards and targets for various services, as we have discovered in the rest of the book, these are essential to process delivery and control but are meaningless in the absence of a clear purpose. It is fulfilment of purpose that is the measure of success.

Drucker (1986) writes of the need for public services of all sorts to be entrepreneurial, to innovate, but recognises that they can only do so when they have a clear sense of purpose; that is, when innovation and entrepreneurialism are expressed in terms of the outcome to be achieved. Clarity of purpose enables all of the other criteria of the Intelligent Organisation to be addressed:

- Who are the customers?
- What are the outcomes they expect?
- What do the processes need to be to achieve those outcomes?
- What behaviours and values are appropriate?
- How much is 'enough'?
- How can we manage, adapt, develop the organisation?

In the absence of clearly defined purpose, effectiveness cannot be addressed and the question of efficiency is an irrelevance. In that case, then, we cannot reasonably expect public sector organisations, or the people employed in them, to deliver the outcomes we want. We cannot have what we have not defined.

## Doing more with less

There is, in many countries, pressure for 'public sector reform', usually translated as 'doing more for less'. This is not the place for a political debate about the appropriateness of that, but it is interesting to consider.

Political survival in a position of governance over the medium to long term perhaps depends as much on economic well-being as it does on the state responding (or not) to the broader wishes of the people. However, like any organisation, the state must over time spend less than it receives in order to be financially viable.

There is of course scope for ideological debate about the range and extent to which any level of government should provide services to and on behalf of its population of citizens as a whole, though that is not the purpose here. There can be little doubt though that public services (whether national or local) should consider themselves under an obligation to manage those services to provide the maximum benefit to citizens (customer outcome) at the lowest cost. There is no such thing in most states as 'public money', since for the most part any money spent or invested by the state is obtained from individuals and corporate bodies through taxation.

In the absence of clarity of purpose, a typical examination of any budget leads to a cost reduction focus, considering either marginal activity (what can we stop doing?) or 'big ticket' items. Emphasis will be on reducing the operating budget and, because the biggest budget numbers in any service-oriented organisation are staff costs, that usually translates into reductions in headcount. That in turn either limits the number of the population whose needs can be met, reduces the share of activity that each customer receives or, sometimes, displaces cost to another service. Such phenomena have been reported in the UK press with general practitioners (GPs) protesting at levels of funding and reducing the service provided locally to patients, displacing those patients to the Accident and Emergency (A&E) departments. The GPs' waiting times are thereby 'managed'; their costs are reduced. Meanwhile, the A&E waiting times and costs are increased, the patient suffers. The costs have not been reduced, just displaced. The 'head office' need for reduced spending may or may not be met, but the service fails to the extent that its purpose is not fulfilled.

Public services in many countries, including the UK, are commonly hierarchical and functionally oriented. They are operated in a manner focused on internal adherence to procedure and the delivery of, often bureaucratic, output rather than the customer outcome. The overall design of state services, in general, reflects this and we find this functional structure replicated in local authorities, healthcare, education, policing and so on. Any citizen, the customer of the state administration, must then have multiple interactions with the functionally organised state. If 'the customer outcome' should be the focus of the organisation, then we need to organise things from the customer's perspective and functional, internally oriented organisations cannot do that.

The greater part of any population is affected by the organisation of state or local authority functions. We pay our taxes, send our children to school, have our bins emptied, receive healthcare and eventually collect our pensions. The system mainly works but is 'customer inefficient'; we have to deal with multiple agencies and multiple ways of working, a plethora of forms. It could, should, be better.

If everyone fitted a standard pattern then we could, perhaps, deliver significant improvements whilst working within the established structures. However, and this will always be the case, there are a wide range of individuals and families with a wide range of needs. While the majority may place little demand on the various systems, a relatively small proportion of the whole population need support and engagement from a wide variety of services, often in parallel, to cope with the demands and complexities of contemporary life. Those who are fortunate should not fool themselves into thinking that coping is simple.

The provision of services to this latter few requires careful consideration. Their needs are likely to be complex and they will be in continuing contact with multiple arms of the state – healthcare, social services, adult services, children's services, police and welfare. The conventional way of dealing with these individuals and families has been through multi-agency working, that is the 'pushing' of individual services through a combined and agreed strategy but with continuing individual service engagement, i.e. the overall approach is agreed but the parts are delivered separately. While this may deliver some benefit, it is both costly and inefficient to manage 'internally' through the functionally arranged delivery organisations. It absorbs resources in both direct and indirect (management) activity. It is possible, if not probable, that the cost possibly outweighs the benefit when the 'cost' to the customer, whose life is still peppered with multiple visits from multiple agencies, is taken into account. Overall, this coordinated approach should be some degrees better than an uncoordinated one, but it is customer inefficient. Designed from the perspective of the provider, not the consumer, it may have an element of self-protection for those providers built into it, 'we all worked together and did our best'.

Perhaps, it is time to really challenge what the process and organisations should look like. If we design the service delivery backwards from the customer and to deal with the full range of demands, we would be sure to develop a single 'touch point'. That is a point at which the state as provider connects with the customer as consumer and which acts as the focus for all of their interactions. That means that customer 'demand' would pull through the system those services and interactions needed (and yes, some people will always need support to identify when they require help). The internal processes, decision systems and hierarchies would exist only to enable the continuing interaction, not to 'manage' or 'control' it – and certainly not to 'ration' the service or add it to the 'postcode lottery'. The key to 'better' for the majority of clients perhaps rests in three dimensions:

- Processes aligned to deliver the customer outcomes – efficiently for both parties;
- Effective capture and use of information – about the customer, the process and its control;

• Adoption of an organisational form in which process improvement, expressed in terms of customer outcome and fulfilment of purpose, is embedded.

Much reform, in both the private and public sectors, fails because it attempts to overlay process on a functional structure rather than replacing it. The upshot is that cost is added and effectiveness is reduced because more of the resources of the organisation are devoted to managing itself. Our desire should be that state organisations be (or become) Intelligent Organisations. If levied taxes, in all forms, fund value-enabling activities at the national and local levels, then each and every such organisation should seek to fulfil its purpose at the lowest possible cost. The 'savings' can be applied to value-generating activity, and that means as with any organisation, to sustainably do more with less. While the absolute costs of provision of state services may increase as a function of population, it should be managed in a manner that continually seeks to meet the desired customer outcome while lowering the cost per transaction.

## Organisational inertia

We have already established that very large organisations are difficult, if not impossible, to communicate through and with. Functional hierarchies and centralisation of control compound the problem, yet that is how many state organisations are arranged.

Long-established institutional structures also mean that such organisations are often unconsciously profligate. That is, rooted in Weberian bureaucracy, legitimate 'rational–legal' authority (Pugh & Hickson, 1989), they have no mechanism by which they can be conscious of waste. Waste, or inefficiency, is embedded in the interfaces between long-established procedures in such a manner as to be invisible. Managed essentially the way they have been managed for 100 years or more, they are bureaucratic (in the pejorative sense), fragmented, siloed – and might be considered as 'suprahumanly autopoietic' (Robb, 1989) – beyond human control. In extreme cases, because they have an undefined or unclear sense of 'purpose' (why they exist), they are driven by 'what' and 'how', they become administratively focused. Such organisations will typically not only fail to deliver the customer outcomes that they could, they also fail to get the best from the people they employ, the processes they utilise and the information systems they procure. Their costs, embedded in the inefficiency of historic structures, cannot even be meaningfully identified, let alone reduced. This is, of course, not a new phenomenon. For the history buffs, take a look at the diaries of Samuel Pepys (Latham & Williams, 1978).

Whilst there has been much change in recent years, that change has essentially been delivered within the established model of organisation. It is likely therefore that if or when the pressure for change is relieved or there is a change of political will, then the 'system', paradigm unchallenged, will revert to its previous state; that is, the organisation will revert to the pursuit of its own ends (pathological autopoiesis) and as a result the costs will grow and services will deteriorate. Unless we act to change the underlying process, the system behaviour will reassert itself.

A recent and very personal story might let us see what we can learn. This story is not a critique of individuals, who all did their best within the constraints of the system, or of the clinical process itself, which clearly worked, but to illustrate the potential for improvement that could arise from more effective use of information.

## I waited . . .

*Experiencing severe gastric discomfort, I contacted the National Health Service (NHS) Helpline at around 4:00 in the morning. The call centre operator asked a series of scripted questions and could be heard writing down the answers. He asked me to wait and could be heard typing those answers.*

*I waited for transfer to a paramedic who could 'give advice'.*

*The paramedic repeated the script, wrote down the answers, asked me to wait and again was heard typing those answers. The 'advice' given was to carry on doing what I had been doing for the previous 48 hours (it doesn't do to call in too much of a hurry). There was no benefit.*

*Around 8 am, feeling worse, we sought an emergency appointment with the GP. Seen within 40 minutes from the start of the telephone call (good!), the GP repeated the essential 'script' used by the helpline operator, accompanied by a little prodding and poking, wrote down the answers and diagnosed the problem as being, probably, gallstones. I waited, he typed.*

*He contacted the hospital and spoke to a surgeon, outlined the symptoms and his diagnosis (I could not hear the surgeon's end of the conversation but imagined him writing and then typing). Immediate emergency admission was agreed. I waited, he typed.*

*Arriving at A&E as instructed, I presented the letter from the GP, provided my name, address and symptoms and took a seat. I waited.*

*After waiting some time I was taken into the 'triage' area. The nurse followed the script (fourth person, same questions), writing the answers down on a scrap of paper. I waited, he typed.*

*Asked whether he had read the letter from the GP, he had not. I suggested that it might be helpful, he replied that he had to follow process. Standard clinical observations were taken, my blood pressure was at this point dangerously high – though whether that was caused by the illness or the process I cannot now say.*

*I waited.*

*Sent to the 'clinical decision unit' (CDU), I waited. The CDU doctor followed the same script. I was now fully confident in my answers and yes, 'it is worse now than before'. Answers were written down. I waited, he typed.*

*Handed over from CDU to a surgical team, same script, same answers, written down. I waited, he typed.*

*Actions now; pain relief; ultrasound scan. Late afternoon, I was informed that I would indeed be admitted 'as soon as a bed is available' and that I would require surgery. I waited.*

*Eventually, around 6 pm, I was admitted. Same questions, same answers, written down. I waited, he typed.*

*Left until the surgeon arrived. I waited.*

*Whilst waiting, some critical procedures had to be followed; check for MRSA, regular observations of blood pressure, temperature and so on. The MRSA check never got completed, the staff member was called away, the daily injection, 'to reduce the risk of blood clots through immobility', was delivered only on day one. I waited.*

*Observations ('obs') were taken (6 times per day), but no member of staff ever completed one patient before being pulled away to do something else. On each occasion, the results of the 'obs' were written on a scrap of paper, shoved in a uniform pocket and, presumably, added to a patient record at some later time. Were they added to my record or somebody else's?*

*Pain relieved, I was well enough to observe what was happening around me. Most obviously, the two senior nursing staff seemed to be spending all of their time negotiating with other parts of the hospital over admission and discharge of patients.*

*Operated on late on the second day (things had gotten a little more urgent!)*

*I was then discharged by the surgeon on the third morning at around 9 o'clock.*

*I waited, somebody typed. Mid-afternoon the 'discharge letter' was completed and the necessary medicines had been ordered from and delivered by the hospital pharmacy.*

What can we learn from this?

I repeat, this was a clinically effective process leading to complete and rapid recovery. The staff were excellent. Organisationally and informationally, it was not so effective. The functional orientation of the NHS generated:

- two organisational handovers – helpline, GP, hospital;
- four clinical handovers – operator, paramedic, A&E, CDU, surgeon;
- seven 'data capture' sessions, each one duplicated;
- data stored but not, seemingly, used.

The processes were 'production–push' not 'consumption–pull' and apparently optimised to the functional unit target, not the patient outcome. There appeared to be no ability to use the data and convert it into information to support the process delivery *or* either clinical or operational decision making. The inability to generate information and use it to close the process loops means that there is no mechanism for organisational learning. The system is unconsciously profligate with no mechanism for realising or changing that.

This experience suggests an organisation designed from the head down, not the bottom up, from the producer forwards rather than the customer backwards. Its 'production–push' focus guarantees both that there is waste (delay) in the system and that much of the cost (time, money, health) is borne by the patient. While each individual part of the process may be internally efficient when we look at the whole system and include the waiting time and other costs imparted to the patient (waste), then we must conclude that the overall process (a transformation of a sick person into a well person perhaps) is systemically inefficient. The functional form of the organisation, coupled to the institutional and legal boundaries to each, ensure that the process cannot be efficient, effective or adaptive. Failure has been built in.

The public sector is not alone in exporting process inefficiency to its customers. Supermarkets and other retailers use 'self-scan' tills, ostensibly as a means of reducing queuing with the beneficial effect (for them) of outsourcing the cost of labour to the customer. They have not reduced waste in the system or its overall cost, they have simply displaced some elements of it to the customer. Online retailers, in some cases, offer 'low-cost' delivery by providing collection points in local shops or other areas. Again, they have not reduced the cost, they have displaced it so that it is now borne by the customer in terms of time.

Perhaps the salvation of the NHS and the desire for reform for other public services would be achieved by them being managed as Intelligent Organisations, instead of being major employers of good staff let down by a bad system they are powerless to change.

## Information systems

It is always comical when, following some failure or another (it matters not what, the list is endless), a minister of the state is reported in the press, usually apologising and pronouncing that 'lessons will be learned'. Well, guess what? They won't. Lessons often cannot be learned, or where they might be learned they cannot be implemented. The institutional structures and the information systems (or lack of them) get in the way. If the information systems are not designed to enable and support learning (by both individuals and the organisation), and the system of incentives acts to keep things the same, then the only sure bet is that another, very similar, failure will happen in the future.

Reviewing this chapter just before submission, I pondered the continued relevance of the opening quote and the previous paragraph. Then, in March 2015, the UK government announced another failed IT project (payments to farmers) after spending £150m or thereabouts!

Nothing here should suggest that public sector organisations have not attempted to change. There are examples of successful investment in information systems which have delivered significant gains. Though it probably pains any UK taxpayer to say so, the changes in HMRC (tax collection) systems over recent years have indeed made the process of paying our taxes much simpler and more transparent, even if not entirely painless. So, it can be done.

However, this short list of examples and their financial scale demonstrate the point being made here:

- C-Nomis (National Offender Management Information System), budget £234m, spent £700m, abandoned;
- NHS National IT Programme, budget £2.3bn, spent £12.4bn, dismantled;
- National Identity Card Scheme, estimated cost £5.4bn, scrapped on repeal of act of parliament.

I could go on, but I won't.

We appear always to be trying to solve process and information problems with technology solutions. That is bound to fail. If we are to revolutionise public services then as information-hungry, information-driven organisations, we need to get the basic things right. I do believe that effective investment in information is the best way to transform public services in any country. But 'effective' is the key. If the investments are to be effective then we cannot make them, or make them work, without understanding:

- The needs and wants of the citizens that the services address;
- The purpose of the particular public service, the outcomes required;
- The decisions that need to be made *and* the information required to make them;
- The processes, tasks, procedures, skills and behaviours that are required to fulfil the purpose;
- The data structure necessary to underpin decisions, processes, tasks and procedures;
- The mapping of the informational and organisational architectures;
- How to separate the information structure (which like the organisation is semi-fixed) from the variable data that flow through it.

We cannot do that within the existing, centralising, functional structures. We must change the system!

## Public sector: revolution

It may be that public sector organisations are trapped in 'managing the present' because there is no mechanism, internal to them, through which they can 'create the future', because those decisions are reserved to others. Good people are doing their best despite the system, rather than because of it. There is substantial pressure, driven by 'austerity measures' (or their local equivalent) to 'do more with less' and that translates, most often, into reducing the number of hierarchical levels, consolidation of small units into larger ones, outsourcing of some elements and reduced numbers of staff working harder to produce the same outputs. Some of which might be reasonable, much of which might not.

When . . .

- A chief constable announces that his force will be bankrupt in three years;
- A local authority reduces the frequency of bin emptying;
- An ambulance service, sanctioned by government, reclassifies types of emergency so that it achieves targets;
- A railway decrees that a train is 'on time' as long as it is no more than ten minutes late;
- A health authority 'rations' one treatment and records a surplus on another;

. . . then something is wrong, the attention of the organisation is focused on itself, not its customers. The system reports better performance while the service gets worse.

Effective change requires a customer-oriented, structural, processual, informational and behavioural revolution. We must learn to do the right thing right, not the wrong thing better.

What is needed to drive public sector transformation is not an improved version of 'what is' but a coherent vision of 'what could be'. Managers and leaders must not continue to be imprisoned in an inadequate 'MoS' that simply delivers budget cuts (compliance to procedure) but liberated into thinking about what is possible, about realising the potential of the organisation in terms that meet the outcomes for customers.

In the absence of a guiding mind from government, the leaders of the various organisations must develop that vision of what could be, propose it as the way forward and then make it happen. This will require government to liberate these leaders to become active co-creators of the future rather than passive administrators. While it may be thought that ministers hold the power, they can only make choices about 'what' between the options that they are presented with by their party or by policy advisers. The 'how' is in the gift of the public administration, and that is where the opportunity for change resides. Government must decide, with the electorate, whether to provide a particular service and how much of it there will be. Public servants can determine how and how well it is done.

Public services are always, at the organisational level, value enabling. They are there to let the rest of the country function – its commerce, utilities, enterprise and so on. Internally, though, they are split like any other organisation. They have elements which are value generating, that deliver current services to current customers to meet current outcomes. Some are focused on value enabling, supporting the provision of current services, developing future services and products, preparing things for tomorrow and enabling national adaptation to changes in the world. Whole functions of government must be reorganised to reflect this and, it may be that in considering this, the functional split of public services needs to be challenged. There might be more effective ways of organising public service to be both more effective and more efficient. In the UK, the consolidation of HM Inland Revenue and HM Customs into HM Revenue and Customs appears to have delivered such benefits. Work is going on in 2015 to integrate some aspects of health and social care provision at both national and local levels. Perhaps there is scope for more?

## Summary

This chapter has looked briefly at some particular challenges faced by public sector organisations, considering in particular their freedom to act, clarity (and breadth) of purpose, their structures and the ways in which information is, and could be, used. The potential for change has been highlighted.

It is difficult, in the abstract, to say how much might be gained in performance. My hospital experience suggests that, simply by eradicating duplication of data capture and enhancing information provision, a change of the order of 20% could be achieved. That is, if data were captured once and only verified (not repeated) on a clinical handover, we would save each individual 20% or thereabouts of their work. That benefit would be amplified by reductions in delays; information being more readily available, decisions could be made more quickly. Transmission (or sharing) of data between clinical functions would also reduce delays (waste), as documents would no longer need to be transported. Savings would start to arise in other parts of the system in consequence. Seddon (2005, 2008) frequently refers to 'waste' in the public sector and provides examples. His case studies are well worth reading, rooted as they are in a systemic approach to reform. He gives this example (2005):

> he estimated he and his staff spent only 40% of their time organizing services for drug users – the rest of their time was consumed by producing paper plans and reports for Whitehall.

Some public services are 'pure' information processers (e.g. pensions, social security), others use information to drive processes (e.g. clinical decision making), but *all* must become Intelligent Organisations. They must examine the interaction of their structures, processes, behaviours and information, challenge established practices and synthesise a whole new way of being. That is how they will, sustainably, do more with less.

# 14

# DISSOLVING THE CHALLENGE

There is nothing more difficult to carry out, nor more doubtful of success, nor more dangerous to handle, than to initiate a new order of things.

Machiavelli, *The Prince* (1513)

## Introduction

The Intelligent Organisation is an idealised way of thinking about how we should manage organisations today. Pursuing this ideal is not about achieving a finite end. It is instead about creating a set of organisational conditions, structural, informational and behavioural, which allow and enable the continual evolution of the organisation in concert with its environment and particularly its current and future customers. The thinking is nonconformist, even heretical (even if it now looks like common sense to you and me). So, if you decide to pursue it, don't expect to be popular or be given an easy time!

This chapter shows how to apply the thinking to your own organisation or one you know well. I suggest you have a pad and pen handy to capture your thoughts and ideas. Thinking about a specific organisation will help to make the ideas real for you, my words are necessarily abstract. You will certainly find it helpful to refer back to some of the diagrams in previous chapters and adopt those conventions to help you think and sketch your own organisation.

The chapter presents the methodology as an iterative process, a homeostat, from which the desired outcome is changes in the state of your knowledge about the organisation. The essential, simple cycle sits at the centre of Figure 14.1 and is described as:

- Exploration:  collecting data about the organisation;
- Synthesis:  collating that data into an overall understanding;
- Comparison:  comparing that with the principles of the Intelligent Organisation.

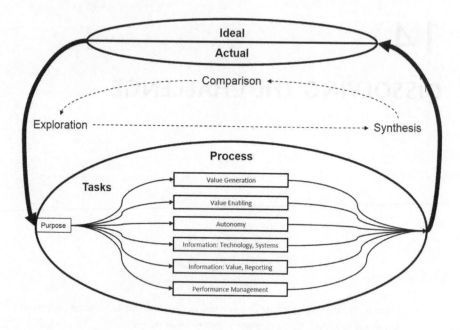

**FIGURE 14.1** Diagnostic process

Note please that I use the word 'synthesis' rather than 'analysis'. Analysis is concerned with the separation of things into their constituent elements; it breaks them down. Synthesis is concerned with their integration, the combination of elements and their interactions from which something new, in this case the emergent understanding of your chosen organisation as intelligent (or not!), emerges. Only when a synthesis has been achieved is it appropriate to engage in detailed analytical work to design and deliver the desired changes. I have subsumed analysis into synthesis since it is that which creates the context that renders it meaningful.

Wrapped around the outside of that simple cycle is the fuller process of study which embraces all of the key aspects of the Intelligent Organisation. The aim is to compare what we find in our exploration of the organisation with the idealised model, the gap being the basis for change. We will use this model throughout the chapter to structure our work and classify the findings.

The intention is to stimulate your thinking. It will not lead you to an easy answer or a prescription, but to a more useful way of thinking about your organisation and how it might be better. That will be the measure of usefulness of the model.

## Engaging the organisation

Before we start that diagnostic process, a few words about engagement. I have chosen in writing to assume that you are, as is so often the case, working alone in the first instance. Perhaps worried about performance, maybe charged with delivering some project or other, maybe even intrigued by the art of the possible laid out for you. Whichever it may be, working alone will not suffice for the long term.

My experience of this approach with a variety of organisations around the world is that once the gaps and potential are understood and accepted, many of the challenges of Intelligent Organisation are dissolved. Shared knowledge, common understanding, a different way of thinking, disseminated throughout the organisation, changes the situation. Collective understanding is often a large part of any solution. Achieving that understanding necessitates authentic inclusion of people throughout the organisation, the involved population increasing as the dialogue evolves. It is vitally important, even if the process commences with a 1–2–1 discussion as it usually does, to rapidly move to an inclusive dialogue. These parties must include:

> those 'involved' (client, decision taker, designer) and those 'affected' but not involved (witnesses).
>
> *Flood and Jackson (1991) on Ulrich (1983)*

This inclusive dialogue matters for two reasons:

First, in order for the Intelligent Organisation to be survival worthy, the human actors who create its "collective consciousness" (Durkheim, 1893) through their interactions need to be in alignment with its espoused purpose and values. What better way is there to ensure this than to include those human actors in defining them? This does not mean the abandonment of the organisational goals and ideals to the crowd; it does not suggest an abdication of leadership by those in charge. It rather requires that leaders who wish to be effective must adopt a position and engage others in it. There must be a collective sharing of the purpose, goals, values and ideals of the organisation to minimise active resistance.

This is at heart pragmatic. People aligned with the organisational purpose and values are likely to be more highly motivated around the delivery of the desired outcome. People not aligned with them need to be given the opportunity to understand them and may then apply their individual autonomy to join in or not, possibly seeking work elsewhere. Nonaligned people remaining within the organisation and either actively or passively resisting its future will be damaging to themselves and their host; after all, to quote Benjamin Tucker:

> Passive resistance is the most potent weapon ever wielded by man.
>
> *Tucker (1887)*

The second reason is even more pragmatic. The people who populate the organisation know far more about what customer outcomes are required and how to deliver them than those in positions of management. Engaging them in the process of design just makes sense.

Rather than taking a 'big bang' approach, it is probably appropriate to develop engagement over time, so that as conversations evolve more people are participating.

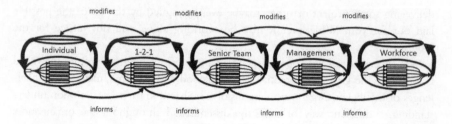

**FIGURE 14.2** Developing engagement

Assuming at each stage that a level of agreement is reached about the nature of the challenges, opportunities and emerging solutions, it could develop like this:

- Individual exploration;
- 1–2–1 discussion with a trusted colleague or two;
- Engagement of wider senior team;
- Engagement of management;
- Engagement of workforce.

That says nothing of the technical or analytical content of the work to be done, but whatever that technical content is, it needs ultimately to be exposed to, explored and tested with those who really know how the business works!

Simplifying, it may look a little like Figure 14.2.

So the conversations are progressively opened up to include others in the organisation, to expose the work already undertaken and the ideas developed genuinely test the thinking and engage that wider population in redefining both the questions and the answers. In a large organisation, this conversation is likely to include multiple groups in multiple locations.

## Global engagement

*In one organisation where this process was followed, an initial series of events with the Board was widened to the Regional Directors and their management teams and, when there was a general level of agreement about the diagnosis, the whole organisation, every member of staff, was involved in the discussion – a truly big conversation. Overall about 180 events were held and, at one stage, 42 identical events were held, one with every location individually to understand and explore what it meant just for them. This was a huge commitment, but when the attempt is being made to change the whole organisation globally, such commitment is rather important! The benefits of that investment have been clear in the subsequent performance turnaround achieved by the organisation, which has been both substantial and sustained over seven years.*

The word 'event' is chosen deliberately. These are not 'presentations' or 'show and tell' sales pitches, they are not and cannot be configured as 'meetings'. In the

Intelligent Organisation, wisdom is emerging from the crowd at least as much as it is descending from the 'C suite'. The events must be designed (specifically to each circumstance) to ask, explore and answer questions about the individuals and the organisation which will enable understanding of the challenges it faces and possible choices about its future. They are always work, they are usually enjoyable and they need to be managed to produce useful customer outcomes, which might be measured first in terms of engagement and action plans and second in terms of the change brought about in the organisation over time.

Ultimately, if we want to create a truly Intelligent Organisation, then the leaders and the led must be working in harmony towards a common purpose, and that implies shared values. That can only be achieved if everyone is genuinely engaged in and contributing towards it.

For every element that follows, capture the evidence! What is it you are finding, or being told, that gives you reassurance, or concerns you? Examine that evidence, use it to stimulate further questions. The Intelligent Organisation will be able to show that information is integral to everything, valued and valuable.

## Exploration, synthesis, comparison: the diagnostic process

Diagnosis lets you consider the challenges any organisation faces and understand the future it is currently in. A thorough diagnosis will also often indicate what might be done to improve things; the answers rest in asking the right questions, the challenge dissolves itself in the process.

The process essentially follows the pattern of the book, which is why it was written that way! So, where do we start? It is important to imagine that you are approaching the organisation for the first time, to see it afresh.

## Purpose

Now you can look at the organisation itself. Is there a clear sense of purpose? Can people articulate to you the reasons the organisation exists, the need or opportunity it seeks to fulfil (beyond the constraint of profit, surplus or budget)?

It is all too common when addressing this question that the response is expressed in terms of short-term outputs, the products or services. It is more helpful in diagnosis to think about it from the customer's perspective, because that helps to broaden organisational thinking about both short- and long-term success. For example, an oil company may define itself in terms of its products (and here I simplify again) of petrol and diesel, and in doing so lock its future into its past. If on the other hand it defines itself in terms of its customers' needs, it could conceive of itself as 'a provider of energy' because 'energy' is the need that is fulfilled, the specific product is not in the long term important. In making that choice, the oil company shows a greater understanding of its customer and, at the same time, opens itself up to new ways of fulfilling that need in the future, for example, in a low-carbon economy.

Identification of a clear understanding of the reason for the existence of the organisation, the need it exists to fulfil, expresses the 'why' that gives meaning to the 'what' and 'how' of the things that are done. That 'why' and the measurement of the achievement of the desired customer outcome gives the basis for thinking about effectiveness and efficiency. That in turn provides the basis for the provision of resources. After all, if the organisation has no clear statement of purpose, it cannot know whether it has sufficient resources or is applying them appropriately since it doesn't know what it is trying to do. Such a definition of purpose must, at least, be developed through an understanding of customers' needs, engagement of the workforce and agreement with the leadership. In the absence of a clear purpose, demand will always be infinite and the resources inadequate. Even in the case of what the marketing folk would characterise as a 'distress purchase', such as the payment of taxes or petrol for a car, defining the desired customer outcome (and including the customer in the process of definition) is critical.

The statement of purpose is not a 'mission statement' or a 'vision', it is a straightforward operational definition. This is important because such a definition will bound the organisation and its activities since, once agreed, it provides legitimacy for many other actions. For example, if we look at the railway purely as a railway then we might consider the purpose to be:

> to move people and goods to and from locations on the system.
>
> *Beckford and Dora, 2013 (webref 8)*

This definition codifies the aim, determines who/what the customer is (people and goods) and limits the range (locations on the system). In making this suggestion, and for absolute clarity, it is not one which has been discussed or agreed with the railway, we are limiting our purpose to the railway itself, we have no concern with the rest of the journey of the people or the goods beyond the 'locations'. So, our measure of effectiveness would be concerned with the success of the rail journey and our measure of efficiency would be the minimisation of the resources used:

> maximum benefit to travellers at the lowest cost.

Having settled the question of purpose, definitions of effectiveness and efficiency are embedded.

If we are only concerned with the rail element of the journey, then treating it just as a railway is relatively easy. However, if we think about this from the traveller's perspective, it can be considered inadequate. It is rare that the railway will provide the whole of a journey for a traveller. For most, the railway will be a single element in a journey, which might include walking, a flight, a car journey, a bus or a bicycle. So, if we are looking at this from the perspective of the traveller, or the government (as representing the sociopolitical level of governance), then our definition must be richer – we must embrace the customer outcome, which is a completed journey. The railway definition then sits inside something more abstract – the 'journey process' which is made up of all the possible elements of any journey. The railway section is a 'task' within the journey 'process'.

So, the definition of purpose still works, but its performance must be measured both in terms of how well it contributes to the overall journey and how well it delivers the railway element. If this is to work for the traveller and not just the operator, it implies some serious thinking about modes of travel, integration of services, e.g. aligning bus and train timetables, colocation of termini and even integrated ticketing.

Beer (1985) argued that "the purpose of the system is what it does", so in making our diagnosis we need to identify the impacts that the organisation has on its customers and its environment, as well as recognise the intent of those who purport to own or manage the system. There is often a gap between the actual outcome and the intent and that provides the first opportunity for change.

## Generating value

A process ends with delivery of an outcome for the customer (typically by way of a product or service) and starts at the other end of the organisation. Typical value-generating processes include sales, manufacturing or assembly, service or customer support. You might like to consider whether these are appropriate ways of achieving customer outcomes and whether the process(es) as designed are capable of meeting them. It is critical in considering processes to follow them backwards to the start and not be limited by functional or organisational boundaries. While this may be relatively simple for some organisations, it is more difficult for others. As you pursue this thinking in your target organisation, try sketching the high-level processes (and their embedded tasks) and use them to visualise how things fit together (or don't). If they can be made available, it is worth reviewing the organisation charts, they will allow you to understand how the organisation fits to the processes.

If we take the paper mills that we reviewed in earlier parts of the book, then they have a simple process running backwards from new paper through conversion and production to raw materials. A motor dealership probably does two things that deliver customer outcomes: 'sell cars' and 'service cars'. At the process level, these can be seen as available to all customers, though there is of course a difference of timing and, critically, both contribute to the same customer outcome and, arguably, to the success of the dealership through retained customers. A police force perhaps has two processes: prevention of harm and crime and the detection and arrest of criminals. This is interesting, because the better they are at the first, the less they will have to do of the second. If we compare the functional organisation of a police force with these two suggested processes, I wonder if they would align?

This gets more difficult again if we shift our attention to larger and more complex organisations. Perhaps your desired customer outcome is 'propulsion' and your organisation, being an international conglomerate, has processes that run backwards through manufacturing and design to raw materials extraction. Clearly it would be difficult to manage this as a single process, so, having defined its existence, it is then useful to break it down into manageable process segments (what we called tasks earlier in the book). In this case you need to consider how these segments align with each other. Is there, organisationally, a clear process being followed (joined up by information systems)? Is somebody, somewhere, managing and balancing the whole process or are they functionally split so that each can separately claim success (or not)? How do the 'handovers' between elements of the process work? Do they work?

Similarly, your organisation may address the same customer need but in multiple locations (branches, shops, countries). The process is supposedly the same everywhere (think fast food), but it is not a single instance, it is many instances of the same thing replicated. Again, it cannot be managed as a single process, so how is it broken down? Should it be by geography, market, customer or product? For banking customers it may be by type of customer (high net worth, mass market, small business, big business) or some combination of these.

Here we are trying to understand whether things are organised in such a way that the individuals responsible for a process have been provided with the information, skills, knowledge and, importantly, authority to both manage current performance and locally adapt it to its future. If any of these elements are absent or weak, then either the process will be failing in one or more ways or the higher order management will be compensating by intervening more than should be necessary.

It is often the case that 'senior' managers feel the need to intervene – it is useful at this point to understand why. It is often characterised as reflecting the inadequacy of the process manager but, upon examination, it is often found to be an inadequacy of some aspect of the overall process design.

If there are chains of activity in the value-generating process, then it is also necessary to look (consider the task and process levels of Figure 3.6) at the same questions for each point where there is a horizontal (procedure to procedure or task to task) or vertical (when control shifts across the levels) handover.

Consider the way the organisation is presented particularly by the organisation charts. Is it internally, functionally arranged to be easy to control, designed from the head downwards, or is it focused on the customer? It is always a good test to ask someone to describe or draw the organisation. If they start with the Chief Executive and work downwards, then you can be pretty sure that the organisation is internally focused. Listening to the people in the organisation is good throughout. How is their language focused – is it expressed in terms of customer needs and outcomes or on internal compliance to process and task? Are they looking at outputs or outcomes?

Even with a functional organisation, does it make sense? Consider whether there is a clear identification and separation of value-generating activity from value-enabling activity or does it all appear to be mixed in together?

When considering the core value-generating processes (and there may well be more than one of them), ask how the organisation delivers value to customers. Is it clear that there is a process that does that or are there a series of functional steps, separately managed in their vertical silos with all the implications of hand-overs, delays and, potentially, waste? It is worth looking at a process performance report if such a thing exists. Is it integrated, covering multiple aspects of performance, or are there a series of separate, functional reports which, added together by the manager, make up the overall view?

Identify what is the lowest level at which 'process decisions' can be brought together. A clue here – if it is at director or head of function level, or worse, CEO level, then the organisation is not oriented towards its customer but towards itself. Think then about what that tells you of decision making and autonomy. If routine decisions are being made high up the organisational tree, then autonomy is necessarily limited at lower levels. Does that suggest something about the directors? Are they all people with enormous brains and infinite capacity for work? If not, then they are probably being overworked if not overwhelmed, decision power may be too remote from the value-generating process. Consider what impact that may be having on the customers.

## Enabling value

The logic of the value-enabling processes is the same as that of the value-generating processes; identify the customer (in this case the value-generating processes) and consider whether the outcome achieved supports them appropriately. If not, then there is a fundamental problem. You need to consider all aspects of the value-enabling process, including the understanding of the desired outcome, the process design itself (Is it capable of delivering the outcome?), the skills, knowledge and behaviours of the relevant workforce and the information provision. If any one of those elements is misaligned or inappropriate, it compromises the performance of the whole.

Typical value-enabling processes include Human Resources, Finance, Information Services, Technology, Systems, Procurement, Property, Quality, Health and Safety and so on. They are often clustered (IT and Procurement with Finance, for example) and are most usually managed functionally rather than in an integrated manner.

There are some processes which can be interpreted either as value generating or value enabling. A good example of this can be found in the supply chain, e.g. the provision of materials into a manufacturing flow. The determination of where to place them rests on a couple of criteria. The first is to consider the extent to which the supply chain is integrated (organisationally and informationally) to the value-generating process flow itself. If the organisation is operating a 'just-in-time' fully integrated model, then most benefit will be obtained from treating the supply chain as part of the value-generating activity. If on the other hand the flows are disaggregated, i.e. there is a need for a storage or warehousing phase or the process demand on the supply chain is stochastic or random, then most benefit might be obtained from dealing with them separately. The second is to consider whether the enabling process is, at least in principle, capable of independent existence, i.e. it could be, or be provided by, another completely separate organisation. Here we might think about plant maintenance as an example. While the plant itself must be maintained in order for the value-generating process to be sustained, there are genuine choices to be made about whether that maintenance is undertaken within the value-generating suite of activities or within value enabling. This is an area where both synthesis and analysis are useful. Analysis might suggest that greater efficiency can be obtained from treating this as a supplier, a value-enabling activity that can be, in effect, bought in. This of course assumes that the needs can be specified in a form that will ensure that every need is met; that is only possible in an 'output' orientation, not one focused on 'outcomes'. Integrating maintenance, on the other hand, while offering an approach much more likely to be flexible in meeting changing needs, has the disadvantage that some degree of clarity is lost. It may be less efficient but more effective. This challenge does need some thinking about!

Enabling processes also look outward into the unknown and problematic future, see for example Figure 5.3, so further questions apply. We need to look at the extent to which, if at all, the enabling processes investigate the problematic environment of the organisation, comprehend the challenges and opportunities surrounding it (in relation to all of the enabling processes already mentioned, but also including product development, marketing, people development and so on). It is not enough in our Intelligent Organisation to be looking inwards and improving, we need to be looking outwards and learning. So, we need to find out whether future-oriented work is being undertaken in a systematic, ordered and thoughtful manner which is offering new opportunities for the future or, if it happens at all, is it mainly reactive to adverse events either in the wider environment or the organisation itself. It is useful at this point to unearth some of the myths and stories that pervade the atmosphere of every organisation; these tell us much about 'the way things are done around here'!

We also need to understand how the organisation brings together information from the 'outward-looking' enabling process and the 'inward-looking' enabling process into a dialogue in which decisions can be made about things to do in the future. Is that being done with a sense of integration of the 'whole system' or are partial or functional decisions being made which optimise one element while damaging another? We should be asking what the mechanisms are by which these conversations happen, if they happen at all, and how the implications of one with another are understood and resolved. In a perfect world, we will of course find an ongoing and coherent conversation about the whole future as the basis of all decision making. We are more likely to find presentation of functionally oriented business cases to Boards and/or Executive teams, in which proposals compete for time and money (winners and losers) rather than complement for enhanced effectiveness. Lots of analysis will have been done, but no synthesis.

If value-enabling work is being well done and brought to bear properly, then there will be tensions between 'managing the present' and 'creating the future'. If these tensions are present, we need to establish whether they are being resolved by reference back to our starting point, the definition of purpose. If not present, then how are tensions resolved? The trialogue, Figure 5.5, is the mechanism by which this conversation ought to be taking place. If it is not, then you need to determine how it *is* being done.

This requires a considered view of how the organisation actually makes these sorts of decisions. Indeed, it might require you to consider whether it does before you can think about how. The common responses to these questions are that the only point at which the whole organisation comes together as a coherent whole is in the board meeting, that the tensions are not actively managed and that measurement of performance is all about short-term financial results and has little, if anything, to do with long-term sustainability.

Looking at the enabling activities. A note of caution here, sometimes they don't exist (or not in a meaningful way). In some organisations they will have been isolated into Head Office departments or projects and will hand down tablets of 'strategy' to the masses. In others they may have been lost altogether into a focus on short-term incremental improvement (this is relatively common). In yet others, there may be a segmentation of value-enabling activity into 'operational' and 'strategic' elements and they are not joined together. You should seek to determine whether the organisation has a specified strategy both corporately and for individual elements and assess whether it is aligned around delivering it. It is common to find that one half will be battling hard to deliver today while the other will be wondering why nobody is listening or acting! How does it all come together – the present, the future and the purpose in a single, multi-party conversation about resolving the tension between the present and the future? In most organisations, it doesn't.

## Autonomy

That can lead us back to look at how autonomy is being managed. Is it being managed, or is there just an embedded, historically driven 'scheme of delegation' which acts as its proxy? A scheme of delegation is important, but it also has to be meaningful.

This needs to be considered in the context of the decision points in the structure – do they align? Are they consistent? Are too many requests for permission being passed up and down the command chain (particularly where they cross functional boundaries) or, alternatively, is too much local action being taken either despite the rules or in the absence of any?

It is rare to find in any organisation that a deliberate and conscious decision has been made about levels of autonomy other than in relation to delegation of financial decision making (and it is common to find with finance that the cash sums are small). It is worth investigating the extent to which this has been thought about and to determine the real scope of autonomy and whether that is understood.

## Practical autonomy and invisible outcome

*In one organisation I considered, a particular individual had signing authority for cash disbursements up to £500 – a reasonable but modest sum which allowed for local purchases of essential material supplies. However, his practical autonomy, the real difference he could make to the organisation, rested in his ability to decide other things. In the particular instance, as a Health & Safety Manager, he was responsible for determining the frequency of refresh training for a number of key processes (manual handling, working at heights, safe methods of working) in an organisation where process failure could easily kill. In reviewing this he had determined, without reference to anyone else, that the frequency of refresh training should be doubled, i.e. that each individual should attend a half-day workshop on each topic twice per annum instead of once. The implication of that was a doubling of the amount of training to be provided, a doubling of the backfill required to ensure that work was completed and a commensurate increase in overtime working to compensate. The 'cash cost' of the decision was around £250k per annum, some 500 times his signing authority for expenditure. I cannot say whether his judgement was right or wrong; I can say that his decision was made without any assessment of the financial consequences (or any other organisational consequences, e.g. disrupted shift patterns) of the proposed change and without reference to the legal and regulatory requirements with which his particular organisation was bound to comply.*

This is but one of many instances where autonomy may be inappropriately used. It is far more common to find that it is unnecessarily constrained. Consider using the framework for autonomy provided in Chapter 7 as the basis of assessing this aspect.

## Information: technology and systems

The next area for consideration is the information systems and technology, that is, the software applications and the hardware employed by the organisation. You need to determine first whether these are consistent with the orientation of the organisation – functionally oriented organisations usually have functionally oriented IT! The real challenge arises when one is functionally oriented and the other process oriented. If that is the case, then how does the organisation join it all together? It may be done through a 'business warehouse' or 'business intelligence' application; more likely it is done by individuals using spreadsheets. It is important to grasp how this is done and to understand the consequences for workload, cost and decision integrity (if the information is badly put together, what consequences are there for decisions taken using it?).

You should also at this point take a look at the technology hardware. Does it appear to be consistent with the needs of the users? Do people complain about their various devices? About the speed of response of the systems? Is the hardware in use compatible with the way that the processes need to be operated or does it either get in the way (people have invented workarounds) or does it make things simple and easy for them? Again, a good source of information is to enquire about recent information system and technology projects in the organisation. How did they go? Do people have better information as a result of them and therefore find it easier to do their jobs or are they simply following the old process on a new machine? That is *not* to say that new machines are always a bad idea, far from it, but what you are trying to understand is what information benefit is being achieved from the investments. Information provision is the point of the systems and the hardware.

A further test is that of data integrity. Does every application that uses a particular data set share it or are there multiple versions of the truth? Are there multiple applications dedicated to carrying out similar activities (or separate aspects of the same activity)? How is the data brought together? Are there different ways of measuring or characterising something depending on who is using it and for what purpose – and if there are, do those differences make sense? Is each complete and accurate in its own right or are there evident weaknesses? How is information provided and brought together in a coherent manner to inform decisions? Is it brought together in that way?

## Information: value and reporting

This is a critical area.

Given that information, the way it is captured, stored and utilised, generates the potential opportunity for becoming an Intelligent Organisation, you need to consider whether the information systems are fully aligned and integrated to the organisational processes. Or do they sit alongside them, useful, but not fully embedded? Ask about the last two or three information system projects, were they technically biased, organisationally biased or informationally biased? In preparing this chapter, I asked a group of Masters students about the most recent information systems projects in their nine separate organisations. Every one of them had delivered a 'technology' improvement, none had delivered any information benefit.

Given the answers to those first questions, explore how information is valued by the organisation. Does it recognise it as having value in its own right? Does it, or has it, explicitly made an issue of exploiting the value of its information *and* accounted for value realisation in any change or improvement projects it has undertaken? Is there an understanding or appreciation of the value of the information they hold and how it is exploited by the business? Ask someone to demonstrate that value and how it has been or is being realised.

Now we can consider the outputs of the system – and here we should avoid being sucked into particular parts or technology or applications. A helpful starting point is to gain sight of the last set of management reports. Are you presented with a neat set of management accounts, perhaps accompanied by output reports from each function (HR, Safety, Operations, Sales, Production) or a set which are customer process oriented and integrated, dealing with all aspects of the process and addressing the customer outcomes? Are customers represented as a 'nuisance' or the whole reason the organisation exists? I know which is most likely. If you found a functionally oriented organisation chart, it is highly likely you will get functionally oriented reports. Ask how the reports are compiled. Are they produced in a single operation from a single source or are they formulated in freeform documents in which the data has, in effect, become unstructured because it is embedded in the story telling? The evidence builds, it demonstrates a consistent picture.

## Performance management

Finally, although you probably know the answer by now because you have seen the reports, have a look at how performance is being managed. Is it aggregated into an overall view of process performance or presented in separate, functionally oriented reports? Is it backward looking and reactive or forward looking and pre-emptive? Consider, if you can, the agenda for any management meeting, or take a look at the minutes of the last one. What was the focus of concern, was it explanation of the past or preparation for the future? If both, where was the balance of attention? How was information about past performance used to help think about and understand performance in the future?

A common finding is that decisions are, primarily, made using only the financial data and it is that for which individuals are held to account. However, as has been suggested earlier in the book, financial outcomes are a consequence of other activities, so it is important to find out how those other activities are included in the dialogue. It is not uncommon to find that they are not.

## Synthesis

While that is necessarily a quick romp through the exploration, your version should be much richer in data than mine! The exploration element of the diagnosis is roughly complete at this point. Enough can be known through the questions asked (and all the others that will fall out of asking them) to be able to offer a prognosis of the future of the organisation. I cannot speak for your particular example, but in all those I have looked at, there has always been a substantial gap between where they are and where they could be – and that gap has always contained more than enough value to compensate for the cost of closing it.

It is usually most helpful as you complete the first iteration to line up your thoughts around a few themes. In each case, adopt a position *and* have reasons:

• Is the business orientated to itself or its customer?
• Is it managed functionally or through its processes?
• Is the language used internally or externally focused?

- Is information provision considered in terms of its cost or its value?
- Is information functionally segregated or integrated with processes?
- Is control centralised or distributed?
- What is the focus of management? Is it biased towards fixing the past or creating the future?

Some of your views will be subjective, but much will be evidenced by the things you have found out on the way through.

Compare your findings with the idealised Intelligent Organisation in all its aspects and reflect on the gap (if any!). You have enough information to determine whether or not the organisation responds to those principles and, if it doesn't, you have a good initial idea of the opportunity. Essentially, and being deliberately extreme, you should be able to make one of two statements:

> This is an organisation whose people and processes are customer oriented; it understands and exploits the value of integrated information and uses it to distribute control. It has a healthy balance of managing the present and creating the future and tensions are resolved through a strong sense of identity.
>
> Insert your evidence here . . .

Or

> This is an organisation whose people and functions are internally oriented; it regards information provision as a cost and seeks to minimise it to the detriment of effective decision making, with those decisions mainly made remotely from the customer. It is focused on the identification and rectification of past mistakes and as a consequence is prone to being overtaken by events.
>
> Insert your evidence here . . .

Most organisations will, of course, have elements of both. As you build the evidence base to support the assertion, it is ok to modify the overall thinking!

By understanding the dynamics of the situation as you perceive it and in the light of your knowledge of what could be, you should now be able to make a number of useful, evidence-based assertions about the future of the organisation.

## How would it be if . . .

Before you proceed to share your thoughts and findings with a colleague (or two), it is probably worth at least beginning to think about the future. It is one thing to be able to offer a critique of the current situation; it is another matter again to offer a way forward and your colleagues will respond more positively. Nobody likes to be told they are doing a bad job; most will enjoy a vivid picture of a better future.

Rooted in the critique you have just created, you can develop an initial vision of the future. Think about what success would look like and make that vivid, bring it to life with examples of things that would happen and of things that would no longer happen. Understand and express how it would address identified deficiencies and create new opportunities and, very importantly, begin to develop an idea of the financial consequences of the things that you think should change. But remember that there are consequences, products of change in other aspects of the organisation. The finances cannot be delivered without the process, behavioural, structural and informational changes that enable them.

Think also about how you will engage people. How will you share your concerns and explore theirs? How will you validate your work so far, how will you challenge 'the way we do things round here' and develop a robust business case for change? What do you believe will (or should) be the hard and soft benefits and how will they be achieved?

For me, the opportunity for most organisations is immense, but so is the challenge!

## Conclusion

These same questions drive each iteration of the engagement methodology. They are the key substance of the events and can be asked at every organisational level (whole organisation, process, task, procedure) and with every level of employee. So, whether we are considering the whole organisation, one process, factory or unit, or looking at an individual part or single employee, we have a language and process for diagnosis.

As you progress through the cycles of investigation, the detail underpinning each element should become clearer. However, it is important to realise in undertaking this process of enquiry that simply by asking the questions we have influenced the organisation.

I like to imagine an organisation existing in a state of Zen-like calm. Reality will be that the co-evolution of the organisational environment and the organisation itself must be dynamic and that those of us charged with managing must learn to deal with that dynamism. We are not, though, victims of circumstance. By taking responsibility for leadership, by understanding and holding to the purpose of the organisation, by active management to anticipate, provoke and guide the response to external changes, we can evolve towards Intelligent Organisation.

# REFERENCES

Ackoff, R.L., 1981. *Creating the corporate future*. New York: Wiley.

Ansoff, I., 1987. *Corporate strategy*. London: Penguin.

Ashby, W.R., 1952. *Design for a brain*. London: Chapman Hall.

Beckford, J., 1993. *The viable system model: A more adequate tool for practising management?* Ph.D. Thesis, The University of Hull, UK.

Beckford, J., 2010. *Quality*. 3rd ed. London: Routledge.

Beer, S., 1959. *Cybernetics and management*. New York: Wiley.

Beer, S., 1966. *Decision and control*. Chichester, UK: Wiley.

Beer, S., 1974. *Designing freedom*. Chichester, UK: Wiley.

Beer, S., 1979. *The heart of enterprise*. Chichester, UK: Wiley.

Beer, S., 1981. *Brain of the firm*. Chichester, UK: Wiley.

Beer, S., 1985. *Diagnosing the system for organisations*. Chichester, UK: Wiley.

Beer, S., 1993. World in torment: A time whose idea must come. Presidential Address to the Triennial Conference of the World Organisation of Systems and Cybernetics, New Delhi, India.

Bender, R. and Ward, K., 2008. *Corporate financial strategy*. 3rd ed. Oxford: Elsevier Butterworth-Heinemman.

Beynon-Davies, P., 2013. *Business information systems*. London: Palgrave MacMillan.

Borges, J.L., 1962. The Library of Babel in *Labyrinths*. Translated by D.A. Yates and J.E. Irby. New York: New Directions.

Box, G.E.P., 1979. Robustness in the strategy of scientific model building. In: R.L. Launer and G.N. Wilkinson, eds. *Robustness in statistics: Proceedings of a workshop*. New York: Academic Press. pp. 201–236.

Brynjolfsson, E. and McAfee, A., 2014. *The second machine age*. New York: Norton.

Carr, N., 2003. IT doesn't matter. *Harvard Business Review*, 81(5).

Checkland, P.B., 1981. *Systems thinking, systems practice*. Chichester, UK: Wiley.

Conant, R.C. and Ashby, W.R., 1970. Every good regulator of a system must be a model of that system. *International Journal of Systems Science*, 1(2), pp. 89–97.

Deming, W.E., 1986. *Out of the crisis*. Cambridge, UK: The Press Syndicate.

Dennis, P., 2007. *Lean production simplified*. New York: Productivity Press.

Drucker, P., 1969. *The age of discontinuity*. London: Heinemann.

Drucker, P., 1986. *Innovation and entrepreneurship*. London: Pan Books.

Dudley, P., 2000. *'Quality management or management quality?' An adaptive model of organisation as the basis of organisational learning and quality provision*. PhD Thesis, The University of Hull, UK.

Durkheim, E., 1893. *Division of labour in society*. Translated by W.D. Halls, 1997. New York: Free Press.

Einstein, A. 1946. Atomic education urged by Einstein. *The New York Times*, 25th May.

Eliot, T.S., 1934. *The rock*. London: Faber and Faber.

Every time, 2011. *Daily Telegraph*, 30th September.

Fayol, H., 1916. *General and industrial management*. Translated by Constance Storrs, 1949. London: Pitman.

Feigenbaum, A.V., 1986. *Total quality control*. New York: McGraw-Hill.

Flood, R.L. and Jackson, M., 1991. *Creative problem solving*. Chichester, UK: Wiley.

Goldacre, B., 2013. *Bad pharma*. London: Fourth Estate.

Goodwin, P. and Wright, G., 2004. *Decision analysis for management judgement*. Chichester, UK: Wiley.

Hammer, M. and Champy, J., 1993. *Reengineering the corporation*. London: Nicholas Brealey.

Handy, C., 1985. *The future of work*. Oxford, UK: Blackwell.

Handy, C., 1989. *The age of unreason*. London: Century Hutchinson.

Harper, W.M. and Lim, H.C., 1982. *Operational research*. London: Pitman.

Herzberg, F., Mauser, B. and Synderman, B.B., 1959. *The motivation to work*. 2nd ed. New York: Wiley.

Hislop, D., 2013. *Knowledge management in organisations: A critical introduction*. Oxford, UK: Oxford University Press.

Huff, D., 1991. *How to lie with statistics*. London: Penguin.

Hutber, P., 1970s. City Pages, *Daily Telegraph*.

Jackson, T.W., 2015. *The connected jungle and the digital tree*. Inaugural Lecture, Loughborough University.

Jashapara, A., 2010. *Knowledge management: An integrated approach*. Harlow, UK: Pearson.

Johnson, G. and Scholes, K., 1989. *Exploring corporate strategy*. London: Prentice Hall.

Joseph Rowntree Reform Trust, 2009. Cited in *Daily Telegraph*, March.

Kahnemann, D., 2011. *Thinking, fast and slow*. New York: Penguin.

Kaplan, R.S. and Norton, D.P., 1992. The balanced scorecard: Measures that drive performance. *Harvard Business Review*, January–February, pp. 71–79.

Knott, G., 1991. *Financial management*. London: MacMillan.

Kotler, P. and Armstrong, G., 2015. *Principles of marketing*. 16th ed. Harlow, UK: Pearson.

Latham, R. and Williams, M., 1978. *The illustrated Pepys*. Berkeley and Los Angeles: University of California Press.

Lewin, K., 1947. Frontiers in group dynamics. In: D. Cartwright, ed. *Field theory in social science*. London: Social Science Paperbacks.

Lindsay, A.D., 1906. *Plato, The Republic*. Translated. London: Everyman.

Lorenzo, O. et al., 2011. *The long conversation*. London: Palgrave Macmillan.

Lynn, M., 2015. Taking over the world? Tech giants blowing billions. *Daily Telegraph*, Business Section, London, 20th February.

MacCormick, J., 2012. *9 algorithms that changed the future*. Princeton, NJ: Princeton University Press.

Machiavelli, N., 1513. *The Prince*. Translated by G. Bull, 1961. London: Penguin.

Malachowski, A.R., 2001. *Business ethics: Critical perspectives on business and management*. London: Routledge.

Maltz, M., 2001. *The new psycho-cybernetics.* New York: Prentice Hall.

Maslow, A., 1970. *Motivation and personality.* 2nd ed. New York: Harper and Row.

Maturana, H.R. and Varela, F.J., 1987. *The tree of knowledge.* Boston: Shambhala.

Mayo, E., 1949. *The social problems of an industrial civilisation.* London: Routledge & Kegan Paul.

McGregor, D., 1960. Theory x and theory y. In: D.S. Pugh, ed., *Organization theory, selected readings.* 3rd ed., 1990. London: Penguin.

Mill, J.S., 1974. *On liberty.* London: Pelican.

Mischel, W., 2014. *The marshmallow test.* London: Bantam Press.

Moore, G.E. 1965. Cramming more components onto integrated circuits. *Electronics,* 38(8), pp. 114–117.

Moore, P., 1986. *Basic operational research.* 3rd ed. London: Pitman.

Murphy, Paul A., 2005. *The cult of personality testing.* New York: Free Press.

News, 2014. *Times Higher Education,* (2,181), p. 10, 4th December.

Oakland, J.S., 2003. *Total quality management.* Oxford, UK: Butterworth-Heinemann.

O'Donohue, J., 2007. *Benedictus: A book of blessings.* London: Bantam Press.

Ohno, T., 1988. *Toyota production system.* New York: Productivity Press.

Paddock, S.S., 2003. *Appreciative inquiry in the Catholic church.* Plano, TX: Thin Book Publishing.

Peters, S., 2012. *The chimp paradox.* London: Vermilion.

Peters, T. and Waterman, R., 1982. *In search of excellence.* New York: Harper Collins.

Plato, 390 BC approx., Alcibiades.

Porter, M., 1980. *Competitive strategy.* Free Press. New York: Macmillan.

Pugh, D.S. and Hickson, D.J., 1989. *Writers on organisations.* London: Penguin.

Reichheld, F. and Markey, R., 2011. *The ultimate question 2.0.* Boston: Harvard Business Review Press.

Robb, F., 1989. Cybernetics and suprahuman autopoietic systems. *Systems Practice,* 2(1). New York: Plenum.

Roethlisberger, F.J. and Dickson, W.J., 1939. *Management and the worker: An account of a research program conducted by the Western Electric Company, Hawthorne Works, Chicago.* Cambridge, MA: Harvard University Press.

Sampson, A., 1993. *The essential anatomy of Britain.* London: Coronet.

Schein, E., 1988. *Organisational psychology.* New York: Prentice Hall.

Seddon, J., 2005. *Freedom from command and control.* New York: Productivity Press.

Seddon, J., 2008. *Systems thinking in the public sector.* Axminster, UK: Triarchy Press.

Senge, P., 1993. *The fifth discipline.* London: Century Business.

Shingo, S., 1987. *The sayings of Shigeo Shingo.* Translated by A.P. Dillon. New York: Productivity Press.

Silver, N., 2012. *The signal and the noise.* London: Penguin.

Slack, N. et al., 1995. *Operations management.* London: Pitman.

Smith, A., 1776. *The wealth of nations.* Everyman ed. 1991. London: Random Century.

Taleb, N., 2010. *The black swan.* London: Penguin.

Taylor, F., 1911. *The principles of scientific management.* Norwood, MA: Plimpton Press.

Tennent, J. and Friend, G., 2005. *Guide to business modelling.* London: Profile Books.

The week in higher education, 2014. *Times Higher Education,* 14th August.

Torrington, D., Hall, L. and Taylor, S., 2008. *Human resource management.* 7th ed. Harlow, UK: Pearson.

Tucker, B., 1887. The method of anarchy. *Liberty,* 18th June.

Tucker, M., 1996. *Successful process management in a week.* London: Headway-Hodder & Stoughton.

Ulrich, W., 1983. *Critical heuristics of social planning.* Berne: Haupt.

Vose, D., 1996. *Quantitative risk analysis.* Chichester, UK: Wiley.

Weber, M., 1924. Legitimate authority and bureaucracy. In: D.S. Pugh, ed. *Organisation theory, selected readings.* 3rd ed., 1990. London: Penguin.

Wiener, N., 1948. *Cybernetics: Or control and communication in the animal and the machine.* Cambridge, MA: MIT Press.

Wilde, O., 1890. *The picture of Dorian Gray. Lippincott's Monthly Magazine.*

Wilson, T.D., 2002. *Strangers to ourselves, discovering the adaptive unconscious.* Cambridge, MA: Harvard University Press.

Woodward, J., 1965. *Industrial organization: Theory and practice.* London: Oxford University Press.

## Web references

1. http://www.enterpriseappstoday.com/business-intelligence/why-most-business-intelligence-projects-fail-1.html, Accessed 02/04/2015
2. http://www.cfo.com/printable/article.cfm/3006814, Accessed 02/04/2015
3. http://corporate.walmart.com/our-story/our-business/locations/, Accessed 02/04/2015
4. http://www.microsoft.com/en-us/news/inside_ms.aspx, Accessed 02/04/2015
5. http://www.jaguarlandrover.com/media/23076/jlr_company_information.pdf, Accessed 02/04/2015
6. http://beckfordconsulting.com/wp-content/uploads/2014/03/Introducing-VSMethod.pdf, Accessed 02/04/2015
7. http://www.oxforddictionaries.com/definition/english/managerialism, Accessed 02/04/2015
8. http://beckfordconsulting.com/wp-content/uploads/2014/05/Reimagining-the-Railway-VF.pdf, Accessed 02/04/2015

# INDEX